About the Cover

*"In 1997, I coined the phrase Continuous Partial Attention to describe what I observed in the world around me, at Microsoft where I was a researcher and later a Vice President, with customers, and at NYU where I was adjunct faculty in a graduate program. We all seemed to be paying partial attention—continuously. NYU students had their screens tiled to display multiple instant messaging windows, email, WORD documents, and more. My colleagues in high technology did their best to give the appearance of paying attention to a conversation, all the while, also attending to caller I.D., Tetris and BrickOut on their cell phones, and other people in range. **Every stray input was a firefly. And every firefly was examined to determine if it burned more brightly than the one in hand.**"*

—Researcher Linda Stone, quoted by Henry Jenkins (2010)[1]

Cognitively, we have all become catchers of fireflies.

KO: For the leaders with whom we work every day, who inspire me with their courage, wisdom, toughness, and ingenuity.

VB: For our families for their love and support and for students, the future of mindful schools.

"The art of being a mindful leader requires just one thing, and that is cultivating the art of living mindfully. Truly being there for ourselves is the best way to bring positive change to our family, our colleagues, and our students—the future of our planet. I am convinced that happy teachers will change the world. This book offers simple practices for nourishing mindful leaders."

Thich Nhat Hanh is a monk, poet, and peace activist and was nominated for the Nobel Peace Prize by Martin Luther King, Jr., in 1967. His many books include *Living Buddha, Living Christ, Peace Is Every Step,* and *The Miracle of Mindfulness.* He lives in Plum Village, a monastic community in France, and travels worldwide leading retreats on "the art of mindful living."

"When school leaders are stressed, their tensions radiate to their staff. When teachers are stressed, their students reap the turbulent ripples. When students' brains are stressed, optimal learning is unlikely. This book offers inspirational and practical advice to school leaders for calming their waters and spawning ripples of clarity and serenity throughout the school pond."

Jay McTighe, Co-author, the Understanding by Design® series

"Leadership of any sort is demanding work, and nowhere more so than in our schools. What do school leaders need if they are to lead well? Technical knowledge and skill, of course. But equally critical to good leadership is a capacity for 'mindfulness' which helps leaders see more clearly what's going on around and within them so they can navigate complex terrain without getting lost. This important book—beautifully written, illustrated with case studies, and full of practical guidance—can help school leaders find their bearings in ways that allow them to serve the urgent needs of teachers, students, and the larger society."

Parker J. Palmer, Author of *Healing the Heart of Democracy,*
The Courage to Teach, A Hidden Wholeness, and Let Your Life Speak

"This is a book with deep wisdom on every page. While it draws its examples and targets its practical recommendations to educators, there is so much here of benefit to people in all manner of pursuits, pedagogical or otherwise. For me, this profoundly necessary book serves as a guide to being human in a world that seems determined to sap the humanity from us. And imagine the impact on our future that a more present and aware population of educators will make. Pay attention to this book, and it will teach you how to truly pay attention."

Steve Heller, Program Director, Leadership Coaching Certificate Program
Georgetown University Institute for Transformational Leadership

"In June of 2013, as I was leaving Baltimore City Public Schools, I wrote a letter to all students in which I paraphrased Tolstoy's beautiful parable, 'The Three Questions': Now was the most important time, because it was the only time when we have power. The person with you was the most important person, because you didn't know if you would ever have the chance to be true to that person. And the most important thing was to do good in the moment, because that was our fundamental purpose in life. This immensely wonderful book, full of practical lessons and next steps, as well as of stories by practitioners in the field, kept reminding me of the lessons in that parable, and why I had chosen them as my final words to my students— leadership, like all life, demands mindfulness, not only for the sake of ourselves as individuals, but in order to be true to the purpose of making life better for those we work with and those we lead. I recommend it enthusiastically for those seeking to lead in our increasingly difficult school and community settings."

Andres A. Alonso, Former Superintendent of Baltimore City Public Schools
and Deputy Chancellor of New York City Public Schools, Currently Professor
of Practice, Harvard Graduate School of Education

"A 'must-get' book for school leaders looking for help to handle the daunting stress of their work. Brimming with hope and practical advice, this inspiring book combines fascinating portraits of real leaders with down-to-earth mindfulness practices that work. Brown and Olson—longtime practitioners of mindfulness, seasoned coaches, and wise observers of the education scene—offer balm for the soul of school leaders who today are giving their all to realize their dreams."

Jerome T. Murphy, Howe Research Professor of Education and
Dean Emeritus, Harvard Graduate School of Education

"In school environments where thick tension and palpable stress levels are all too common thanks to the pressures of high-stakes accountability, administrators struggle daily to navigate challenging terrain. This practical and hope-filled book by Valerie Brown and Kirsten Olson guides school leaders on a path toward transforming their practice in meaningful, mindful ways—and, in so doing, transforming their schools. The message here is simple yet powerful: To promote equitable and lasting change in America's classrooms, we have to begin within."

Gregory Michie, Author of *Holler If You Hear Me: The Education of a Teacher and His Students*

"Leaders looking to reach higher or who feel like they are drowning amidst conflicting responsibilities often feel like they have no time to grab a ladder or a lifeline, even though they know those tools would help them achieve their goals. This book is both ladder and lifeline, and I would encourage all leaders to take the time to reach for it."

James E. Ryan, Dean of the Faculty of Education,
Charles William Eliot Professor, Harvard Graduate School of Education

"Fireflies, cursing, conflict, and clarity—The Mindful School Leader stitches honest stories from everyday school leaders with practical guides and the most up to date research on mindfulness. I saw much of my own struggles and

learning in its pages, and I suspect many educational leader will find resonance and helpful guidance for the ongoing challenges of growing our own souls and skills."

Scott Nine, Former Director of the Institute for Democratic Education in America

"An important support for school leaders, this book is comprehensive, and well-thought-out. The personal stories within are compelling and encouraging. The Mindful School Leader *is a tremendous asset to leaders worldwide to foster greater understanding and compassion within themselves and within schools."*

Sharon Salzberg, Co-Founder, Insight Meditation Society

"This book is a must-read for all school leaders. Given the high stakes testing environment and shrinking budgets of schools today, educators are under more stress than ever. This book will help school leaders find the equanimity needed to lead with calm, clarity, and effectiveness in the midst of the storm."

Kristin Neff, Associate Professor
Educational Psychology Department, University of Texas at Austin

"In The Mindful School Leader, *Brown and Olson offer with remarkable clarity and depth a thorough introduction to the practice of meditation, the science behind its benefits, and many firsthand accounts of lives and work situations transformed through this practice. Although this book was written for those in leadership roles in education, it will be inspiring for anyone interested in understanding their own minds and finding more ease in life and work."*

Joseph Goldstein, Author of *Mindfulness:*
***A Practical Guide to Awakening, A Heart Full of Peace,* and Others**

"Courageous, visionary, caring leadership is crucial to building and sustaining positive learning environments in schools. Such leaders recognize that to promote optimal social-emotional and academic learning, collaboration is essential and ongoing. Given the unrelenting, complex demands of our education system, The Mindful School Leader *is an indispensable resource for all who exercise leadership in schools. From school leaders with formal authority (e.g. principals) to pre-service teachers, this book presents compelling evidence, and specific practices (e.g. Mindfulness Practice Aids) that can help all educators to both develop resilience and cultivate optimal learning in schools."*

Deborah Donahue-Keegan, Co-Founder and Lead Organizer, Massachusetts Consortium
for Social-Emotional Learning in Teacher Education and Lecturer, Tufts University

"This inspiring book makes a strong case for school leaders to include mindfulness in their personal and professional lives. Based on solid research and enhanced by compelling examples of real people, it shows how school leaders can feel more grounded, connected, clear, and focused. Mindfulness makes leaders more effective with relatively little effort, but be advised that the benefits can be contagious, transforming your school from the inside out."

Christopher Germer, Clinical Instructor, Harvard Medical School

"Masterfully practical, rich with wisdom and the heartfelt experiences of scholars and leaders in the field, this is the handbook to keep at your side if you wish to become more evolved, insightful, nimble, and better prepared, in general, to address the challenges of teaching and leading. "

Dianne E Horgan, Associate Director, Center for Mindfulness in
Medicine, Health Care, and Society, UMASS Medical School

"How can K–12 schools possibly thrive today without wholehearted leadership? With The Mindful School Leader, *Brown and Olson offer a sourcebook for bringing the age-old wisdom of mindfulness to current school leaders with compelling stories of people at work, current research, and simple, specific practices to apply. This book delivers an essential resource to the courageous school leader."*

Terry Chadsey, Executive Director, Center for Courage & Renewal

"Finally, after serving for fourteen years as a school leader and reading everything I could find, this is the book that I've been searching for. By deftly weaving together mindfulness theory, poignant personal portraits, and imminently practical advice regarding specific methods, the authors provide the antidote to the frenetic and oppressive toxins of contemporary education; they remind us that we should stop 'Racing to the Top' and take the time instead to plumb the depths of our own hearts and souls. This is a book that will join a select few on my shelf, as one I know I will return to again and again."

Paul Freedman, Founding Director, Salmonberry School, Eastsound, WA

The Mindful School Leader

Practices to Transform Your Leadership and School

Valerie Brown ○ **Kirsten Olson**
Foreword by Richard Brady

FOR INFORMATION:

Corwin

A SAGE Company

2455 Teller Road

Thousand Oaks, California 91320

(800) 233-9936

www.corwin.com

SAGE Publications Ltd.

1 Oliver's Yard

55 City Road

London EC1Y 1SP

United Kingdom

SAGE Publications India Pvt. Ltd.

B 1/I 1 Mohan Cooperative Industrial Area

Mathura Road, New Delhi 110 044

India

SAGE Publications Asia-Pacific Pte. Ltd.

3 Church Street

#10-04 Samsung Hub

Singapore 049483

Executive Editor: Arnis Burvikovs

Associate Editor: Desirée A. Bartlett

Editorial Assistants: Ariel Price and
Andrew Olson

Project Editor: Veronica Stapleton Hooper

Copy Editor: Melinda Masson

Typesetter: C&M Digitals (P) Ltd.

Proofreader: Ellen Howard

Indexer: Jean Casalegno

Cover Designer: Candice Harman

Marketing Manager: Lisa Lysne

Copyright © 2015 by Valerie Brown and Kirsten Olson

Printed in the United States of America.

ISBN 978-1-4833-0308-6

Library of Congress Control Number: 2014959323

This book is printed on acid-free paper.

16 17 18 19 20 10 9 8 7 6 5 4 3 2

Contents

Additional materials and resources related to *The Mindful School Leader: Practices to Transform Your Leadership and School* can be found at Resources.corwin.com/BrownMindfulLeader

Chapter 2. The Science of Mindfulness   47

Additional materials and resources related to *The Mindful School Leader: Practices to Transform Your Leadership and School* can be found at Resources.corwin.com/BrownMindfulLeader

Additional materials and resources related to *The Mindful School Leader: Practices to Transform Your Leadership and School* can be found at Resources.corwin.com/BrownMindfulLeader

Additional materials and resources related to *The Mindful School Leader: Practices to Transform Your Leadership and School* can be found at Resources.corwin.com/BrownMindfulLeader

Additional materials and resources related to *The Mindful School Leader: Practices to Transform Your Leadership and School* can be found at Resources.corwin.com/BrownMindfulLeader

Additional materials and resources related to *The Mindful School Leader: Practices to Transform Your Leadership and School* can be found at Resources.corwin.com/BrownMindfulLeader

Additional materials and resources related to *The Mindful School Leader: Practices to Transform Your Leadership and School* can be found at Resources.corwin.com/BrownMindfulLeader

Please visit us on Facebook at https://www.facebook.com/TheMindfulSchoolLeader.

Foreword

When my friends Valerie and Kirsten first told me they were writing a book on mindfulness for school leaders, I so wished their book had been available when I began to practice mindfulness. In 1984, during a silent meal at a Quaker retreat center, someone read a passage on how to eat a tangerine. It was from *The Miracle of Mindfulness* by Thich Nhat Hanh. I had never heard of contemplating one's food while eating. I bought the book. Later, when I read the first lesson in it about how to have unlimited time for oneself, I felt compelled to read the whole book to my high school math students. At that time, reading about mindfulness was like reading science fiction. I knew no one who practiced mindfulness, inside or outside the classroom. It seemed impossible to get to the life I was reading about from where I was. Perhaps this describes your situation. Where do you start? What do you do?

The Mindful School Leader is an ideal place to start. By the time you've finished reading it, you'll likely have some next steps. I lacked a guide like Valerie and Kirsten's book, but I was fortunate to be able to attend a retreat with Thich Nhat Hanh in person in 1989. This experience inspired me to begin a personal mindfulness practice. But for years I kept my personal practice separate from my life as an educator.

Over the last thirty years, numerous books on mindfulness have been written. Early books, like *When Things Fall Apart* by Pema Chödrön, focus on mindfulness practices. They were written primarily by Buddhist monastics and lay teachers. As research began to reveal the neuroplasticity of the brain, books on brain science and the effects of mindfulness on mental and physical well-being, such as *Train Your Mind, Change Your Brain* by Sharon Begley, began to be written by scientists and science writers. Meanwhile, Jon Kabat-Zinn, the creator of what might be termed "applied mindfulness," was establishing mindfulness-based stress-reduction (MBSR) programs and, starting in 1990 with *Full Catastrophe Living*, writing books about his work.

People in the field of education discovered mindfulness relatively recently. The Center for Contemplative Mind in Society began awarding contemplative practice fellowships to academics only in 1997. In 2005, the center held its first conference and contemplative curriculum development workshop. In 2001, a group of K–12 educators and academics founded the Mindfulness in Education Network (MiEN) to enable educators interested in mindfulness to be part of an online community. Early K–12 mindfulness programs include Susan Kaiser Greenland's "Inner Kids" program in Los Angeles, established in 2005, and Mindful Schools in Oakland, established in 2007 by Laurie Grossman, Richard Shankman, and Megan Cowan. In 2005, the Garrison Institute issued its report *Contemplation and Education— Current Status of Programs Using Contemplative Techniques in K–12 Educational Settings.* The first books on mindfulness in education appeared in 2009: *Tuning In: Mindfulness in Teaching and Learning* edited by Irene McHenry and Richard Brady, followed by Deborah Schoeberlein and Suki Sheth's *Mindful Teaching and Teaching Mindfulness.*

In spite of Parker J. Palmer's observation that "We teach who we are," the student, not the teacher, is the focus of most mindfulness programs in education. A notable exception is Garrison Institute's CARE for Teachers, *a unique program designed to help teachers reduce stress and enliven their teaching by promoting awareness, presence, compassion, reflection, and inspiration—the inner resources they need to help students flourish, socially, emotionally, and academically.*[2] With a few small modifications, this description applies perfectly to the book you're now reading, *The Mindful School Leader.* Here, Valerie and Kirsten, aided by the school leaders they interview, paint a rich picture of many ways leaders can transform their personal and professional lives and, in so doing, transform their institutions. In the process, the authors also present research that substantiates the positive impact of mindfulness practice on mental and physical health.

I vividly recall sitting in a circle of 32 participants at the opening of the Center for Contemplative Mind in Society's first contemplative curriculum development workshop. I had come to develop a contemplative component for my tenth-grade geometry course. One by one, we introduced ourselves and spoke briefly about a course we would be working on. Two participants reported they had already introduced contemplative practices in their courses the previous year.

Both had received the highest ratings of their careers from students. Hearing this, my remaining doubt about the rightness of bringing mindfulness to my school was dispelled. This is what I'd been missing—success stories from other educators. This is what makes *The Mindful School Leader* compelling and unique, the stories of school leaders who have used mindfulness practice to become more focused, avoid burnout, improve communication, relieve their staffs' stress, and meet a host of other challenges. The trials these leaders faced are common. The ways these leaders addressed them are not. Valerie and Kirsten's skillful rendering of the practices these leaders employ now makes them available to you, the reader. The rest is up to you.

Richard Brady
President, Mindfulness in Education Network

Acknowledgments

Valerie's Acknowledgments

The Hindu tale of Indra's Net speaks of a vast cosmic web that reaches in infinite directions across the universe with an infinite number of sparkling jewels at every juncture in the net with each jewel reflecting the brilliance of all the other jewels. Each gem is intrinsically connected to the others such that touching one affects all the others. The tale is often used as a metaphor for speaking of the essential interconnectedness of all things.

Writing this book has been a process of deep reflection and deep interconnectedness. The interconnections begin with Kirsten Olson, my friend and colleague, spiritual and learning partner along the journey in life. From the day we met while studying at the Center for Courage & Renewal, I knew I met a soul friend for life. I want to acknowledge not only her but her family for their gracious and loving support during the process of writing this book.

My family has always been a source of inspiration of love and generosity. I want to thank them and especially my brothers Trevor, Lloyd, and Milton; my father Lewis; my nieces and nephews Jemal, Jason, Katie Lynne, Kyle, Amy, and Chris; and my great nieces Maya and Sophia. My love and appreciation go to my husband John, for offering his quiet support.

I am grateful to supportive friends who offered their kindness at just the right moment, especially Karen L. Erlichman, Sharon Victor, Abraham Leibson, Marisela Gomez, Oliver Bartlett, and Brenda Harrington. To my dear yoga and meditation teachers Nibhe Kaur and Mahan Rishi Singh Khalsa, who have nurtured and supported me over many years, I am grateful. Every week for nearly 20 years we have sat in meditation together, and their compassionate and loving support and guidance has always been an inspiration to me.

These interconnections have reflected brilliantly in my life and in this book.

This book began with a short essay that was published in *Education Week*, and I would like to thank Elizabeth Rich and her staff for their vision and energy to encourage this writing.

I want to express my gratitude to my Dharma friends at Blue Cliff Monastery, the monks and nuns and especially Sister True Vow and Brother Phap Khoi and Phap Khong; New York Insight Meditation Center, especially Gina Sharpe; Plum Village, especially my friend, Sister Peace; Deer Park Monastery; and Old Path Sangha for being a place of refuge, love, and support. Thank you to the Deeps Group for our monthly calls and spiritual friendship. The Quaker communities of Pendle Hill, Solebury Monthly Meeting, and Philadelphia Yearly Meeting have been foundational in awakening spiritual transformation in my life. Thank you to Jennifer Karsten and John Meyer of Pendle Hill, to Margaret Cooley of Woolman Hill, and to Debra M. Hepler and Stephen Picha of Ghost Ranch for supporting my work and for providing a place of deep beauty and rest.

I recognize the importance of having a spiritual home, a place of refuge, peace, and deep reflection, and am grateful to have found several, including Ghost Ranch, Pendle Hill, the Center for Mindfulness in Medicine, Health Care, and Society/University of Massachusetts Medical School, the Community of St. John Baptist, St. Philip's Chapel, Khalsa Healing Arts and Yoga Center, Columcille, the Chalfonte Hotel, Bowman's Hill Wildflower Preserve, and Chanticleer.

My work, my writing, and my life have been profoundly transformed by my study at Center for Courage & Renewal (CCR), and I want to especially acknowledge Parker J. Palmer for his support and wise guidance. I am grateful to CCR staffers and, especially, Terry Chadsey, Marcy and Rick Jackson, Rose Yu, Shelly Francis, and Karen Rauppius. Boundless gratitudes to Carol Kortsch, a wonderful learning partner and friend; Penny Williamson, a CCR colleague and creative partner; Judy Brown, a beloved poet and CCR colleague; Ken Saxon, Caryl Hurtig Casbon, Susan Plummer, and John Fenner for their generosity of heart and mind, as well as Bev Coleman, a CCR mentor who has always been willing to lend a listening ear and wise counsel. I cannot capture in words how deeply I have been touched by the CCR work and mission and these people. Their brilliant light penetrates the world.

To Zen Master Thich Nhat Hanh and the international community of Plum Village and monasteries worldwide, I acknowledge the profound depth of teachings that inspired this book and my life.

I am grateful to the Corwin staff for their extraordinary support, especially Arnis Burvikovs, Ariel Price, Desirée A. Bartlett, Veronica Stapleton Hooper, Melinda Masson, Lisa Lysne, Andrew Olson, Cassandra Seibel, and Candice Harman. For fine developmental editing, I am grateful to Susan Walker, and I am indebted to Tom Rocha for his extraordinary skill in reading this manuscript and suggesting important improvements. To Gaelle Desbordes for her close reading and reviewing Chapter 2, and her expertise and insight, thank you.

Thank you to Richard Brady for reading an early version of the manuscript and for writing a truly heartfelt foreword, and to Jerry Murphy, I am grateful for his early review of the manuscript and his support. Finally, I am grateful to the school leaders across the globe who have shared their stories and their lives with us. They are living examples of Indra's Net. Their work is intrinsically connected to the work of leaders throughout the world.

Kirsten's Acknowledgments

Wendy Palmer writes in *Leadership Embodiment*, "Great leaders with a strong leadership presence can create the feeling of inclusion wherever they are—a meeting room, a big auditorium, a playing field, and even on a conference call. Everyone included in their expanded personal space has a felt-sense that they are *part of something bigger than themselves.*"[3]

Writing this book has been an experience of that: feeling myself part of something much larger than me. Rather than leading it, I have been included in it. Every step of the way, this book, and the process of writing it, has been my teacher.

First I acknowledge Valerie Brown, my co-author and partner in this journey of writing—and living. Valerie is a deep and mindful soul, a spiritual force. As we fling drafts back and forth, discuss Keynote slides, and talk about important life passages and font sizes, all in the course of one short, punctual phone call, I am grateful for all she is. Valerie's tremendous personal depth, and her ongoing quest to be more present, more real, and more herself, inspires and teaches me every day. With incredible respect and love, this really is for you, Val.

Some of our mutual friends have supported our friendship and writing especially. I wish to thank Karen Erlichman, our thought-partner and sister-in-the-work, who is present with us whenever we say anything that makes sense, is funny, or observes the absurdity of life. Our friends and mentors at the Center for Courage & Renewal, especially Parker J. Palmer, Terry Chadsey, Pamela Seigle, Sally Hare, Sharlene Cochrane, Lisa Santkowski, and our original facilitator training group, inform every page. They have nurtured our friendships and understandings, and our grasp of the paradoxical simplicity of mindfulness.

My yoga practice group at Baptiste Yoga in Brookline is especially important to me in my daily journey of mindfulness and presence, and I especially thank Mark Finneran, Rachel Lappen, Nick Dickenson, Samuel Robinson, Pilar Caso, Gregor Singleton, and Paula Harvey, each a gifted and authentic teacher who deeply cares about how we show up on the mat. I also thank Abby Erdmann, who had my back (literally) as I began my current yogic journey, and Anna Mulholland, whose somatic genius and intuitive practice are part of my somatic mindful journey.

So many of my extraordinary colleagues and clients appear in these pages it is impossible to call them out individually. In great brevity, all my colleagues and friends from the Georgetown coaching program and the Institute for Transformational Leadership, especially Mike McGinley, Lloyd Raines, Alexander Caillet, Kelly Lewis, Rozlyn Kay, Chris Wahl, Kristi Hedges, and Kate Ebner, are extraordinary human beings, gifted leadership coaches, and organizational consultants. Colleagues and friends such as these are beyond description, and the generosity of each is ever-present to me.

Tara Brach, Kristin Neff and Christopher Germer, Paul Gilbert, Dan Leven at Kripalu, and Tami Simon at Sounds True (who has offered hundreds of experiences at no charge through her amazing organization) are all central spiritual teachers and mentors, and I thank them for their presence and generosity.

My educational co-collaborators and co-conspirators are at the heart of my work and my beliefs about the necessary transformation of the education sector. I am grateful for Richard Elmore, my profound learning partner; and the whole crew at IDEA, particularly Scott Nine, Dana Bennis, Jonah Canner, Melia Dicker, Santiago Rincon Gallardo, Natalia Rosado, Shawn Strader, Justo Mendez, Robert Davis, and Kwesi Rollins. Cooperative Catalyst, especially Chad Sansing, Paula White, David Loitz, and Paul Freedman, has meant so much to me. Beth Anderson, Sarah Miller, and their teams at Phoenix Charter Academy Network; Stacy Spector and her leaders at Juvenile Court and Community Schools in San Diego; and Antonia Rudenstine at reDesign are part of my "heart team." And too many colleagues to name at the Harvard Graduate School of Education, I thank you. With deep gratitude for you, you are all equity warriors every one.

This book began with a short essay that was published in *Education Week,* and Valerie and I together thank Elizabeth Rich and her staff for their vision and energy to encourage this writing. I am grateful to the Corwin staff for their extraordinary support, especially Arnis Burvikovs, Ariel Price, Desirée A. Bartlett, Candice Harman, Lisa Lysne, Veronica Stapleton Hooper, Melinda Masson, and Andrew Olson. For careful and path-correcting developmental editing, we are thankful for Susan Walker, and we are both especially indebted to Tom Rocha for his extraordinary skill in reading this manuscript and suggesting important improvements.

Thank you to Richard Brady for reading an early version of the manuscript and for writing a truly heartfelt foreword, and to Jerry Murphy, I am grateful for his early review of the manuscript and his support.

Both Valerie and I are also profoundly grateful to the individuals we interviewed for this book who were willing to speak with us in depth about their own mindfulness practices: Tanishia Williams Minor, Leslie J. Dangerfield, Ben Marcune, Miles Dunmore, Larry Ward, Mary F. Spence, Pilar Aguilera, Sophia Isako Wong, Philip Altmann, Robin Correll, Peter Godard, Todd D. Cantrell, Nicole A. Falconer, Cornelia Cannon Holden, Dan Huston, Lucretia M. Wells, Irene McHenry, Anita Garcia Morales, Shantum Seth, and Diana Chapman Walsh. We learned a great deal from every conversation, and honor their practice-knowledge.

My beloved family, Jon and Nancy Olson; Jean Olson and Tom Bryan; Nathan, Toby, and Amy Elmore; Greta, Eric, and Beatriz Olson, and Erika Bjerstrom; Henry, Cole, Lily, and Samuel Lanier, you are my best and most grounded teachers, and I thank you for your patient support in all my many activities, enthusiasms, "great ideas!," and interests. Finally, my beloved Richard. Thank you for your partnership, endless coexploration, vision, generosity, and love.

Thank you, too, Louis Armstrong, Pug and Chief Operating Officer of Old Sow Intergalactic. Your attentiveness and constant companionship are the mindful background snores of my days at home writing.

Publisher's Acknowledgments

Corwin gratefully acknowledges the contributions of the following reviewers:

Lorin W. Anderson
Carolina Distinguished Professor Emeritus
University of South Carolina
Columbia, SC

Sally Bennett
Superintendent
Armorel School District
Armorel, AR

Jennifer A. Boone
Principal
EARTHS Magnet School
Newbury Park, CA

Roberta J. Cramer
Executive Director
Michigan Science Teachers Association
Ann Arbor, MI

Lanelle Gordin
Educator
Riverside County Office of Education
Riverside, CA

Carol A. Kochhar-Bryant
Associate Dean, Graduate School of Education and Human
Development
George Washington University
Washington, DC

Audrey F. Lakin
Induction and Mentoring Coordinator; Independent Educational
Consultant
Community Unit School District #300
Carpentersville, IL

Donna Marie Norton
Executive Director for Data and Accountability
North Syracuse Central School District
North Syracuse, NY

Paul Parkison
Associate Professor
University of Southern Indiana
Evansville, IN

Lyne Ssebikindu
Assistant Principal
Shelby County Schools
Cordova, TN

Sharon Sweet
Principal
LAUSD, Elizabeth Learning Center
Cudahy, CA

Jason Thompson
Assistant Principal
Jefferson Elementary School
Schenectady, NY

Bonnie Tryon
Mentor Coach
School Administrators Association of New York State (SAANYS)
Latham, NY

Denise J. Uitto
Retired Assistant Professor
The University of Akron Wayne College
Orrville, OH

About the Authors

 **Kirsten Olson** has worked in the transformational learning sector for over twenty-five years. After becoming too involved in co-leading a cooperative school for her own four children, she received a masters and doctorate from the Harvard Graduate School of Education, where she studied large-scale educational improvement and the relationships between race, class and educational achievement in the United States. After starting on a conventional academic path, and authoring several books and many articles on education, *Wounded by School: Recapturing the Joy in Learning and Standing Up To Old School Culture* (Teachers College Press, 2009) and *Schools as Colonizers* (Verlag, 2008) among them, she realized she was most interested in working with the students, teachers and leaders involved in creating educational transformation. Kirsten is now Chief Listening Officer at Old Sow Coaching and Consulting, where she works with educational and learning-sector leaders involved in the daily work of influencing their complex, dynamic, rapidly-shifting organizations. The new demands of leadership are at the center of her vision. Kirsten is an ICF-certified leadership coach trained at Georgetown University's Institute for Transformational Leadership, and also trained as a facilitator at the Center for Courage and Renewal with Parker Palmer, where she met Valerie. Kirsten is a founding board member of the Institute for Democratic Education in America (IDEA), a national not-for-profit organized to create greater educational equity, social justice, and to foster passionate learning. Beauty Baths (Practice 2.4) every day help Kirsten savor and appreciate the world around us.

 **Valerie Brown** has studied and practiced mindfulness meditation in the Plum Village tradition since 1995 and was ordained as a member of the Tiep Hien Order by Zen Master Thich Nhat Hanh in 2003. She is an educational consultant and ICF-accredited leadership coach of Lead Smart Coaching, LLC, specializing in leadership and mindfulness training for educational leaders (www.leadsmartcoaching.com). Valerie's life and work is a blending of career paths and disciplines, having devoted her early career as an attorney and lobbyist, representing educational institutions. She holds JD, MA, and BA degrees, and has trained extensively with the Center for Courage & Renewal, Georgetown University's Institute for Transformational Leadership, and the Center for Mindfulness in Medicine, Health Care, and Society/University of Massachusetts Medical School. As a certified Kundalini yoga teacher, she engages the wisdom of the mind-body connection to support vibrant, healthy leaders and teams. She shares her global vision of a society that is interconnected through mindful awareness and compassionate action in her first book, *The Road That Teaches: Lessons in Transformation Through Travel* (QuakerBridge Media, 2012). She firmly believes that ice cream and carousel rides are critical to a better world!

Introduction

In the spring of 2013, we, Kirsten and Valerie, were leading a workshop for school leaders at a beautiful retreat center outside of Boston. On this particular day, the sun was shining; daffodils were blooming; the sky was blue; and overhead, it was nearly cloudless. In the early afternoon as we were strolling outside on a break, we suddenly and unexpectedly received word that a horrific and terrible bombing had just occurred at the finish line of the Boston Marathon only a few miles away. The Boston Marathon, always held on Patriots' Day, is traditionally a day of celebration and civic pride in Boston, a day filled with families on the streets cheering other family members and friends—everyone is friends!—shouting out and supporting each other all along the race route as participants run for heroic causes and sometimes show superhuman efforts to finish the race. The tragic events of April 15, 2013, transformed this sunny day. At the retreat center, uncertainty, anxiety, and a sense of fear spread throughout the classroom as participants scurried to their devices to check on news and loved ones and to respond to messages of concern. The conference environment was, understandably, torn and shattered. We all wondered what to do. Adjourn the conference? Break for the day? Sit together watching the news and the emerging reports on our laptops and iPads?

Because this was a workshop on mindfulness for school leaders—many of the participants had come to describe the mindfulness practices they brought to their school and academic settings, and the effect these practices had on learning and leadership—someone suggested we sit together and begin a loving-kindness meditation. Loving-kindness meditations can help evoke compassion and friendliness toward oneself and others, and are central practices for those who wish to increase their capacity to feel love for tenderness, kindness, and a sense of generosity toward oneself and others. The loving-kindness meditation is about "planting the seeds of loving wishes over and over in our hearts," as described by the acclaimed mindfulness teacher Jack Kornfield. This meditation often begins with an embrace of oneself, moving outward to imagining love and compassion for others and the world.[1] This meditation seemed especially appropriate at this moment of fear and uncertainty, a moment when so many were filled with a sense of the unknown and potential danger. (We personally had a friend, a young physician-in-training, who had volunteered to work in the medical tent at the finish line that day. We were unable to get in touch with him at that moment because cell phone signals were jammed and overwhelmed.)

Committed to a new course of action, we gathered our group together and explained our plan. Without much discussion a wave of quiet moved over the group. We sat in a circle, and began to breathe gently, reciting the words, "May I be filled with loving-kindness." We stilled our bodies (which was difficult to do at that moment) and, beginning with deep, rhythmic breathing, tried to listen to our beating hearts and to be compassionate toward ourselves in this fearful moment. Slowly, with a sense of easing in the area around our hearts and chests, we moved to picturing someone or something we loved—a child, a dog, a grandmother or grandfather we felt especially close to—evoking a visual image of this person smiling at us and filled with love. We said the words quietly to ourselves, "May she be filled with loving-kindness, may she be safe from outer dangers . . ." Gradually, encouraging our bodies to relax and our minds to quiet, and easing into the gentle in and out of our inhalation and exhalation, we moved to picturing all the people at the Boston Marathon finish line site, where so much chaos and trauma was occurring at that moment. "May they find safety. May they not be too afraid. May they get the medical and spiritual help they need. May their helpers know what to do." We envisioned all the spectators on the sidelines, and the wider world, hearing this news of the bombings, and breathed into the idea that eventually individuals might find a way to make sense of this event, and to heal. "May they also find the help they need. May they find the psychological support they need. May we find a way of understanding this. May we find a way of healing this." Finally we came back to ourselves, once again wishing compassion for ourselves in our fear, and exhaling a sense of calm into the room and over each other. "May I be filled with loving-kindness. May I be filled with understanding and compassion. May my sense of peace extend outward to the world."

Because we have a preference for visual meditations, we pictured a circle of energy, beginning in our breath and moving toward the finish line of the marathon, finally moving outward across the world. As we together imagined not only the intense scene at the finish line, the scene of mayhem and chaos and blood, we were also imagining peace, connection, and the possibility of forgiveness amid the terrible tragedies of that day. Our meditation was a way of finding meaning around this event, creating peacefulness and connectedness in ourselves, and trying to do some good in the world while we sat in our small circle. The next day we talked about what we had noticed during the meditation. Many of us observed that we emerged from the circle feeling more grounded, more connected to ourselves, and more able to move forward into the grueling week that was to come, during which some of the attendees would be dealing with the tragic deaths that had occurred within their own school communities and neighborhoods.[2]

The School Leader's Dilemma

Our schools—and the larger world in which we and our pupils navigate—grow increasingly complex and unpredictable. Buffeted by global happenings, and the speed and pace at which we operate in school as information and connection are increasingly available at every moment, our leadership selves can be sorely tested and profoundly challenged. Not only are our leadership selves asked to grow bigger by sometimes tragic external events like the marathon bombings, but the complexity of our leadership environments and accountability systems, and the new *turned-on-ness* of our reality in which we are expected to respond to this complexity almost immediately, challenges us intellectually and spiritually in ways that are unprecedented in human life. This complexity, immediacy, overabundance of information, and potential for distraction has consequences for everyone, but we feel perhaps most particularly for school leaders, because they must lead and show the way forward during a period in which the education sector is undergoing transformational and truly groundbreaking change. In our view, the parameters of the learning sector are profoundly transforming: How we define learning is dramatically shifting, when and where learning may occur is being redefined, and the ways in which educational systems should respond to these shifts are all profound and pressing questions. Readers of this book know and feel this complexity every day. As a recent informal study by Jerry Murphy, former dean of the Harvard Graduate School of Education, reveals,[3] school leaders experience professional stress at extraordinarily high rates, and in myriad ways. At a professional development meeting convened by Murphy at the Harvard Graduate School of Education, a group of school leaders reported that

- 89% felt overwhelmed;
- 84% neglected to take care of themselves in the midst of stress; and
- 80% scolded themselves when they performed less than perfectly—conditions under which few of us are primed to feel our best or do our best work.

How are educational leaders expected to reflect and renew, and avoid the "sacrifice syndrome" that spirals leaders downward into coping and putting up with, rather than devising creative solutions to, the problems that beset their buildings, their districts, and their organizations?[4] Can the practices of mindfulness positively affect the learning environments in which school leaders operate? What does mindfulness help us do, at an individual and organizational level? How can the "soft" practices of mindfulness increase our leadership effectiveness, our capacity to grow our educational programs and the individuals within them, to achieve the results demanded by our accountability environments and ourselves? These are the questions we explore in this book through the following chapters, with portraits of practice from the leaders with whom we work, and with stories from our own lives as mindfulness practitioners.

This Book Is for Educational Leaders

The effectiveness of mindfulness practices on students and teachers has been demonstrated now by hundreds of empirical studies (only some of which are featured in this book) and supported by many organizations that specialize in helping teachers and students bring mindfulness practices to the classroom and other learning environments. But we feel school leaders themselves, in their daily leadership lives, are underserved.

Our several decades of work with school leaders, as organizational consultants, researchers, retreat leaders, and leadership coaches, suggest that our clients—those trying to lead wildly shifting organizations in the midst of profound cultural and technological change—are extraordinarily stressed and frequently lack resources and supports for building and nurturing their own leadership practices.

Often the leaders we work with feel unauthorized even to consider what *they* might need to be the leaders they feel they should be during challenging times. ("It's selfish, and self-indulgent to think about me," they tell us, and we understand why they feel this way.) But we also observe that after years of habitual stress and pedal-to-the-metal coping, their leadership decisions often suffer. Former high performers find themselves slipping into simply maintaining the status quo, or coping day to day and hoping that external events will bring a change.

Ironically, we believe that difficulty, stress, and even crisis are invitations to grow, to expand our ways of understanding ourselves and our habitual reactions. Through body attunement practices, contemplation exercises, and other kinds of integrative practices we outline in this book, we believe leaders can learn some of the fundamental building blocks of sustainable and coherent mindful leadership, and use these tools to reboot themselves on the job, enjoy their leadership lives more, and lead more boldly and with more support from others around them and within themselves. We are honored to begin this journey with you.

Who We Are—Mindfully

We, Kirsten and Valerie, met many years ago while training at the Center for Courage & Renewal with Parker J. Palmer and his team. For several decades, philosopher and educator Palmer, and an inspiring group of collaborators, have created uniquely contemplative, thoughtful, transforming retreats in which leaders can contemplate the challenges and paradoxes of leadership in the 21st century. We engaged in this training to learn how to create spaces in which a leader's true values, soul, and inner teacher might emerge, and of course to deepen our own practices and self understandings. Among many other things, we learned facilitation techniques that put a high premium on self-disclosure, self-reflection, and vulnerability. So although we tell you more about our training and the experiences we've had throughout the book, here is a brief introduction to our mindfulness stories, as educators and leaders ourselves. We want you to understand how our own mindfulness practices arose not out of special knowledge, particular insights, or "gifts from the East" but in response to real professional and personal challenges in our own lives. We notice a pattern in the lives of those we've had the privilege to coach and teach: that we are opened to these practices through difficulty, often through failure, trauma, and disappointment with the ways we have chosen to live our lives. Our stories tell the same narrative.

Kirsten Olson

Fifteen years ago, I attended a workshop and retreat sponsored by the Omega Institute for Holistic Studies in Rhinebeck, New York, taught by Jon Kabat-Zinn, the pioneering mindfulness-based stress-reduction trainer and physician mentioned in Chapter 1, pages 19, 21. The retreat was held in a windowless hotel ballroom set up banquet style, which swallowed up the attendees and gave us all a weary, ghoulish look even though it was only 10 in the morning. Although Kabat-Zinn already was well known in many alternative medicine circles and in pain research, at that time, he was just beginning to take his emerging ideas—that meditation should not be confined to the cushion—to a broad public. Emerging clinical studies made it clear that mindfulness meditation might have revolutionary healing and well-being implications for medicine and other health and wellness endeavors, and popular interest in stress reduction was growing.

At this retreat, doctors, nurses and other health care professionals gathered, as did alternative healers, longtime meditators, and people like me, in attendance for much more prosaic personal reasons. I decided to attend this retreat because I was looking for a break from my life, and I heard from a respected friend that this Omega retreat might offer something restful, peaceful, and intriguing on an autumn weekend. I longed for some silence and peacefulness, and the idea of simply being in a hotel room by myself felt like a retreat and a vacation. This was a particularly challenging period in my life. My 15-year marriage was coming to an end, and I was in the midst of completing a doctorate in a highly competitive graduate school program that required extensive commuting. I was the mother of four young children. Lying in an already-made bed, with an opportunity to raid the minibar, seemed an alluring and exotic part of the retreat.

Chomping on M&M's from the minibar and considering the last several years of my life, in many ways so blessed and in many ways also so rushed and too full, I felt roiling anxiety about my precarious financial future and my unknown professional life, and tremendous concern about my capacity to support these children and be the mother, teacher, and leader I wished to be. Most of all, I noticed the pace I was keeping: sleeping only three to four hours a night, composing constant and punishing to-do lists, feeling pervaded by a constant sense of never having done enough. This sense of incompletion and falling behind was accompanied by withering internal self-criticism (my inner critic was a medieval executioner, as well as the sternest academic ever!). From the outside, I appeared to be coping well and keeping up with an overabundant number of commitments—in fact, I took great pride in being "remarkable!" and resilient. Inside, of course, I was in turmoil: The rising tide of self-criticism and the lack of self-compassion would drive me to new heights of achievement, and I found it difficult to ask for help or to find people to whom I could really open up. After all, wasn't I the one coping so well? Stepping off my pedestal of strength and perfection felt very threatening, even inconceivable, yet keeping myself there sometimes required more effort than I could muster. Like many people around me, I was exhausted and overwhelmed, inside and out. But I took great pride in not showing it.

Kabat-Zinn began the retreat by asking us to create a circle of chairs and the quiet ring of a bell. He spoke a little about his own journey though mindfulness and meditation, an abundantly documented story that he recounts in a beautiful interview you can listen to on Sounds True.[5] With an earnest commitment to laying aside my academic skepticism, I listened to Jon attentively, openly, and uncomprehendingly; at a deeper level, I hardly understood a word of what he was saying. Then he began to lead us through a body scan (described in this book in Chapter 2, page 62). As it happened, the room where we were doing this exploration and body scan was directly adjacent to a kitchen, and there was loud pop music playing as the kitchen staff moved into full gear to prepare lunch for the retreat's hungry visitors. As we began to quiet ourselves and focus on our feet, beginning to move up through the various places in our bodies, suddenly, someone in the kitchen dropped a pile of lunch plates and silverware, and shouted, *"Oh shit!* Goddammit to hell!" Jon gently looked up at us, smiled quietly, and said, "Everything that comes to us is part of the meditation, part of life. Enjoy all the sights and sounds the world presents to you as you meditate and know that perfect silence and stillness is not required."

My journey with mindfulness began with that cursing. Through the years of building a mindfulness practice, and many other forms of complementary training including a vigorous daily yoga practice, frequent Beauty Baths (see Mindfulness Practice Aid 2.4, "The Beauty Bath," in Chapter 2, page 65), and mindful walking, talking, and listening (listening perhaps most of all), I am constantly relearning that perfect silence and the ideal conditions for mindfulness are not required for contemplative practice. I find that looking up at the sky; closely observing leaves on trees; engaging in a hot, sweaty yoga routine; and deeply joining with my clients by listening to them, are gifts of mindfulness to myself, and help attune me to my own needs and feelings, so I am more available for others. Since those early days, all the practices described in this book have helped me become more myself everyday: less frantic, more able to be realistic and truthful, and more attentive to moments of *alrightness* and the sacred and pleasurable gifts of being alive. These practices help bring me back to myself when I am far away.

We want the same for others, which is why we wrote this book.

Valerie Brown

When I passed the New Jersey bar exam in 1983, I had no intention of practicing mindfulness. Back then, I was mindful of very little, except my determination to get a job, make money, and get out of Brooklyn, which was at that time very much a ghetto. I actually began practicing mindfulness years later, in 1991, when, by chance, I drove past a storefront in my new neighborhood. The sign read: Meditation and Mindfulness.

I was at a low point. I was going through a divorce, ending a marriage that had lasted a very short and tumultuous year. My former husband said he wanted a divorce because I never listened to him. And he was right. The big-shot lawyer, the expert, I had it all figured out, and I didn't have time to listen anyway. The split left me looking for a place to live, and facing surgery. I was convinced that all this emotional turmoil had contributed to the stress I felt and to my getting sick. A classic type A personality, I was always moving fast. I drove fast; I parked my car headlights facing out for a quick getaway. I talked fast, I walked fast, and my thinking was fast, too.

The unexpected surgery brought all that fast talking, fast walking, and fast driving to an abrupt halt, and I found myself laid up, barely able to walk for weeks. It wasn't pretty. Several months after my divorce and the surgery, I decided I needed a vacation and went hiking in the mountains of northern New Mexico, a place I felt deeply connected. When I reached the top of a high mountain, at a clearing in the woods, I sat on a log and looked up at the sky. I watched as the clouds inched along, fascinated by this slow-motion dance. I had been so disconnected from nature, so rushed and hurried in my daily life, that I had forgotten to look up at the sky; I hadn't done so in months, maybe years. I had forgotten that clouds move. I realized then how disconnected I was from the natural world around me, and from myself.

I had missed so much. This was an important moment of recognition, a turning point.

I left New Mexico with a new passion to understand myself and regain a sense of balance in my life. Out of this experience, I learned an important lesson about mindfulness: Mindfulness is about being present, showing up for one's self and for others, for life. I could not mentally think my way over the walls I had created. I had to find another way around the wall, or disassemble it brick by brick.

I went back to that storefront for the first night of a meditation class, an event that stays with me even now. The instruction that night was simple: "Let go of thoughts as they arise. See them like clouds floating in the sky." I wrestled with myself through the experience of meditation. My mind raced nearly out of control, feeling like it was going to crash and burn. I noticed that my back hurt, and I felt a strange ache behind my knees. I felt sleepy. I wanted gum. The whole thing tormented me, and I wondered when it would end. Finally, after two hours, the bell rang and the meditation ended. It felt like a disaster. But I came back the next week to try to get it right. And I have been coming back to Monday night meditation for almost two decades, learning ways of extending mindfulness into my daily life.

Little did I know that the year of crisis, watching the clouds move on that day on the top of a mountain, and that night of trying out meditation would set me on a new course, a new direction. I was learning, the hard way, the art of stopping, a fundamental practice of meditation and mindfulness. I became a lawyer as a way to escape poverty and the damage of childhood: the broken home, a life of penny pinching, scrimping, and saving every dime. Paradoxically, as my mindfulness practice grew steadier, I began to recognize just how out of control I was: my fear, my anger, running—always on the run—the hiding. I attended a daylong retreat with Thich Nhat Hanh, a Buddhist monk and Master of Zen meditation, at the Riverside Church in Manhattan. Instinctively, I knew I had gotten lucky yet again and had met someone very special, who would have a profound impact on me. Nhat Hanh's words were so simple and yet so profound. He talked about feeling alive in this moment, about recognizing what is happening right now: that I am breathing, that I am sitting here, my sense of well-being. This was radical for me. So much of my life as a lawyer-lobbyist was about the mental satisfaction of ticking off the next thing on my to-do list, only to have it replaced with yet another thing. My high-powered career had left me with little time even to recognize my own breath. Since that first retreat with Nhat Hanh, I have trained myself to do just one thing at a time.

When I eat a meal, I don't read or talk on the phone. When I cook at home, I don't watch TV. When I talk with someone on the phone, I just talk on the phone.

Remembering to live in mindfulness is not a once-and-done proposition; it is about recommitting myself every day and every hour of every day. My life now is very different from the one I lived with my all-consuming lawyer-lobbyist job. Today, working as a leadership coach and educational consultant, I create the life I want, at a human scale and at a human pace. I still struggle with days when I am overly busy, moving from project to project. I sometimes find it difficult to say "no" to a new project. I coax myself into asking for help from others, and not just offering help. I notice the impulse to hide my true self from others, recognizing this familiar pattern, its origin and purpose. Being mindful creates a kind of internal space that allows me to hold these difficult feelings and thoughts, and to feel deep appreciation and compassion for my personal journey, a journey that is not unlike the journeys traveled by the many people you will encounter in this book.

Benefits of Mindfulness—To the Leader (and Your Team)

If you're wondering what mindfulness can do for _you_, consider some of the benefits of engaging in a regular mindfulness practice based on our experiences of working with many educational leaders.

- **Improved ability to notice and slow down, or stop, automatic reactions.** In the highly stressful, 12- to 14-hour-a-day leadership cycles most school leaders face, many educational leaders fall into habitual patterns of behavior, in part simply because they have too little time to reflect on these patterns. One person we recently interviewed for this book said, "I used to be late and arrive stressed to nearly every meeting. Working with a coach who is also a mindfulness practitioner, I developed an explicit 'pause' practice three to four times a day, where I regrouped and then spent a little time looking at my schedule in my office and breathing. At first this felt incredibly weird, but now I count on it and it's almost become automatic. I am now coming to meetings much calmer and more focused. This means I can notice what's going on in meetings better, and I think our team tends to make better decisions and waste less time. That helps everyone, not just me. And everyone also spends less time tangled up with me, and dealing with my issues!"

- **Increased capacity to respond to complex and difficult situations.** A West Coast superintendent described being tangled in ongoing power skirmishes between a prominent union member and a few school board leaders. "This conflict was sapping everyone's energy and focus. After I began a morning practice of 'Count Your Blessings Pause, Dwell in Your Victories, and Show Up as Your Bigger Self (CVS)' [see Mindfulness Practice Aid 7.2 in Chapter 7, page 199], I found myself much less activated by the maneuvering and tension. Increasingly, I felt that I could choose whether or not to get involved, and how. Finally, I was able to name the power struggle as a source of dysfunction, face to face between the two parties—which took a lot of courage for me. Oddly, the parties involved started to take more responsibility for their behavior. I never would have predicted that." Mindfulness practices actually helped this superintendent bravely face up to an ongoing leadership dysfunction and pivot the parties into taking greater responsibility for it themselves. "I had to feel pretty grounded in myself to do this. My CVS practice [see Mindfulness Practice Aid 7.2, page 199] helped me show up as my bigger self, just like it says."

- **Ability to see situations more clearly, or many dimensions of a situation.** An executive director of a charter school in the Northeast told us, "We were constantly struggling with teacher turnover at our charter school. Whole groups of teachers would leave every year, which dramatically affected our learning climate and performance results. I felt frantic every spring, and would actually feel like I was having panic attacks driving to school in the morning. A friend recommended that I try some breathing practices, which I read about through Dr. Andrew Weil's website. Through the breathing, and practicing it when I was driving, I was able to slow down a little and begin thinking about what I was modeling. I began to ask myself, 'Is what we are asking people to do really a sustainable pace? Is it a sustainable leadership pace for me?'" That pace question, and the breath practice, actually began to change things for this leader, and for her school culture. Ultimately, teacher turnover began to drop— remarkable given such a small intervention.

- **Becoming more creative at designing solutions to complex dilemmas.** As we've said, many of our clients come to mindfulness through a difficult event: a pitched public battle over an educational issue that spills into the media, a staff crisis, or a divorce or an event with a child or family member that is so disturbing or shaking that they are moved to explore new kinds of healing and comfort. As one leader in the midst of a divorce told us, "The intensity of that situation, the difficulties I was having in accepting feelings and being present to difficult emotions at that time made me need to find something." He began a yoga practice, which eventually led him to a regular meditation practice, and now he teaches a course on mindful communication in addition to his educational leadership duties. "It has transformed my life, and now I teach these practices to others. At a moment when I thought my life had come to an end, that was when my life really began."

- **Ability to achieve balance and greater resilience at work and at home.** Many of the individuals we work with are eager, sometimes desperate, to find ways to feel more grounded and less distracted, given the demands of work, family, and personal life. Not enough time for career development, children, spouses, personal renewal, professional reading, and hobbies is an omnipresent dilemma. We have found, through working with hundreds of people, however, that pausing even for a few moments a day to stop and quiet oneself—to relax the nervous system, body, and mind, can reduce feelings of stress and the sense of time famine and not enough of "you." Paradoxically, this sometimes creates more time, more energy, a sense of greater resources. As one principal told us, "I used to believe that time completely ran me. Now I see much more that I am in charge of my time, that I'm more in control than I think I am. I also feel much clearer about what I can give up, so as not to get so hijacked during the day and to enjoy the moments I am with my kids, my husband." Even just the stopping to observe a thing of beauty (in our practice we call this taking a Beauty Bath, described in Mindfulness Practice Aid 2.4 in Chapter 2, page 65) can offer powerful benefits, and our clients are often surprised that these small events can make them happier and more contented, less frenzied and more balanced. "I've discovered that it's really small little practices in the day that have changed my perceptions and made me a more effective leader. Who knew? They sure didn't teach you this in graduate school," said the same principal.

Every chapter of our book discusses practical day-to-day mindful leadership applications and includes mindful practice exercises. We explain how to engage in each practice, and describe the exercises sequentially so that you can start with a most basic practice and progress if you wish. (Please remember that these practices take time, and the shifts are usually subtle . . . so hang with us.)

One special education program leader concluded her story around her journey into mindfulness and other contemplative practices in this way: "Personally, I meditate twice a day. I do a morning meditation and an evening meditation—perhaps a loving-kindness meditation in the evening and calming my breath in the morning. I spend about 20 minutes doing each meditation, but I don't set an alarm anymore; I can just manage it. I have found that in my own life, through a recent divorce, breast cancer, and having a special needs child of my own, I've been able to stay much more calm. I'm not as reactive, I do much less ruminating, I'm more resilient. People say to me, 'You really help us stay grounded,' and I attribute that to my practice," she told us. "I also find that mindfulness training helps my teachers and me be more in touch with our bodies, be more engaged in work, to trust ourselves. It changes everything. I think mindfulness training changes the world. It changed my world."

We believe mindfulness practices really do change the world, for educational leaders, their learning organization, and eventually all communities around them. In the next chapters, we invite you to come on this exploration of mindfulness practices with us to see how real school leaders are incorporating these practices into their leadership lives.

We also invite you to please come check in with us at Facebook .com/TheMindfulSchoolLeader to

- share your own mindful leadership story,
- get valuable advice and resources from the authors and other educational leaders, and
- create a community of practitioners who share their practices for creating more coherent and gratifying professional and personal lives.

 Additional materials and resources related to *The Mindful School Leader: Practices to Transform Your Leadership and School* can be found at Resources.corwin.com/BrownMindfulLeader

1

Why Mindfulness?

The School Leader's Life

"Once a person has consciously embraced his or her leadership role and embarked on an inner journey to stay in touch with the soul's imperatives, life can and usually does get challenging. . . . Quietude and clarity are both doorways into and destinations of an inner journey. They name what leaders most need: a path that can take us toward our own lives."

—Parker J. Palmer, Introduction to
Leading From Within (2007)[1]

"Becoming a great leader demands tremendous self-awareness."

—Jeff Jordan, former president of PayPal (2014)[2]

A School Leader Practicing Mindfulness

Albert is driving to his district offices at 6:20 a.m. As the superintendent of a large public school system in the Southwest, his day routinely starts at 5 a.m., a time when he used to review emails and briefing notes for the 8–10 meetings he participates in every day as a part of his regular professional routine. "To be honest, my mornings used to start like cannon fire, almost with a sense of panic. The alarm would go off and I'd leap out of bed, already engaged in intense thinking and worry about what was coming in the day. As I prepared coffee and let the dog out, I'd glance through my phone at emails and often I'd start feeling this sense of dread . . . like something bad was coming or bad news was on its way. Often that feeling, a kind of undertow, used to be there churning in me through the whole day. I just assumed this was how professional life was. I used that anxiety. I thought, 'I need this anxiety to be productive, to stay ahead of the game.'"

After Albert was promoted to superintendent, however, he realized that the pace of his professional life was not going to change—there would never be a natural letup. "It wasn't about changing 'what was out there' in my leadership life, it was about altering my own responses to my life." He realized he had achieved some of his goals and created some personal stability, but wondered whether this was the example of extreme busyness and multitasking he wanted to set for his students and staff. "Was I living my life the way I wanted to? Some *honest* feedback from my wife and kids about my irritability and negative moods helped make me ready for some new possibilities, but I also had a sense that I wanted to live my life in a different way. That became stronger."

SOME HONEST FEEDBACK

"Some *honest* feedback from my wife and kids about my irritability and negative moods helped make me ready for some new possibilities, but I also had a sense that I wanted to live life in a different way. That became stronger."

—*Superintendent in the Southwest*

Are you living your life as you want to right now? Can you relate to these feelings of wanting to "live life in a different way"? What is your dream for your professional life?

About the same time, Albert happened to hear a mindfulness coach speak about the benefits of a regular mindfulness practice at a regional professional development meeting. Though initially wary and skeptical, Albert bought a couple of CDs on mindfulness and began listening to them in his car. Then he bought a workbook of practical, mindfulness-based stress-reduction (MBSR) exercises, which, in very tangible ways, helped him notice his stressors and how they were affecting the people in his life. He began doing some of the exercises in the workbook; one was a worksheet he used to assign a numerical rating to the kind of stress he felt every day in various situations.[3] Albert realized he was laying the foundation for a mindfulness practice when he noticed himself more able to observe what set him off in work conversations, for instance, and that he could observe this and calm himself down more easily before he got too triggered. This led to a couple of sessions with a mindfulness coach, who helped him put several practices together and gave him a place to talk about his leadership practice.

Now Albert begins his day at 5 a.m. by sitting quietly at the edge of his bed, observing and taking in the silence and peace of his house before his wife and three teenage children have woken. He feels a moment of gratitude for the peace of his home, and he encourages himself to experience his love for the people (and dogs!) sleeping in it, and is grateful for the quiet. Underneath the shades of his bedroom windows he notices that the sun is just starting to rise, which gives him a feeling of pleasant anticipation about the day. Then, as he's learned from the mindfulness podcasts and tapes and his workbook that support his practice, he focuses on his breath. He takes in three deep belly breaths (see Mindfulness Practice Aid 1.2, "Three-Minute Focused Breathing Practice," page 35), paying close attention to the flow of air in and out of his body, starting at his mouth and moving down into his belly. Albert has begun to understand and actually feel that each breath is an anchor that brings him to the present, right there at that moment, and his body has begun to respond to this breathing by relaxing. With practice, he feels his "mind and body working more together." In that moment, as he is waking, Albert says he feels himself "grounding into the day" and sinking into the feeling of "being there, not dreading the day ahead."

Albert then takes a moment to ask himself what he's feeling, and he explores those sensations and feelings with a greater sense of acceptance. (His mindfulness coach has encouraged him to think of difficult emotions as natural, and not to try to avoid them as he has in the past.) He's worried about the upcoming school board meeting that evening, which is bound to be contentious and watched closely on this city's local cable access station. He's also concerned about his daughter's rocky adjustment to sixth grade, and her transition to her new middle school, especially after what she told him last night about "stuff on the bus with a group of girls." She's shy and quiet, and he wonders about the complexity of tween interactions. Albert also observes his new role at home: His wife recently began her own graduate program, so she's out of the house much more often in the evenings, and Albert now has additional child care and household responsibilities. He also checks in with his anxiety about the district budget meetings that will consume his afternoon. Negotiating between state funding cuts and his district's strong union representatives is part of what he calls his professional world of "riding the rapids of tough choices." He accepts those feelings without deciding whether they're right or wrong, but with a sense of observing them—yes, there they are, he notes; there is worry, there is anxiety. He says to himself, "This is OK," and he feels those feelings in his body, letting out a deep exhale. Using techniques he learned from another mindfulness practice, about "taking in the good,"[4] Albert appreciates all that is comforting and pleasant about the sensations of sitting in the quiet morning peace, and with a final deep, calming breath, and some thoughts about things that help him feel strong (he remembers times he's successfully negotiated a day just like this), he says, "I am capable, I will be alright." Then he gets up and starts making coffee. This routine takes three minutes. (Albert is also using the R.A.I.N. practice for self-inquiry into stress and anxiety, explained at Mindfulness Practice Aid 4.2, "R.A.I.N.," page 123.)

NEED A RESET?

Use one of Albert's visualization techniques for resetting mood, like imagining someone you love in a very happy moment or recalling an appreciative comment someone recently made about you. Then watch Louie Schwartzberg's 2011 TED Talk on the beauty of everyday things.[5]

Benefits of Practice

Why does Albert engage in these practices? "What I notice," says Albert, "is that the morning drive, and the whole day following, feel much more stable after these simple breathing, investigating, savoring, and gratitude practices. I am able to notice the beauty of the day more as I'm driving into the district offices, not thinking about a thousand different things. I see the way the trees look blowing in the wind in the morning, the colors of the sunrise, the garden outside the house where I make this right turn. I often have a sense of promise and pleasant anticipation of the day now. It makes a big difference."

Albert also notices that since he began practicing, he loses his temper much less frequently in meetings, and he feels he is able to come back to himself more rapidly when things get confusing and contentious in negotiations. "I am more able to take some steps back and think, is there something here we haven't thought of? Are there other alternatives? I feel more balanced and less thrown off by small things, and sometimes even able to handle more with greater efficiency. I waste less time worrying about things I can't control."

Most of all, Albert notices he is more energetic throughout the day, because he feels less rushed. His mindfulness coach has asked him to practice S.T.O.P. (Stop. Take a breath. Observe. Proceed., explained in Mindfulness Practice Aid 1.1, "Stopping, Pausing, and Observing," page 35) twice a day, and often he uses S.T.O.P. more frequently when the day is really busy, like today will be. "This is becoming a habit. I programmed the pauses into my phone [for a complete list of mindfulness apps, see Appendix C, online, page 17], but I now do the practice whenever I need to. I notice that when I pause, my team also is starting to slow up. I feel like we don't hurtle into decisions so quickly, and we're able to explore more options. We're making fewer decisions just out of fear or covering our as*. This has made a big difference for us as we face a state budget crisis and cuts to our budget everywhere. Really, I do feel the difference, and I'm motivated to keep going with these practices."

What Is Mindfulness?

"Mindfulness is awareness, cultivated by paying attention on purpose, in the present moment, non-judgmentally."

—Jon Kabat-Zinn, author of *Mindfulness for Beginners* (2012)[6] and founder of the Stress Reduction Program and the Center for Mindfulness in Medicine, Health Care, and Society at the University of Massachusetts Medical School. Kabat-Zinn is considered a foundational presence in the rise of the practice of mindfulness around the world.

As you already are aware, we are in the midst of a mindfulness revolution.[7] Sometimes it seems impossible to open a newspaper or read a blog or magazine without finding a reference to new mindfulness practices and the innovative ways in which they are being applied. In the West, practices once considered alternative and associated with Buddhism have captured attention in virtually every sector of our culture, far beyond their initial Western applications in medicine. (We ourselves have several colleagues who are publishing books on mindful leadership. Whew!) Staying abreast of the mindfulness literature can make one not-mindful.

Training in mindfulness—*the intentional cultivation of moment-by-moment nonjudgmental, focused attention and awareness*—also seems to be everywhere. Managers at General Mills and Luckstone building products are being taught the benefits of the thoughtful pause. Global economic leaders stopped for moments of silence at the World Economic Forum in Davos, Switzerland, in 2013. The U.S. Marine Corps is now studying how to train its troops through meditative practices based on mindfulness, in a course called "M-Fit" at Camp Pendleton, California.[8] Deepak Chopra and Oprah Winfrey offer online meditation programs for beginners at least three times a year. And increasingly these practices are being regarded as essential for leaders and others, for cognitive fitness and focus. Jeffery Bearor, the executive deputy of Marine Corps training and education command at Quantico, Virginia, who supports M-Fit, notes, "Some people might say these are Eastern-based religious practices but this goes way beyond that. This is not tied to any religious practice. This is about mental preparation to better handle stress."[9]

Like training for an athletic event, you do mindfulness by practicing. With gentle and relatively frequent practice—and a belief that this might be helpful—mindfulness can alter the neural architectures and reaction patterns of our brains and shift the ways in which we regard ourselves, our lives, and the contexts in which we operate as leaders. With practice, mindfulness can allow educational leaders to "disengage from habitual reactions," as one superintendent said, and become more able to observe oneself in action and to act more effectively in the midst of chaos, overstimulation, and threat, a condition of the lives of many educational leaders. As we explained in the introduction to this chapter, mindfulness practices helped one particular educational leader with a tendency toward anxiety. Albert observed, "I realized that every time that school board member called me I didn't have to assume that it was a disaster. That's my choice and that's my story. I can work with what's going on in another way. Through the breath practice, and taking a daily couple of pauses to look around me and observe quietly, I am becoming more peaceful and happier as I face the never-ending challenges of my job. I just don't feel buffeted and blown around by everything the way I used to." As nearly everyone who writes about mindfulness now points out, the practice of mindfulness is not a religion, and it is not about learning how to clear the mind of all thoughts, nor is it a "relaxation technique." Mindfulness is not a substitute for appropriate medical care and treatment (if you are experiencing consistent and extreme negative thoughts and feelings, consult an appropriate mental health professional). Rather, mindfulness practices help us understand and become aware of our habitual reactions, emotional triggers, and narratives—to calm our minds and support our bodies for greater clarity, focus, agility, and personal satisfaction—which, in a truly virtuous circle, makes us more effective and powerful leaders.

WHAT IS MBSR?

Mindfulness-based stress-reduction, or MBSR, was originally developed in a modest clinic in a spare room of the University of Massachusetts Medical School by Jon Kabat-Zinn in 1979. From this humble beginning, MBSR has grown into a worldwide movement. Currently, more than 500 MBSR programs are offered in medical centers, hospitals, and clinics around the world. More than 20,000 people have completed the MBSR program at the University of Massachusetts Stress Reduction clinic and other locations. Hundreds, perhaps thousands, of businesses have made mindfulness-based training available within their organizations. Mindful Schools, a mindfulness training program for students and teachers, has presented its in-school program to more than 18,000 students in 53 schools since 2007.[10] Mindfulness, in the words of Jon Kabat-Zinn, "has a big future."[11]

Mindfulness can be practiced both formally and informally, and we will describe both ways of conceiving of these practices in the subsequent chapters. Formal practice usually involves mindful breathing, a body scan, sitting meditation, loving-kindness meditation, and mindful movement. The informal practice of mindfulness involves bringing the many daily activities of life—making the bed, shaving, washing the dishes, walking the dog, making a cup of tea, applying mascara—into a kind of present-centered focus in which we simply observe and experience the qualities of each of these activities.[12] As described in the University of Massachusetts MBSR programs, this sense of being present—*of being here now*—helps us **not believe** all our thoughts (our mind thinks many things that simply aren't true), and with practice allows us to become a bit like weather reporters of what's happening in our minds, observing the weather fronts that are blowing in without reacting to them or moving immediately to action or reaction to them. And, in our view, this capacity for meta-reflection—to be aware of one's own thoughts and to practice regarding them in less judgmental ways ("oh, that's a terrible thought; I'm a bad person") or not believing that everything we think is true—is a critical leadership and learning skill. For us, mindfulness practice has offered a way of returning to our center, of finding true self or "the inner teacher," as our mentor Parker J. Palmer describes it, throughout our own full and frequently overflowing lives. Both of us find, through mindfulness practice, that we are much better able to observe our own ingrained stories, our narratives and habitual thought patterns, and to decide whether they have truth for us at that moment, rather than being ordered around and seized by them. We find this makes life a lot more pleasant and relaxed, and we are able to be more playful and laugh at ourselves, even when we are (simultaneously) late for a meeting, have just said something that landed with a thud, or made a mistake on our budget that just caused our proposal to get rejected, and our spouse is also angry with us. Ever been there?

Practice Pause—Do You Need a Mindfulness Practice?

"How often do you look at the time, see that it is 6 p.m. and feel very tired from running around all day, [yet] don't really know where the time went or what you did with all that time? How often do you find yourself just doing something, anything, to get it off the 'to do' list rather than finding the optimal choice?"

—Janet Marturano, Institute for Mindful Leadership (2013)[13]

Why Do Leaders Need a Mindfulness Practice?

"In 1997, I coined the phrase Continuous Partial Attention to describe what I observed in the world around me, at Microsoft where I was a researcher and later a Vice President, with customers, and at NYU where I was adjunct faculty in a graduate program. We all seemed to be paying partial attention—continuously. NYU students had their screens tiled to display multiple instant messaging windows, email, WORD documents, and more. My colleagues in high technology did their best to give the appearance of paying attention to a conversation, all the while, also attending to caller I.D., Tetris and BrickOut on their cell phones, and other people in range.

"Every stray input was a firefly. And every firefly was examined
to determine if it burned more brightly than the one in hand."

—Researcher Linda Stone, quoted by
Henry Jenkins (2010)[14]

Cognitively, we have all become catchers of fireflies.[15] Like the
beautiful Linda Stone image in the front of this book, the rise of interest in mindfulness throughout the world, we believe, is tied to at least
two critical features of contemporary life. First, **the effect of stress and
cognitive overload** of our always-on, always-connected lives means
we must find new ways to respond to the conditions of our daily lives,
as we juggle ever-more-intense leadership environments with all the
other things that fill our existences: family commitments, community
service, the needs of children and aging parents, exercise, professional
learning, play, and relaxation. The second and much more invitational
part of our global interest in mindfulness is **our ever-expanding
understanding of** *neuroplasticity,* **Richard Davidson's (and others')
term for the brain's ability to change, develop, and grow throughout
the life span**. Since the late 1990s, Richard Davidson, professor of psychology and psychiatry at the University of Wisconsin-Madison as
well as founder and chair of the Center for Investigating Healthy
Minds, and many other researchers, have demonstrated that to a
much greater degree than previously understood, we have capacity to
train our minds to respond better and more skillfully to environmental
and emotional stimulation, meaning we also have new opportunities
and ways to manage our changing—and challenging—emotional and
cognitive environments. (That's what this book is about.)

Real Overload: "Everything Is Urgent"

As we've already described, part of this mounting pressure on
leaders, as tracked by stress-related health conditions and insurance
claims, is biological, and an equal share is cultural. As the pressure to
close the achievement gap, transform our outdated organizational
infrastructures, and meet accountability goals has mounted in the education sector, for many, educational leadership has become an always-
on, round-the-clock, nonstop work ecology, without letup and without
organizational structures that give us any time for thinking or resetting.
As a recent *Teachers College Record* research study on principal renewal
observed, "the principalship is one of the most difficult, complex and
challenging jobs in the nation," and the need for resetting and reflection
for most individuals in the role is profound, and unmet.[16]

Given the demands of leadership, many educational leaders we work with say they feel they can't leave the building or the office (which we regard as a critical leadership problem), and several have struggled hard to declare even one day of their weekend email and text-free. One charter school leader we work with described receiving texts from the chairman of her board at 1:30 a.m. (he was a night owl) that woke her up with worrisome requests and concerns, and made it impossible for her to sleep. She also observed that her son's Saturday football games were constantly interrupted by her director of data's phone questions about a state accountability report, and by her dean of students' weekend catch-up. We understood this leader felt she could not ignore these messages, but her weekend was hardly restful or restorative. Institutional underperformance too means more stress. As another executive director of a no-excuses charter school network said to us recently, "Leaders with bad test scores don't get vacations." Yet ironically, we find these stressed and overwhelmed leaders are the ones who would most benefit from mindful pauses and opportunities to reflect on their work. And we also recognize everyone truly is doing the best he or she can.

Always connected and always expected to be responsive, overload and attention fracturing is real, and it comes from everywhere. We were recently visiting schools across the country with a group of talented, highly committed educators on a senior leadership team. We had carefully planned and carved out school visits to focus explicitly on instructional practice and honing the team's discourse around instructional practice. We observed how much these leaders wished to be present for the classroom visits and in discussions with teachers and school leaders, and also how they were simultaneously and constantly pulled away from focus on these conversations because they were scanning their phones for messages and texts about potential other brewing critical matters. In our leadership consulting, we notice how phone and device scanning has become habitual and oddly comfortable (I'm here, but I'm not really here)—as we feel the sense that we're "managing" things by constantly responding (often poorly and incompletely). In our view, this contributes to tremendously diminished leadership focus in our sector, and a lost sense of satisfaction in our work. (We know because we observe this in ourselves as well.)

Globally, of course, this phenomenon of over-connection and over-responsiveness is also real and hardly limited to the education sector. We attended a mindfulness conference recently where a mindfulness trainer asked the audience to guess what time period this set of statistics represented: 2 million Google searches, 6 million Facebook views, 204 million emails sent, 30 hours of video uploaded.[17] The time period? A global minute. (Those who guessed correctly were awarded a plastic brain, which said, "Be Here Now!") Much closer to home, we sat with the leader of a high-performing all-girls' charter school in a coaching meeting in which she explained to us how many emails and texts she receives a day (sometimes up to 300), and the difficulties in getting focused time for work or rest when "everything is urgent, and parents, the Board, or my staff all need answers immediately. Sometimes I work late, late into the night and fall asleep in my clothes—too tired to take them off—simply trying to respond to everyone. It's no wonder I sometimes lose focus or make mistakes." We agree.

Leadership Challenges to Our Sector

Amid this common picture of too-much-ness, and fractured and incomplete attention, which itself is debilitating and can affect mood (the neurobiological effects of stress will be covered more extensively in Chapter 2), in our view the very meaning of being an educational leader is also undergoing significant shift and redefinition.[18] The meaning and purpose of our work as learning leaders is shifting as definitions of learning, and where and how it occurs, evolve. Public confidence in educational leaders and understanding of what they do, and the ways in which our work is measured, have never been more contested and challenging. The introduction of the Common Core, new teacher and leader evaluation accountabilities, much more intense public scrutiny of the value and purpose of public education, and the need to be more and more responsive to our many and varied constituencies while working within bureaucratic structures—as well as a true and dawning sense of the reinvention of the learning sector altogether[19]— mean that we are working in very challenging times in which change is constant. For many of our clients, that may mean "Blorft," as Tina Fey calls it. "'Blorft' is an adjective I just made up," Fey writes in *Bossypants*, "that means, 'Completely overwhelmed but proceeding as if everything is fine and reacting to the stress with the torpor of a possum.'"[20] We truly believe, however, that in the midst of these challenges lies the possibility of reinvention and renewal. The strains and seismic shifts we are experiencing sector-wide and as individual leaders may also be opportunities for rethinking and reframing the conditions in which we experience, our work as educational leaders. We believe the practices we outline in this book are central to this reinvention.

WHAT DOES IT MEAN TO BE A MINDFUL LEADER?

"The journey of developing the ability to observe oneself in the moment can be viewed as a process of shrinking the amount of time that it takes us to notice what is happening to us and how we respond. By focusing my attention on my ability to observe myself, I will, over time, move from 'As I look back on what happened in that meeting last week, I can now see how my behavior . . .' to realizing upon walking out of a meeting, 'Oh no, I just did it again!' to noticing in the moment, 'Ooh, I just got triggered!' and finally, to thinking, 'Here comes the trigger. I can be at choice with . . . how I respond.' This capacity is central to the disciplines of doing leadership. We must be intentional about developing and strengthening this capacity in ourselves."

—Steve Heller, Director of the Georgetown University
Leadership Coaching Program (2013)[21]

Knowing When to Disengage and Recharge

What does all this mean for us? The leaders we work with are tasked with guiding and inspiring others to accomplish the organization's goals, while simultaneously enforcing policy (often created by others) and encouraging cohesion and collaboration. They must communicate clearly and stirringly, and maintain high levels of efficiency and focus across a huge variety of tasks. All of this responsibility, in the context of a chaotic and challenging educational leadership environment, in our experience means that most leaders do not prioritize time for renewal and recharge for themselves. It is the last thing on the to-do list and, frequently, the thing they don't get to—with important consequences for the work.

We recently consulted with a superintendent who, after some negotiation, decided she would cease emailing anyone on her senior team or within her organization from 9 p.m. on Friday night until 7 p.m. Sunday night. She was reluctant, but she agreed to try. She herself had a first great weekend (sent us text pictures of herself fishing and going to a baseball game—not working!), and was surprised to observe on reflection later that week that her staff lost little productivity by not receiving emails from her during the weekends, and seemed to arrive on Monday morning much more focused and ready to engage with the challenges of the week. We understood the superintendent's sense of urgency, and her reluctance to reconsider this practice. "How do I communicate my sense of urgency?" she asked us. "The work requires this." But overvaluing attention to our professional lives and under-valuing rest and time off for our personal lives, and the lives of those we lead, can have debilitating long-term professional consequences. This superintendent had a chronic problem with turnover on her senior staff. With some changes to her management habits, she was able to retain much more of her staff in the following year as the jobs in her organization became more sustainable.

Arianna Huffington, founder of the *Huffington Post* and a vocifer-ous crusader for new definitions of cultural and personal success, made this observation at her 2013 commencement address to Smith College: "If we don't redefine success, the personal price we pay will get higher and higher. Right now, America's workplace culture is practically fueled by stress, sleep deprivation, and burnout." At the *Huffington Post,* for instance, Huffington installed nap rooms. At first, employees were hesitant to use them, but "now they are always booked."[22] In light of Jerry Murphy's research on educational leaders, which showed the degree to which leaders felt overwhelmed and stressed (see the Introduction), we know many educational leaders could use a nap room, but we see few organizational cultures where this would be acceptable—yet.

Finally, we frequently find ourselves in coaching situations work-ing with teams or individuals where we are aware that the capacity for reflection on their work—where an initiative stands, what has been successful in a group process, where and what are the true levers of sustainable change within the organization—is underdevel-oped and simply not valued by leaders or individuals. Although many of us are charged with leading *learning* organizations, and learning theory describes the importance of reflection for consolida-tion and scaffolding the next level of insights,[23] culturally in educa-tion we tend not to create pauses for thinking and feeling in our learning and leading, or do so only superficially. (One minute of reflection may not be enough.) "By three methods we may learn wis-dom: first, by reflection, which is noblest; second, by imitation, which is easiest; and third by experience, which is the bitterest," said Confucius. We believe in experiential learning of course, but we think instituting real reflection time as a cultural practice (during com-mutes, scheduled into the weekly calendar, on a mindful walk, in every senior leadership team meeting) is critical; we see the bitter results of too much rushing and too much effort flung in too many unfocused directions. Mindful practices begun at the individual leader level have a way of echoing out from the leader, creating opportunities in meetings and in conversations for groups to slow down, to take a moment to tap the wisdom of the assembled, to move the work to the next level by reinforcing (through thoughtful pausing) what is wise and powerful and helpful. We think this is at the center of growing our effectiveness as a sector.

HOW DO WE DETERMINE EFFECTIVENESS?

"We're always being asked how effective is your work, are you getting results and outcomes? I don't object to that. But I'm really convinced that there's a terrible problem when effectiveness is our only standard and we become utterly obsessed with outcomes and results. When that happens, what else happens is that we keep taking on smaller and smaller tasks because those are the only ones we can get results with."

—Parker J. Palmer, Center for Courage & Renewal (2014)[24]

How do you manage outcomes and results in the overall context of your work? What makes you feel successful and effective?

How Stress Shapes Our Brains

"Mindfulness is a form of brain hygiene. There was a time when we didn't brush our teeth every day, and I think mindfulness practice is a form of brain brushing. Mindfulness is like practicing good hygiene for the mind."

—Dan Siegel, "On the Importance of Mindfulness" (2009)[25]

In addition to our too intensive, too overwhelming work and professional cultures, we're also more aware than ever that how we think about that stress, and our life's other challenges, shapes our brains. (The neurobiological revolution of the last 25 years is charted more extensively in Chapter 2, page 47.) We are ever more aware of how powerful our minds are at shaping our brains—or in the words of Dan Siegel, "The mind can change the brain." We understand now that our patterns of thought affect the very architecture of our brains, and using magnetic resonance imaging (MRI), we are able to demonstrate that we have much more capacity to shape this neural architecture than we ever dreamed possible.[26] This is one of the reasons we have become so interested in mindfulness as a part of leadership practice—because of its potential to sculpt our brains more adaptively to the leadership challenges we face. As the studies cited in this chapter and throughout our book show, a simple, relatively low-commitment, eight-week meditation practice can increase capacity around self-awareness, attention, visual processing, and memory, and help make us less reactive.

THE BRAIN'S PLASTICITY: A STUDY IN THE EFFECTIVENESS OF MINDFULNESS

In a 2011 study by Hölzel and colleagues, published in *Psychiatry Research: Neuroimaging*,[27] meditation group participants spent an average of 27 minutes each day practicing mindfulness exercises. After only eight weeks, their responses to a mindfulness questionnaire indicated significant improvements compared with pre-participation responses. The analysis of MRI, which focused on areas where meditation-associated differences were seen in earlier studies, found increased gray matter density in the hippocampus, known to be important for learning and memory, and in other cortical structures associated with self-awareness, compassion, and introspection. Participant-reported reductions in stress also were correlated with decreased gray matter density in the amygdala, which is known to play an important role in anxiety and stress. Amishi Jha, a University of Miami neuroscientist who was not a part of this study, concluded, "These results shed light on the mechanisms of action of mindfulness-based training. They demonstrate that the first-person experience of stress can not only be reduced with an eight-week mindfulness training program but that this experiential change corresponds with structural changes in the amygdala, a finding that opens doors to many possibilities for further research."[28] Lead author Britta Hölzel observed, commenting on the findings, "It is fascinating to see the brain's plasticity and that, by practicing meditation, we can play an active role in changing the brain and can increase our well-being and quality of life."

The brain's plasticity has huge implications for us as educational leaders. If our seemingly deep-set, "instinctual" leadership habits and reactions—even those that appear to us to be unchangeable—are open to reshaping and redefinition, then we think it's foolish not to investigate these practices. As the acclaimed neuropsychologist Rick Hanson notes in a new work, *Hardwiring Happiness*, "There's a traditional saying that the mind makes its shape from what it rests upon. Based on what we've learned about . . . neuroplasticity, a modern version would be to say that the brain takes its shape from what the mind rests upon. If you keep resting your mind on self-criticism, worries . . . and stress, then your brain will be shaped into greater reactivity, vulnerability to anxiety, and depressed mood. On the other hand, if you keep resting your mind on good events, then over time your brain will take a different shape, one with strength and resilience hardwired into it."[29]

As one of our clients, the chief academic officer of a large school district, said to us with wonderment after engaging in mindfulness practices for several months, "I used to believe that well-being happened by chance or luck. Now I see that it is possible to claim well-being as my right and responsibility." What this means for us as individuals and educational leaders is what Dr. Richard Davidson says in a 2013 video for Mindful Schools—*"Happiness and well-being should be considered skills, like learning to play a musical instrument"*[30]— and very short periods of practice, repeated throughout the day, can bring about significant changes to our neural networks and in how we think, feel, and behave. In other words, we are learning how we can hardwire greater leadership effectiveness and a stronger sense of efficacy in our work—and we believe this is central to the visionary leadership required in our sector.

Mindfulness for Educational Leaders

Yet these mindfulness practices, and their implications for leaders, are still much too unknown, especially in the educational leadership field. Some educational leadership programs are beginning to offer mindfulness studies to students in educational leadership programs; see, for instance, Lesley University's Interdisciplinary Studies in Mindfulness Program,[31] Columbia University's Teachers College Mindfulness and Education Working Group[32] and new Spirituality Mind Body Institute,[33] the University of Virginia's new Contemplative Sciences Center's research-intensive course "Applying Mindfulness Practices to Support School Leadership,"[34] or New York University's Mindfulness Project.[35] Many undergraduate colleges and universities now offer courses in mindfulness for teachers or as part of their pre-service training. Nevertheless, mindfulness training courses and supports for the new or maturing school leader are only beginning to gain popularity. Indeed, some early reviewers of our book cautioned us that a mindfulness-based leadership discussion might be seen as religious or having an Eastern orientation that would make some skeptical about its applicability in an educational leader's context. However, hundreds of mindfulness training programs around the globe emphasize the nonreligious nature of these practices and the practicality and appropriateness of these practices for all people, no matter their ethnicity or religious orientation. Mindfulness, in our view, is a thoroughly secular set of practices and way of being and growing ourselves as educational leaders that should be much more widely supported and embraced.

The premise of our book is simple. As a leader, if you could learn to train yourself to respond to the anxiety and stress of daily life in more productive ways, using practices that make you a clearer and more effective leader and also a calmer and more focused person, doesn't it make sense to explore how? We think this is exactly the promise of mindfulness and the mindfulness practices we teach our leadership clients. We want to offer them to you as encouragement in this book, with stories of real school leaders who use them, and to point you to the hundreds of resources that are now available to you if you decide to explore them more through a mindfulness program, an online resource, or a mindfulness coach.

BE HERE NOW

Mindfulness trainers Bob Stahl and Wendy Millstine note, "When you begin to observe the workings of your mind . . . you may realize that you're generally 'somewhere else' mentally—generally either rehearsing the future or rehashing the past. But consider this: the only moment you ever live in is right now, so why not be here? Mindfulness is never beyond reach; it's as close as your conscious attention. The moment you realize you're not present, you are in fact present."[36]

Your Leadership Practice Matters

"The practice of mindful leadership gives you tools to measure and manage your life as you're living it. It teaches you to pay attention to the present moment, recognizing your feelings and emotions and keeping them under control, especially when faced with highly stressful situations. When you are mindful, you're aware of your presence and the ways you impact other people. You're able to both observe and participate in each moment, while recognizing the implications of your actions for the longer term. And that prevents you from slipping into a life that pulls you away from your values."

—Bill George, professor of management at Harvard Business School and former CEO of Medtronic[37]

Finally, and perhaps most critical in terms of our views of leadership, we believe employing mindfulness practices helps educational leaders develop the most important attribute of all: the capacity to connect with others and themselves. As we know, leading other people is extraordinarily challenging. As one of our clients said to us recently, "When I'm sitting in a chair reading a leadership book, everything makes sense, and I can do it all. But once I'm actually up in front of people running a contentious meeting or giving a difficult presentation, I can easily get triggered by my need for approval or control. I get freaked out and start feeling unsafe, and it gets harder for me to make good decisions." We understand. (Yes, we really do!)

Yet we see effective leaders who are working to develop the capacity to observe themselves and to re-center in the moment, amid the chaos of intense feelings and unanticipated events. The practice of mindfulness helps them grow this capacity. This same leader, quoted above, said, "Some of these mindfulness pauses are helping—helping me to trust myself more. I've noticed people see me as more trustworthy—they actually say that." We know from the work of Wayne Hoy and associates, who developed a metric for evaluating school mindfulness,[38] that trust and mindfulness are inextricably linked, and highly effective schools score high on measures of trust.[39] Trust is linked to student achievement, a sense of leadership coherence, and moral authority, and as described by Hoy and others, organizational mindfulness is a part of creating trust and school mindfulness. "Mindful school climates," says Hoy, lead to a willingness to investigate mistakes, work realistically with organizational weaknesses, and allow for occasional creative reinvention.[40] Due to their capacity to regulate their own moods and manage relationships with others, mindful leaders can ask others more directly for what's needed, describe why this is important to the organization and the individual, and coalesce positive emotions and intentions around workplace goals. The practice of mindfulness, we believe, supports the development of emotional poise and resilience at several levels, and we see this experientially in our coaching practices and in our own lives.

A Leader With a Growing Mindfulness Practice

We work with Natalia, a principal and instructional leader who is unusually skillful at emotional self-regulation and is highly interpersonally self-aware. She knows herself well and is unafraid of describing her faults, and she also holds herself and others to high standards, while managing to be funny, warm, and unassuming. We sometimes watch with wonder as Natalia breaks tension in her staff or between two teachers with a gently funny or self-depreciating remark, and observe how

Natalia is able to connect authentically with those around her because she seems unafraid of being herself. Because of these qualities (and others), Natalia has immense staff loyalty and staff coherence, is able to see problems and crises brewing in the organization long before they become chronic, and has many ways of addressing such problems—like asking her staff members what they think she should do. We also observe that Natalia and her team are creative and risk-taking in their capacity to generate solutions to common problems, especially around lack of time or resources. Natalia and her team tend to be straightforward about what they don't know, frequently describing their lack of knowledge and their need for help from others. When we query Natalia on her stability, high levels of trust, and leadership coherence, Natalia says "self-renewal" is at the center of her leadership vision. She is also a daily yoga practitioner, which she considers central to her work as a manager and leader.

Natalia credits her skill as a leader to the daily "checking in on the mat" and her awareness of emotions as they come up in her body. "I can tell when I'm getting triggered and lost, and I have all these pausing and self-compassion practices I now use, with myself and others. I know this helps me not get sucked into events quite as rapidly as I did in the past." All this makes sense, since we know that self-awareness and creating a sense of "enoughness" is critical to effective leadership and creating a coherent leadership culture, and that magical as this sounds, we all need practical ways of doing this. As we describe in Chapter 3, pages 91–92, we think of somatic awareness, and practices like yoga, aikido, and other forms of mindful movement, as contemplative practices that foster this kind of self-renewal and capacity to be emotionally perceptive of oneself and others, as part of building mindful leadership and gaining access to the wisdom of the entire body.

We know mood matters. As Wharton researchers Shimul Melwani and Sigal Barsade recently found,[41] the emotional climate and mood of a leader have dramatic effects on his or her team. Sour moods have "ripple effects," affecting everyone on the team, both explicitly and subtly, and even relatively subtle emotional cues like "a sarcastic eye roll can have a long-lasting impact on an executive's authority. It can also rock her entire team."[42] On the other hand, having a broad repertoire of emotional intelligence skills and expressing positive emotions tend to enhance the performance of the individual, the group, and the entire organization—sometimes in subtle ways that are difficult to detect. Natalia's warmth, sense of humor, and humility are a part of her skill set, but so too are her sense of being grounded and her ability to be sensitive to others without being rocked by the reactions of others. The educational leaders we work with who value and place a high priority on their own emotional stability, coherence, and emotional presence, supported by mindfulness—like Natalia—are also not surprisingly the highest performers and most innovative leaders.

First Steps: You've Got to Practice

"One of the primary ways you teach mindfulness . . . is just through your presence."

—Megan Cowan, co-founder and
program director, Mindful Schools

If you were calmer, more focused, and less driven by a sense that there is never enough time in the day, would your demeanor have positive effects on your staff and school climate? Would this approach help support a trusting, cohesive school culture and, ultimately, higher student achievement and student efficacy? The purpose of these practices for a school leader is, of course, not only to develop greater clarity, personal poise, and sense of enhanced well-being, but also to become a more skillful leader. So think about Albert, the superintendent presented at the beginning of this chapter. With his growing mindfulness practice, he is better able to "pull his mind and his emotions back to a place where he wants them to be." He is less reactive and more efficient, because he spends less time ruminating about interpersonal reactions and challenges to his ego and ideas. Albert observes that he is more aware of where his thoughts go, and with mindfulness training, he has learned this subtle but important set of skills for getting himself focused on what he thinks is important.

PRACTICE TIP

How mindful are you? Take this quiz: http://greatergood.berkeley.edu/quizzes/take_quiz/4.

For something more extensive, you may also want to visit the self-scored Mindful Attention Awareness Scale developed by Kirk Warren Brown, PhD, at www.mindfulness-extended.nl/content3/wp-content/uploads/2013/07/MAAS-EN.pdf and in Appendix G, online, page 41.

What does it take to become an authentic leader? "You must have practices that you engage in every day."

—His Holiness the Dalai Lama (2012)

Yet unlike so many professional development or leadership trainings we've attended, we cannot buy mindfulness training for our schools or districts, hold a few trainings about it, monitor progress, and assume it is working. Mindfulness cannot be "implemented" in a school culture (or in an individual leader) in a conventional sense, because implementation implies that the result is known and anticipatable. Mindfulness in our leadership practice is rather a commitment to practice, to daily "attentive repetition," with an understanding that for many of us, the benefits of a daily mindfulness commitment are subtle and require a noticing of slight shifts in ourselves and our reactions. As Bill George, professor of management at the Harvard Business School and former CEO of Medtronic, observes about his own meditation and mindfulness practice, it is necessary to commit daily. "I don't use the word 'practice' lightly," George wrote in a highly personal blog post. "In order to gain awareness and clarity about the present moment, you must be able to quiet your mind. That is tremendously difficult and takes a lifetime of practice. In 2012, I had the privilege of presenting my ideas on authentic leadership to his Holiness the Dalai Lama. When I asked him what it took to become an authentic leader, he replied, 'You must have practices that you engage in every day.'"[43]

More than almost any other directive we bring with our book, we believe that educational leaders *must engage with these mindfulness practices themselves to legitimately bring mindfulness initiatives to their schools.* This requires us to commit to the practices ourselves to successfully embody them, as the opening anecdote about Albert indicates. We will take you through formal and informal practice throughout the book, and we urge you to have confidence in yourself as you initiate your journey. We're here with you.

See Mindfulness Practice Aid 1.1, "Stopping, Pausing, and Observing." We urge you to begin—*right now.*

Mindfulness Practice Aids

Mindfulness Practice Aid 1.1: Stopping, Pausing, and Observing

This practice and the breathing practice also in this section are perhaps the most essential building blocks of any mindfulness practice and are so common you can download apps for them into your smartphone (see Appendix C, online, page 17) to tell you when, throughout the day, to practice them.

We learned the pause practice from our MBSR training and thank our teachers Bob Stahl and Wendy Millstine for this particular version of it.[44] There are hundreds of versions and instructions for this practice, from versions designed for children (see, for instance, *Planting Seeds: Practicing Mindfulness With Children* by Thich Nhat Hanh—all books are included in Appendix A, online, page 1) to Jon Kabat-Zinn's lovely instructions in *Mindfulness for Beginners*. Here is ours, from MBSR and the helpful, pragmatic book, *Calming the Rush of Panic* by Bob Stahl and Wendy Millstine.

Because mindfulness is about helping us recognize what's happening in the present moment, to do this practice, you put on hold whatever you're doing for a moment to realize what's going on with you. This pausing practice helps restore your balance, like hitting the reset button on your computer, so you can proceed refreshed and renewed. It's like a little mini-check-in with yourself and your body and the world you are in at the moment.

The acronym S.T.O.P., described by Stahl and Millstine, helps you remember the following steps:

- Stop.
- Take a breath.
- Observe, acknowledge, and allow what's here.
- Proceed and be present.

Many of us, including the authors, have been surprised when we set our phones for an hourly S.T.O.P. practice to discover that we're sitting in an uncomfortable position, we need to go to the bathroom (we didn't even know), we're hungry, or our backs need a stretch. Because we've become acculturated to long meetings or long periods working at the computer, we've actually developed a talent for "checking out" of our bodies so that we can do what we think we're supposed to do and get through our ever-blooming to-do list.

With this S.T.O.P. practice, we recommend that you plan to do this at least twice a day during your workday, and actually set a time of day for it. Remember, like all mindfulness practices, the more you practice it, the more rewarding it becomes (you're rewiring your brain to know how to pause). We observe that the habitual S.T.O.P. practice can help us experience more groundedness in the day—so we can remember what it feels like to be us—and it is especially helpful when we feel moments of anger, panic, or the push of a deadline. For us, pausing can help us feel more expansive and relaxed, and we think this makes us better thinkers and partners in all kinds of work.

Give it a try, and let us know how it feels! We want to hear from you.

Mindfulness Practice Aid 1.2: Three-Minute Focused Breathing Practice

In addition to the S.T.O.P. practice, here is a breath practice to help you begin to alleviate stress, bring greater awareness to how you are breathing, and restore calm. If you wish, you can use one of the mindfulness timers listed in Appendix C, online, page 17, when trying out these practices.

- Sit in a quiet place, with the spine comfortably straight but not rigid, and in a posture that feels dignified.
- Allow your eyes to be open or closed—notice what feels most comfortable.
- Notice how you are sitting without judging yourself
- Feel your feet on the floor.
- Feel your legs, hips, torso, arms, chest, and face.
- Bring your attention to the physical sensation of breathing with a sense of curiosity and openness.
- Locate where you feel the breath in the body.
- Feel the breath come in and go out, accepting things as they are for the moment.
- Observe and feel the in-breath without judgment.
- Follow the breath as it comes into the body.
- Notice the slight pause between the in- and the out-breaths.
- Follow and feel the out-breath, noticing that the out-breath turns into the in-breath.
- Be with the sensations of breathing.
- When you notice that the mind has wandered away from its attention on the breath, gently yet firmly bring the wandering mind back to the direct bodily sensation of breathing.
- Avoid making yourself into a failure or giving yourself grief; pivot your feelings and instead generate a feeling of being OK and accepting yourself as you are.
- Each time the mind wanders, again, gently and firmly bring the mind back to the sensation of the breath, noticing the in-breath and the out-breath, from the very first sensation of the breath coming into the body to the very last sensation of the breath leaving the body.
- After three minutes of practice like this, stretch gently and open your eyes if they are closed.
- Please try this or the other practices listed here daily and notice how you feel.

MINDFUL LEADER PRACTICE CONNECTION

For a beautiful and moving one-hour portrait of Mindful Schools' work in a challenging middle school classroom in San Francisco, please see the 2013 documentary *Room to Breathe*.[45] (The work of Mindful Schools is described in various places in this book.) We think this contains some of the most compelling anecdotal evidence of how mindfulness can be helpful to students, teachers, and schools that we've seen. We hope you'll watch it.

"People who are teaching these methods need to be grounded in a practice."

—Dr. Richard Davidson, "Healthy
Habits of Mind" (2013)[46]

Portraits of Practice

In every chapter of this book we offer you interviews with practicing K–12 or college leaders who are engaged in mindfulness practices. We thank them for agreeing to appear in our book, and hope you can learn from them about their journey of mindful leadership.

1.1: Tanishia Williams Minor, Executive Director

School and Special Education Support Services, District 79, New York City

"When I think of how mindfulness has changed my life, it really boils down to helping me to be my best self, caring for myself spiritually, emotionally, mentally and physically."

Tanishia Williams Minor is a person of boundless energy, and like many heads of educational organizations, she has a nearly nonstop schedule. Finally catching up to her for a phone conversation was well worth it. She begins by describing her work environment.

Tanishia has the challenging responsibility of directing New York City's District 79 special education services. District 79 includes more than 300 alternative schools and programs throughout New York City. The district serves 65,000 over-age, under-credited students whose schooling has been interrupted. The school's population includes adjudicated youth, students with substance abuse issues, a school for adults, and one of New York City's largest high school equivalency testing programs. As she describes the school's population, we sense a deep connection not just to the work, but also to the students she serves.

"District 79 is a school unlike the traditional notion," she says. "Instead, it is a school without walls. One could find one-teacher sites in a recreation room in a public housing facility or a substance abuse treatment program at an agency, or a school-based program at our site on Rikers Island, one of New York City's largest jails. While our population is transient, this movement through the system is exacerbated by the fact that most of our students are in some form of distress. They are in varying stages of distress: Some are teen parents, others are pursuing vocational education services, still others are studying for their high school equivalency diploma, and another group of students is working full time."

We can sense that Tanishia feels a true calling and love for her work, and a real dedication to the students she serves. She describes this dedication as one of the primary reasons she turned toward mindfulness. "When working as a high school principal, I had a very stressful job that was made even more stressful because I really owned the academic success of the 300 students in my school. I wore that ownership like a coat. Actually, I wore it like a second layer of skin.

"Physically, I was tired a lot. I had cramps; I was sluggish. I was living a really fast-paced life: I would leave my house at about 6:30 a.m. and return home around 9:00 p.m. every day. I knew how to cook, but I made a lot of poor food choices, choosing convenience over nutrition. I was young and took my body's ability to process this food for granted. I didn't value the link between the food I ate and my cognitive ability.

"I ate on the go—high calorie, low nutrient—all of the big fast-food chains—quick and easy. I could nibble on a little something and keep thinking about work. I didn't want to lose time trying to find something better. In addition, in many instances, I found solace in the food.

"I started very slowly to change. I realized that I had to take better care of my body to help the students. I completely changed my diet. I started to slow down. I examined why I ate and not just what I ate. I reflected on how I ate. I realized that food started to become synonymous with taking a cognitive break from the stressors at work. And I exploited those tiny breaks as often as I could.

"From examining my eating habits, I started looking at the condition of my physical body. I could keep up with the students—that wasn't a problem. It was my mental stamina and strength—that just wasn't there." Tanishia's voice trails off as she reflects back to this moment. "I could not sustain energy. I realized that I can be a more effective leader and help my kids in school if I take better care of myself.

"I started reading lots of books on mindfulness and meditation. I even attended a mindfulness retreat digitally. I listened to talks on my computer. I learned the importance of being still. This was a revelation. I shifted from thinking, 'What needs to be done next?' to 'How can I do this more efficiently? How can we do this better?' I became aware of my thinking and slowly began to get myself off the endless wheel of looking for what was next. I began to appreciate the small successes in the now. I began to accept that what I had done was enough for that moment." Even in this phone conversation, we can sense that these words resonate deeply within her.

We can hear in her voice a blend of strength, vulnerability, and courage. She says, "Today, I begin each day by sitting quietly for a few minutes, just breathing and noticing how I'm feeling. I practice yoga, and I have adopted a Paleo Diet, which consists mainly of fish, grass-fed pasture-raised meats, eggs, vegetables, fruit, fungi, roots, and nuts, and excludes grains, legumes, dairy products, potatoes, refined salt, refined sugar, and processed oils. I am reminded of my mother's words: 'Eat foods for what they do for your body.'

"'Be your best you' is what I constantly tell myself. When I think of how mindfulness has changed my life, it really boils down to helping me to be my best self, to caring for myself spiritually, emotionally, mentally, and physically."

Tanishia Williams Minor currently serves as the executive director of school and special education support services in District 79 for the New York City Public Schools System Department of Education. She leads the district's efforts to ensure that its teachers, school leaders, and district office staff members are the most effective in the nation. Prior to this appointment, Tanishia served as principal within the District of Columbia Public School System. During her time there, she served as the founding principal of The Washington Metropolitan High School, a premiere alternative school for students who have been disconnected or disengaged throughout their educational tenure.

1.2: Leslie J. Dangerfield, PhD, Assistant Principal

St. Lucie County Public Schools, Florida

"Around here, mindfulness is very outside the box. But we think it's worth doing. And for me, personally, it's been very rewarding."

We recently spoke with Leslie J. Dangerfield, assistant principal of an elementary school in St. Lucie County, Florida, about her emerging mindfulness practice, developed in response to the needs of her school population. Not a longtime practitioner, but a beginner, Dr. Dangerfield's initiation to mindful leadership practice is suggestive about how to begin, how to fit mindfulness practices into a very busy life, and why it's beneficial to a school leader, even if it means getting up a few minutes earlier every morning to do it.

As an assistant principal at a school in southern coastal Florida that serves a population of children who are often struggling with English as a second language, or not living with a biological parent, and are economically challenged—more than 90% receive free or reduced lunches—mindfulness practice for third to fifth graders was not an easy sell to her parent population. "In this neighborhood, mindfulness is completely outside the box. But as a leader, you do anything you can to help your children," Leslie said, as she described how she got started in a mindfulness practice for her students, and inadvertently for herself.

When a guidance counselor at the school first suggested mindfulness practices for staff overwhelmed with the daily stresses of work, Leslie was intrigued. A weekly MBSR (mindfulness-based stress-reduction) training program soon began for interested staff—at no cost. Unfortunately, however, the school's MBSR training program occurred right after school—a time when Leslie wasn't able to participate due to her administrative duties. She did, however, practice on her own, using the resources provided to staff participating in the school's MBSR program. "I started taking the CDs of the meditations home with me at night and listening to them. I began to notice a real difference when I began using them regularly. Starting independently with the guided meditations at the University of California at Los Angeles (UCLA) Mindful Awareness Research Center with Megan Cowan,[47] Leslie also watched the videos of "introduction to mindful awareness" by Diana Winston on the UCLA site.[48] "I had to find the teacher/leader meditation voice that was right for me, and the practices that worked for me. Being a very busy school administrator, with a 24-hour job and three kids, I also had to find a time of day that I could do this."

Most mornings, very early in the morning, Leslie now gets up and meditates before school. "I try to do this every morning, a minimum of two to three times a week for about 10 or 15 minutes. When I first started, I needed all the guidance and the talking, and then more and more I wanted less talking, and more quiet. At first, the full body scan [see Mindfulness Practice Aid 2.3, "The Body Scan: Mindful Awareness of the Body," page 62] was too much for me, and then I started focusing on parts of the body myself, on my own."

What are the big benefits Leslie notices in herself? "I find myself enjoying the peace, and seeking more of it. I find that it's easier for me to focus on what's important, and to let things go that used to bother me . . . you know, laundry, carpooling kids, cooking. It's reduced my headaches and made me more peaceful."

Feeling the personal benefits, she sought additional information to improve her practice. After watching the *Room to Breathe* video from Mindful Schools, she decided to try to expand mindfulness training further at her own school. She wrote a grant to the local school board, which approved it, Leslie says, because its benefits were tied directly to students. She received the grant and was on her way, slowly seeing results with her school's students in the pilot program. "Some kids don't get it, and some do. But really, the message is that you'd do anything to help your kids, and this is important work for us.

"I'm a learner," says Leslie. "Around here, mindfulness is very outside the box. But we think it's worth doing. And for me, personally, it's been very rewarding."

Leslie Dangerfield, PhD, is a school administrator with over twenty years of experience in public schools. She resides in Florida with her husband and three children.

1.3: Ben Marcune, Chemistry Teacher

Alexander Hamilton Preparatory Academy, Elizabeth, New Jersey

"Mindfulness is like a buffer zone between the situation and my response. It gives me a moment to reflect, to notice the gut sense in my body. I come back to my breath, to myself. I check in with myself; then, I know what to do."

Ben Marcune has been a longtime friend, and as we were thinking of people who truly embody mindfulness—the capacity to stay present and focused, with a quiet calm, a true quality of acceptance of whatever shows up in life—we just knew that he should be a part of this book.

We spoke to Ben on a rainy Sunday afternoon. He had just completed five hours of work preparing for the week ahead: reviewing lesson plans, grading papers, making up for the time he spent the day before at an all-day mindfulness retreat offered by a local group in Philadelphia.

Ben begins by talking about his school and the students. He is a chemistry teacher at Alexander Hamilton Preparatory Academy in Elizabeth, New Jersey, a working-class immigrant community. His students are 85% Hispanic, 10% African American, and 5% other designations. We can almost feel the soft-

ness in his voice as he describes "his kids," the students. "They come to me with no math or science skills. They struggle with arithmetic, problem solving, reading, and writing. I have to work on very basic skills just to get them to the point to learn science.

"I'm a new teacher. This is a midlife career change. I spent 17 years as a chemist at Merck, and was laid off. By chance, I ran into a friend who suggested that I might want to apply my science skills in the classroom, teaching kids. I had volunteered a few summers earlier, teaching music for students in my daughter's middle school class, and had a ball. I just knew that teaching was right for me.

"I started practicing meditation with Chan Master Sheng Yen in Corona, Queens, New York, and when I moved to New Jersey, I looked for a place to continue practicing. Meditation gave me so much inner peace of mind in what was a really crazy lifestyle. Music, too, has been a huge part of my life. I have always loved playing guitar, writing music, and improvising with other musicians. Being a musical artist requires a high degree of sensitivity, and being very present. Mindfulness has only heightened my ability as a musician.

"I started practicing mindfulness in 1997 when I met a local group, and I guess you can sense that I am an intuitive person, so again, I just knew this [teaching] was right for me. At the time, I was working at Merck and my life was filled with tremendous stress and pressure, and a lot of fear of layoffs." Ben's voice trails off a bit, recalling the mental and physical toll of his work.

"Mindfulness is huge in helping me realize that everything I do and say can have a profound impact on my kids. Because of mindfulness, I am very aware of my response to my students. I've trained myself to notice my state of mind in any moment, and to minimize negative habits and responses. Mindfulness is like a buffer zone between the situation and my response. It gives me a moment to reflect, to notice the gut sense in my body. I come back to my breath, to myself. I check in with myself; then, I know what to do."

The years of practice and study of mindfulness shine through these words, like a ray of light through cracks in old floorboards, and we sense that this isn't just an idea, a notion for Ben, but, instead, is a way of life.

"About half my job as a teacher is teaching chemistry. The other half is doing my best to motivate and inspire my kids. My work isn't just a paycheck. I give my all to these kids. And, yes, some days, I am totally drained, and yet, it's worth it. I know I have touched them. More importantly, mindfulness has helped me appreciate each student. To be mindful is to be mindful of each person, to really see each person. I have a lot of compassion for these students, for their lives."

Formerly a research chemist for Merck & Co., Ben Marcune now teaches high school chemistry at an inner city high school in Elizabeth, New Jersey. He is also a schooled musician who loves to write, record, and perform his original material. Ben has had a Zen Buddhist practice for over twenty years, studying with Zen Masters Sheng Yen and Thich Nhat Hanh, and has been actualizing the practice through his music and caring for his students.

1.4: Miles Dunmore, English Teacher

The American School in London, United Kingdom

"I am most interested in teacher development, having teachers develop an authentic teaching presence inside and outside

the classroom. This means supporting teachers to cultivate a compassionate and yet firm persona. Because the practice of mindfulness enables us to understand ourselves more deeply and feel more solid and with that more relaxed, the benefits transmit readily to the classroom and the students."

We met Miles Dunmore during Wake Up Schools, an international retreat and course for educators, led by Thich Nhat

Hanh in Barcelona, Spain. Wake Up Schools, an initiative launched by Nhat Hanh and the international Plum Village community, provides educators, students, parents, and the entire school community with mindfulness programs to promote and support a happy and healthy school environment. Miles, along with Pilar Aguilera mentioned in Chapter 2 page 72, is among the leading proponents of mindfulness in Europe. During the retreat, Miles served as a panelist along with Pilar, speaking to an audience of more than 600 educators from throughout Spain to talk about his work as a school leader and about mindfulness in schools. We spoke to Miles just after breakfast while at the University of Barcelona during the five-day Wake Up Schools course.

Miles beams high energy and immediately captures our attention with his boyish enthusiasm and quick British wit. His passion for mindfulness and education, his focused attention from years of practice of mindfulness, and his clarity are apparent and a total delight. On this bright, clear spring morning in Spain, we begin our interview with Miles. He speaks openly about mindfulness and school leadership.

"The work of teachers like Thich Nhat Hanh, Jon Kabat-Zinn, and the Dalai Lama, has laid a strong foundation for mindfulness in schools. Advances in neuroscience have created legitimacy and have opened the door to the possibility of bringing mindfulness into schools. Science now clearly demonstrates the benefits of this approach not just for students and teachers, but for leaders too. We are leaning into a paradigm shift with new discoveries in neuroscience showing how mindfulness affects the workings of the brain and the body, and so learning.

"I first began practicing mindfulness 20 years ago when I worked as a school department head in the United States, where I lived for 17 years. I read a lot about mindfulness, especially books by Thich Nhat Hanh, as well as other teachers. I learned simple mindfulness techniques mainly from the Tibetan tradition. I moved back to London in 2001 and found an established mindfulness community or *sangha*, the Heart of London Sangha, which is still vigorous and growing today. My weekly mindfulness meditation practice with this group is indispensible. I find practice with a group to be foundational. As a long-time department head, some things have become very clear to me. It is important to have a firm understanding of where to take a department and to have really good people skills. But most importantly, my job as a school leader is to inspire and motivate teachers and others in the school community to teach and lead from their most authentic selves and to encourage teachers to develop a classroom presence that is authentic. I found great resources for this in mindfulness practices.

"I am most interested in teacher development, having teachers develop an authentic teaching presence inside and outside the classroom. This means supporting teachers to cultivate a compassionate and yet firm persona. Because the practice of mindfulness enables us to understand ourselves more deeply and feel more solid and with that more relaxed, the benefits transmit readily to the classroom and to the students."

Miles adjusts his seat to avoid the direct, bright sunlight and then continues, his clear blue eyes full of vibrancy. We sense his urgency and passion with each word.

"School leadership demands time and energy. It is complex and requires a constant balancing of constituencies. The development of a personal mindfulness meditation practice gives school leaders a little more space and a little more time. The interesting thing is that taking time for mindfulness makes school leaders feel as if they have more time, not less. And, this translates into greater pleasure in the work and less tension.

"Mindfulness improves our social skills, our ability to relate to others. As school leaders, our interactions with teachers, parents, and students can be tense and pressure filled, but with mindfulness we have a greater ability to calm ourselves, to ease tension within our bodies and minds, and that affects how we interact with others.

"It's really clear to me that with greater appreciation of mindfulness for school leaders, teachers, and students, for the entire school community, we will promote global understanding and prepare students to achieve in a rapidly changing and very complex world, and in the process to live their lives more fully and in a way that makes them feel more free."

Miles has taught in state and independent schools in the United Kingdom and in the United States. A department head for many years, he has a deep interest in how teachers form their teaching selves and in how they deal with challenge and stress. In 2012, he was one of the planners for the United Kingdom Educators' Retreat led by Thich Nhat Hanh. As well as teaching, he now works with educators in building supportive communities together, both as fellow professionals and within their schools.

Please visit us on Facebook at https://www.facebook.com/TheMindfulSchoolLeader.

2

The Science of Mindfulness

"When your mind changes, your brain changes too. . . . And what happens in your brain changes your mind, since the brain and mind are a single, integrated system."

—Richard Hanson, PhD, *Buddha's Brain* (2009)[1]

Practice Snapshot: A School Leader Practicing Mindfulness

Ryan Is Fast

We were in an initial coaching meeting with Ryan, a first-year principal at a suburban middle school in Cleveland, Ohio. We noticed that he was speaking very rapidly, so rapidly we had a hard time keeping up. "Sometimes my wife tells me she can't understand me on the phone," he quipped. Ryan was also a fast meeting chair and observer, and he was a *really, really, really* fast walker as he strode around the building with sparks flying off his shoes (practically). He took pride in working 12- to 14-hour days back when he was a teacher ("If that's what the work requires," he'd say with a tight smile), and now he rarely took vacations, even over the winter and spring breaks. He texted and emailed his teachers until late at night, and Google chatted after midnight with staff. His staff told us they often felt they were underperforming if they left the building before 7 p.m. He prided himself on needing little rest or sleep to keep it all going. While he was excited about the new Common Core and instructional rounds initiatives he had recently brought to his school, he was breathless and described the time leading up to our meeting as "intensely overwhelming." One of his first observations about himself was, "Sometimes I feel like I can't find my breath."

The Science of Mindfulness

Mindfulness and the Brain

In recent years, there has been an explosion of scientific research on mindfulness due to advances in technology that allow scientists to obtain clear, sharp images of the brain and its activity, while at rest, in meditation, and during complex thinking. Contemplative neuroscience, a new and rapidly developing area of the scientific study of how contemplative practices affect the brain and the nervous system, offers convincing evidence on the science behind the practice of mindfulness.[2]

WANT TO KNOW MORE ABOUT CONTEMPLATIVE NEUROSCIENCE?

If you want to learn more about contemplative neuroscience, start with this great 47-minute webinar from the Center for Contemplative Mind in Society at http://vimeo.com/13179421.

Neuroplasticity Defined

Neuroplasticity refers to the brain's ability to change its pattern and structure throughout our lifetime. Your brain is shaped by your environment, your experience, and your beliefs; it is continually maturing and changing. Scientists refer to our brains as "experience-dependent"— meaning they are affected by the experiences we have, even well into adulthood.[3]

The old assumption was that our brains stopped growing by late childhood and started to decline around age 25. We now know that both of these ideas are wrong. Dr. Richard J. Davidson, professor of psychology and psychiatry at the University of Wisconsin–Madison as well as founder and chair of the

Center for Investigating Healthy Minds, has been a major force in the field of neuroscience. In his book, *The Emotional Life of Your Brain*, together with co-author Sharon Begley, he describes how your experiences, mental activity, thinking, and motivation continually change your brain. How you think, and what you experience day to day, can actually change the brain's physical structure. For school leaders, this means that the environment we co-create with teachers, parents, staff, and the entire school community shapes us.

An often-cited study of London's black taxi cab drivers shows how. These cabbies are required to remember the over 25,000 London streets and hundreds of places of interest. The hippocampus is a region of the brain responsible for visual-spatial information and for consolidating short-term memory into long-term memory. When they examined it for this study, researchers found that the hippocampus in the brains of these cabbies was larger than that in the non–taxi drivers' brains, and that the longer one worked as a cabbie, the larger his hippocampus.[4] A similar study published in the journal *Nature* in 2004 showed increased tissue in the brain region controlling spatial perception after several weeks of training in juggling.[5]

The scientific literature makes clear, over and over again, that what matters is not only our experience, but our *thoughts about* our experiences. For some, this notion may be hard to believe: that our brains can change based on our thoughts. Again, Davidson cites in *The Emotional Life of Your Brain* an extraordinary Harvard study in which a group of volunteers learned a simple five-finger piano piece, practicing it repeatedly with their right hand. Using neuroimaging, the scientists determined that the motor cortex was responsible for moving the fingers, finding that the practice correlated with activity in this brain region. The scientists then had the other half of the volunteers merely *imagine* playing the notes. The control group did not touch a piano. The researchers measured the motor cortex and discovered that the region of the brain that controls the fingers of the right hand had changed in these "virtual pianists" just as it had in those who actually played the piano. Amazingly, thinking alone had increased the space in the motor cortex devoted to this specific function.[6]

As most of us in education know, the past 25 years have also seen a neurobiological revolution in the understanding of how the mind, body, and brain work together and function. As Rick Hanson wryly observed in a podcast for Sounds True back in 2009, "We've learned more about the human brain in the last 20 years than we have in the last 200."[7] One of the great scientific revolutions of our times is the stunning advancement in understanding the workings of the human brain over the last three decades.[8] As thousands of publications and neurocognitive studies demonstrate, **we are rapidly gaining insights into the relationships between what we think and how we perform, see the world, feel, and are prompted to act. We think this is part of the next revolution in the design of learning.**

Think About It

A study published in the May 2011 issue of *NeuroImage* suggests that the continual practice of focusing and refocusing our attention—as is done in mindfulness meditation—increases brain connectivity. Researchers at the University of California–Los Angeles compared the brain activity of volunteers who had finished eight weeks of mindfulness-based stress-reduction (MBSR) training with that of volunteers who did not do the training. Brain scans showed stronger connections in several regions of the meditators' brains—especially those regions associated with attention and auditory and visual processing.[9]

At Massachusetts General Hospital, researchers used MRI scans to document before and after changes in the brain's gray matter—where neurons reside—associated with mindfulness meditation. The density of gray matter increased in regions involved in such distinctly different activities as memory, self-awareness, and compassion, and decreased in the amygdala—a part of the brain that can grow with fear and stress.[10]

Stress: A Public Health Risk for Educators

"For me, I've returned to the stressful state of mind. I've got classes almost every day in summertime educational institutions to study math, physics, and chemistry of high school . . . in advance. Maybe it sounds quite unusual for you, but many students do that in order to get more prepared when they enter the next grade."

—15-year-old student from Shanghai, China (2013). Quoted with permission.

We met this student during a 12-day teen mindfulness and leadership summer program at an elite boarding school in the Northeast. We were co-leading the program, and this student was one of many from all over the world. On his return to China, the student shared this message with us. The program was an opportunity for high-achieving teens to experiment with the application of mindfulness in their daily lives, practicing mindful speaking and listening, body awareness, and mindful eating and walking.

Many students come to the United States seeking the advantages of our elite college and university system. Some bear the stress of hyper-competitive cultural environments and come from families that highly value academic success. While these students bring diversity and in some cases much-needed tuition dollars, they also present opportunities for school leaders in understanding these diverse cultures, fostering welcoming environments, and helping these students grow and succeed.

School life and daily living is filled with stressors: a budget crisis, a difficult teacher or student, a delayed flight, losing one's job. Since these daily stressors cannot be avoided, our task as leaders is to change our relationship to stress. Stress is a big deal in the United States: The National Institute of Mental Health (2010)[11] reported that approximately 50 million American adults suffer from anxiety disorders. According to the *New York Times*, diagnosing anxiety and stress is a massive business in the United States, as most of us are aware; for example, doctors wrote 48.7 million prescriptions for Xanax, an anti-anxiety drug, in 2012.[12]

A stressor is anything that takes you out of a state of balance, or homeostasis. The stress response is the body's attempt to reestablish homeostasis. Research nearly 70 years ago by Hans Selye, the godfather of stress physiology, showed that the stress response in humans can be activated not only by physical and psychological events, but also by just thinking about them. Selye developed a three-part view of how the stress response works.[13]

1. The first part of the stress response is the initial alarm stage when your brain notes stress, activating the sympathetic nervous system and the cascade of stress hormones, such as adrenaline and cortisol. Your heart rate and breathing increase.

2. Second, in the adaptation or resistance stage, your body mobilizes the stress response system and seeks to recover balance, and this process is allostasis.

3. Selye calls the third stage, where stress-related disease emerges, *exhaustion,* because hormones secreted during the stress response have depleted the body. You are essentially left with little defense against disease. At this stage, the stress response can become more damaging than the stress itself, especially when the stress is purely psychologica1.[14]

Stressors: When Your Brain Is "Hijacked"

Our brain is constantly evaluating whether it is safe, and we are hardwired to detect stressors. The brain's sentinel, the amygdala, is constantly scanning the brain for threats, and the amygdala is set for a hair-trigger response. When the amygdala is activated, it hijacks the brain, focusing your attention on the threat. With your attention captured by the perceived threat, you have difficulty focusing on work demands. Your ability to think clearly is hijacked, too, so it's hard to innovate and think creatively. And your ability to remember suffers, too. When your brain is hijacked, you rely on overused habits, returning to the way you have responded to threats over and over again. Again, MRIs show that when a person's attention is hijacked, his or her brain flooded with these stress hormones, the amygdala and the prefrontal cortex are highly active.

The body responds in full-blown alarm with the "fight-flight-or-freeze" response (a term coined by physiologist Walter Bradford Cannon), with the amygdala setting off the sympathetic nervous system (SNS) and the hypothalamic-pituitary-adrenal axis (HPAA), flooding the body with stress hormones, mainly cortisol and adrenaline.[15] Obviously, this chain reaction is destructive and sets you up for real problems. It gets worse: Because the amygdala is set for a hair-trigger response, it's often wrong. The amygdala works instantly based on limited information. Other parts of the brain take longer to analyze incoming information. With this incomplete picture, we're prone to mistakes and to incorrect assumptions, leading to overreaction. Again, Dan Goleman in his book *The Brain and Emotional Intelligence: New Insights* points out the top amygdala triggers at work:

- Being treated with disrespect and condescension,
- Being treated unfairly,
- Being underappreciated,
- Feeling that you are not listened to, and
- Being held to unrealistic deadlines.[16]

In our work globally with school leaders, we know many who contend with one or more of these triggers every day, setting them up for chronic stress and anxiety. Given the uncertainty of school budgets and mounting performance pressures, these school leaders may live in a state of chronic flooding, a low-grade hijacking of the amygdala. The result is a very different scenario than when someone is passionate about his or her work. Emotional hijacking is the equivalent to living life close to the boiling point.

When too much cortisol is released, it can damage the brain and the body, whether it is triggered in response to an actual, immediate threat or as a consequence of pathological anxiety. Repeated activation of the SNS and the HPAA further sensitizes the amygdala, increasing rapid arousal and situational anxiety; such continued overstimulation can lead to debilitating chronic anxiety that damages brain and body tissue regardless of context. Frequent SNS/HPAA activation doesn't just exhaust the amygdala; it also wears down the hippocampus, which, as mentioned above, is critical to efficient "storage" of memories.[17] In addition to making us more forgetful, chronic stress increases the risk of contracting diseases; or, if you already have a disease, it increases the risk of the disease overwhelming your body's natural defenses.[18]

Stress-Related Diseases

In his book *Why Zebras Don't Get Ulcers,* biologist Robert M. Sapolsky from Stanford gives the following example to illustrate the use—and misuse—of stress.[19] Think of how a lion in the jungle, chasing its prey, or a zebra running for its life engages physiological mechanisms perfectly suited to deal with short-term stressors in contextually appropriate situations. For the vast majority of animals, stress is a short-term physical crisis: eat or be eaten. For humans, however, constant worry and rumination about life's stressors—work, family relationships, money, traffic, school performance—can activate the same physiological responses, but with dangerous consequences because of their chronic nature. Worry and rumination are examples of low-grade emotional hijacking of the amygdala. Sapolsky notes that disease emerges primarily as a result of the over-activation of physiological systems that have evolved to respond to acute physical emergencies, but have instead been operating on overdrive for days or months at a time. Constant worrying about our retirement plans, relationships, and mortgages, for example, is a consequence of overstimulated mechanisms for managing short-term threats and emergencies. And this doesn't just happen in adults. Our children are worrying, too: about succeeding in school, dealing with bullies, or living stressful home lives.

The Body When Leaders Freeze Under Stress

As leaders, we have all had those deer-in-the-headlights moments, whether we're frozen or boiling-hot mad. We are overloaded with stress hormones (adrenaline, cortisol, and norepinephrine) that flood the prefrontal cortex (PFC). The PFC, informally known as the "thinking brain" or "executive center," controls executive functions, such as problem solving, impulse management, working memory, regulation of attention and focus, complex reasoning, flexibility of response, and cognitive control. The thinking brain's role involves determining what tasks are important to execute, why, and how. The PFC coordinates with the basal ganglia to activate memories that may be relevant to the task at hand, for example, and also networks with the motor cortex to plan and execute physical movements.[20]

Intense stressors can activate a kind of seesaw reaction. When you start feeling the freeze, your limbic system (the emotional center of the brain, also known as the "social brain") is alerting the body to go into the fight-flight-or-freeze response. Stress hormones activated by emotional drivers—take, for example, the perception of "not being treated fairly"—trigger the fight-flight-or-freeze response, which floods the prefrontal cortex with adrenaline, cortisol, and norepinephrine. This process severely distorts higher-level thinking. As the seesaw "goes up" on one side through the onset of stress hormones and emotional drivers, the other side of the seesaw "goes down"; consequently, the rational brain becomes less effective as it is compromised by the fight-flight-or-freeze process. This impedes access to data in long-term memory, thereby freezing the ability to form and articulate fluid, coherent thoughts. The harder a stressed-out leader tries to overcome this reaction, the stronger the emotional drivers become as they push on the PFC's ability to find and access the information that would alleviate the situation. In this state, the leader forgets what he or she was trying to say or do; such leaders may turn to avoiding stimulation and shut down completely.

Mindfulness Alleviates Stress in the Body and Mind

"The only thing that interferes with my learning is my education."

—Albert Einstein, quoted from Gandhi Smriti, New Delhi, India (2014)[21]

Over the past decade, a large number of rigorously designed studies—many using advanced neural imaging—have provided compelling evidence that mindfulness-based contemplative practice reduces psychological stress and improves mental and physical health. Mindfulness helps in alleviating depression, anxiety, loneliness, and chronic pain.[22]

Treatment of these conditions through mindfulness-based interventions is now extremely well documented in research institutes throughout the United States and worldwide. In 1982, the first peer-reviewed scientific paper about mindfulness meditation for chronic pain patients was published in *General Hospital Psychiatry* by Jon Kabat-Zinn, based on data gathered in the first years of the Stress Reduction Program at the University of Massachusetts Medical School. This program, founded in 1979 by Kabat-Zinn and described in Chapter 1, page 21, has conducted extensive randomized clinical trials and laboratory studies on the effects of its classic eight-week course in mindfulness-based stress reduction (MBSR). These studies, which have been published and reported in peer-reviewed journals, demonstrate the effectiveness of mindfulness-based training for a wide range of conditions. In a very early and compelling study conducted at the University of Massachusetts Medical School, a group of 22 medical patients with diagnosed anxiety disorder participated in the eight-week MBSR course. The study concluded "significant improvement in subjective and objective symptoms of anxiety and panic" after the eight-week stress reduction course. Follow-up research conducted three years later on these patients showed that they continued to practice mindfulness-based interventions.[23]

One important key to alleviating stress and the consequent emotional hijacking of the amygdala is the ability to notice—in other words, to pay attention to how you are feeling physically, mentally, and emotionally in the present moment; to stop, pause, breathe, and recognize in the moment that you are in the midst of a mental meltdown. If you are unaware that you are being carried away by feelings of being overwhelmed—if you cannot detect that your heart is racing and your palms are getting sweaty, or that you are feeling really edgy—it's very hard to regain emotional balance. The emotional hijacking may run its course, often leading to actions that you may regret later.

Goleman says in his book *The Brain and Emotional Intelligence: New Insights* that these emotional hijackings can last from a few seconds to hours, days, weeks, or months. Throughout this book, we will offer you tools that you can use in real time to counteract an emotional hijacking, regardless of how long it lasts. A commonsense and oft-cited suggestion—in addition to stopping, pausing, and breathing (see Mindfulness Practice Aid 1.1, "Stopping, Pausing, and Observing," page 35)—is to notice your thinking. Later in the book—see Mindfulness Practice Aid 3.1, "Mindful Sitting With Awareness of Thoughts and Feelings," in Chapter 3, page 83, and the "Managing 'Negative' Emotions" section in Chapter 4, page 119—we talk about the power of your emotions; we have already mentioned how thinking alone can contribute to feeling stressed and anxious. Notice your mind-speak: Are your thoughts in the nature of repetitive rumination, perpetual worrying, and catastrophizing? We've already established that the process of thinking, so often considered to be fleeting and ethereal, can actually result in changes to the structure of the brain. How are *your* thoughts affecting *your* body?

We could devote this entire book to the hundreds of empirical studies and theoretical papers that demonstrate how mindfulness training changes not only your mental state of mind, but also the physical structure of your brain. Here we've listed just a few of the many scientific studies:

- Mindfulness practice increases brain tissue in the insula, a part of the brain that supports self-awareness and empathy for the emotions of others, and in the PFC which helps regulate emotions.[24]
- Mindfulness practice alters activation of the PFC.[25]
- Mindfulness practice reduces activation in the amygdala in response to negative emotions.[26]
- A 2013 report published in *School Psychology Quarterly* (and also referenced in Appendix E, online, page 29) found that teachers who participated in a mindfulness program were better able to manage their classes and to build relationships with students.[27]

This literature calls on school leaders to holistically broaden and deepen our thinking about teaching and learning. As learning is a lifelong process, school leaders can profit from understanding the science of the brain in service of educational leadership. Increasingly, school leaders are called to take in "the big picture" and to reexamine some of the assumptions (now outdated) that have guided instructional design in conventional educational settings for decades. The kind of big-picture engagement that has been the signature of Big Picture schools is now borne out by neuroscientific data, as described by Elliot Washor and Charles Mojkowski. They call for a new reengagement with students and a reexamination of their expectations.[28]

This global picture means understanding the human implications of education not only in terms of curricular and pedagogical theory but also in terms of the very real health and vitality of the basic work of teaching and learning: listening, observing, focusing, reflecting, and so forth. If our brains are shaped by our thoughts and our thoughts catalyze action, it is imperative that we as school leaders recognize and respect the deep and real power of our thoughts. The success of our schools will not be built on antiquated models of learning, but instead will emerge from an approach that honors the whole person. The mind and the intellect cannot be separated from the heart and the spirit. As we come to understand the relationship between how our brain functions and how it is shaped by our thoughts and our actions, we come to a deeper understanding of educating the whole person: body, mind, and spirit. We come to appreciate that learning is rooted not just in the mind but in the heart and that both are interconnected.

We invite you to review Appendix E, online, page 29, for a summary of selected research studies on mindfulness in educational settings.

Neuroscience and Leadership—Using Mindfulness Practices When You Are Stressed Out

"Neuroleadership" is an emerging field of study connecting neuroscientific knowledge with innovative work in the fields of leadership development, management training, and change management, and by consultants and coaches. This cutting-edge science employs what we now know about the brain in order to strengthen leaders' abilities to manage themselves and others, and to influence and motivate others. The NeuroLeadership Institute is a leading force in this area; it helps individuals, teams, and organizations fulfill their potential through a better understanding of how the human brain functions. Mindfulness practices are at the center of a growing movement to bring neuroscientific understanding to the practice of leadership and leadership development. For instance, the Center for Creative Leadership, a national organization at the forefront of leadership development in the United States, describes one of the most significant evolutions in leadership training as the development of neurocognitive practices that help support leaders in calming the fight-flight-or-freeze reactions physiologically programmed into our human bodies. The capacity to regulate your emotions in the moment, to know what you are feeling when you are feeling it, and not to be carried away by strong or difficult emotions not only forms the basis for self-care, but is the basis for wise and skillful action. The center's 2011–2012 annual report notes that the definitions of "leadership support" may increasingly include "a greater emphasis on 'self-support.'"[29] Mindfulness practices can provide daily support and buffer against feeling overwhelmed or helpless.

Let's return again to Ryan, our first-year principal in suburban Cleveland, who over time had developed the unconscious habit of holding his breath. At the copier, while texting and emailing, Ryan held his breath without realizing it, as if bracing himself for the worst. He was unconsciously restricting his breathing by tightening his stomach, leading to bouts of anxiety and stomach pain. Many people hold their breath, or breathe very shallowly, while working or playing in front of a screen, and it is actually a widespread problem. This phenomenon, dubbed "email apnea" by former Microsoft executive Linda Stone (also quoted in Chapter 1, pages 21–22), has been reported in the *Huffington Post* and *New York Times*.[30] This unconscious behavior contributes to stress-related disease. We recommended several practices promoted by the NeuroLeadership Institute to help Ryan learn to slow down, calm his hyper-alert brain, and breathe more fully and consciously. Working with these practices, over time, Ryan gradually became aware of the moments preceding the onset of high stress; he was able to remind himself to take deep breaths into his diaphragm to calm himself.

Behind the breath holding, there is often an intense sense of feeling overwhelmed. We know from our work with school leaders globally that this sense of feeling overwhelmed is a central feature of many school leaders' lives and has truly toxic physical consequences. By developing the capacity to notice how he is feeling in the moment, when he is holding his breath, Ryan began training himself to be more conscious of his body, his habits, and his self-care practices—not in a narcissistic, navel-gazing way—but to acknowledge himself with kind esteem and know that constantly pushing himself won't make him feel good, or lead well. A key element of authentic leadership is being present, and for Ryan, an important element of being present was to recognize that his body was having negative reactions to his thoughts so he could consciously work with it.

Learning to be present, through repeated practice, eventually builds your capacity to notice your wandering attention, bringing it back to where you want it to be, and to be more responsive to your wishes and needs. The capacity to bear witness to your thoughts and emotions, to be a witness instead of an immediate and unconscious reactor, is the essence of mindfulness practice. It is no small matter to recognize and know your state of mind: feelings of edginess, anger, impatience, or contentment; or to know and recognize the state of your body: exhaustion, imbalance, or feeling energized. And, mindfulness is not simply about recognizing these states of mind—these states of your body that are constantly changing; it is also about managing the tendency to mentally grasp onto, push away, or zone out of what is happening in order to feel something different. It is powerful to know what you are feeling as you are feeling it, and not to be lost, overwhelmed, or attached to the thought or emotion. To acknowledge an emotion or a thought, and not be imprisoned by it or cling to it, is like opening a door to freedom—you begin to change your relationship with yourself. And this has huge benefits for leaders, such as enhancing focus and attention, self-awareness, flexibility, and authenticity especially.

Mindfulness of breathing helped Ryan train himself to bring his attention back to where he wanted it. Ryan became better at noticing when he was distracted or holding his breath and then at either bringing his mind back to the task at hand or remembering to breathe. He noticed a greater capacity to be aware, to be focused in everyday tasks. And he observed that during routine tasks he could maintain focus and really concentrate better. This practice and others serve as a mental bench press for the brain's breaking system, the ventro-lateral prefrontal cortex (VLPFC). Mindfulness builds concentration, which supports focused awareness. When you are mindful, you are concentrated. If you are interested in exploring a practice, our recommendation is to begin slowly, with modest amounts of time, and to gradually build up the length of time you spend practicing mindfulness meditation. Obviously, the best time to start is *before* you experience intense stress!

Practice Pause

Shall we try a short meditation? We invite you to close the book and allow your eyes to close gently. Become aware of your breathing and locate where you feel the breath. Place your attention on your breathing. Feel the breath from the moment you notice it come into the body until the moment you notice it go out of the body. Breathe in this way for a few rounds of in- and out-breaths. When you are finished, open your eyes and stretch gently, and notice how you feel.

Mindfulness Practice Aids

Mindfulness Practices: Breathing and the Body Scan

"He who feels it knows it more."

—Bob Marley

Here are several breathing practices to help you alleviate stress, to bring greater awareness to how you are breathing and feeling sensation in the body, and to restore calm. We suggest you use one of the mindfulness timers listed in Appendix C, online, page 17, when trying out these practices.

Mindfulness Practice Aid 2.1: One-Minute Focused Breathing Practice

If you don't have three minutes (see Mindfulness Practice Aid 1.2, "Three-Minute Focused Breathing Practice," page 35), try this abbreviated practice.

- Sit in a comfortable, dignified posture, with the spine straight but not rigid, in a quiet place, and bring your attention and focus to the physical sensation of breathing.
- Allow your eyes to be open or closed—notice what feels most comfortable.
- Bring your attention to the movement of the belly as you breathe.
- Open and close your hands to the movement of the in- and out-breaths.
- Open your hands when the breath goes out of the body, and close your hands when the breath comes in the body.
- Align your hand movements to the rise and fall of your belly, again opening your hands when you breathe out and closing your hands when you breathe in.
- Allow your movements to be very small, and enlarge them if you like.
- When your mind wanders, gently and firmly escort your attention back to the direct, sensory experiences of breathing and moving your hands.
- Avoid making yourself into a failure when you become distracted; instead, generate a feeling of being OK and accepting yourself as you are.

- Simply note that your mind has wandered, and pivot your attention back to the sensation of breathing and moving your hands.
- Practice in this way for one minute daily.
- When you are finished, stretch in any way that is comfortable for you and open your eyes if they are closed.

Mindfulness Practice Aid 2.2:
30-Second Focused Breathing Practice

If you don't have one minute (see Mindfulness Practice Aid 2.1, "One-Minute Focused Breathing Practice," page 60), try this 30-second practice several times daily.

- Sit in a comfortable, dignified posture, with the spine straight but not rigid, in a quiet place, and bring your attention and focus to the physical sensation of breathing.
- Allow your eyes to be open or closed—notice what feels most comfortable.
- Place one hand on your belly and the other hand on your chest.
- Feel the sensations in your body where your hands meet the chest and the belly.
- Feel the sensations of the rise and the fall of the belly, and feel the rise and fall of the chest.
- Observe and feel the expansion and contraction of the chest as the air enters and exits the body.
- Move your hands from the belly and the chest to the sides of the body, feeling the intercostal muscles, the tiny muscles in between the ribs.
- Feel the gentle expansion and contraction of the ribs.
- Feel the movement of the sidewalls of the chest.
- When your mind wanders, gently and firmly escort your attention back to the direct, sensory experiences of breathing and feeling your hands.
- Avoid making yourself into a failure when you become distracted; instead, generate a feeling of being OK and accepting yourself as you are.
- Simply note that your mind has wandered, and pivot your attention back to the sensation of breathing and feeling your hands.
- Continue this practice for 30 seconds.
- When you are finished, stretch in any way that is comfortable for you and open your eyes if they are closed.

We acknowledge and are grateful to the work of Donna Farhi, an internationally recognized registered movement therapist and yoga teacher whose work emphasizes breathing and movement, for the basic framework of these breathing exercises in *The Breathing Book*.[31]

Mindfulness Practice Aid 2.3:
The Body Scan: Mindful Awareness of the Body

The body scan is a foundational mindfulness practice to cultivate present-moment awareness of bodily sensation, and to cultivate a sense of self-care, kindness, and appreciation of the body. It can be done while sitting, standing, or lying down. Please choose the posture that works for you. Although many people practice the body scan lying down, it can easily be done sitting in a chair. If you practice the body scan in the seated posture, the instructions are similar to those below, which are geared toward the lying-down position.

The body scan is time set aside just for you to be with and for yourself. In our hectic lives, this is a gift of time and gentle attention. The instructions to the body scan below are lengthy, and we invite you to visit our Facebook page at www.facebook.com/TheMindful SchoolLeader for a free body scan download. Alternatively, record the instructions yourself.

By directing your attention from one part of the body to another, this foundational mindfulness practice cultivates greater flexibility of attention and awareness. In the body scan, you will build a sense of awareness and acceptance of your body, which aids in identification of sensations—pleasant, unpleasant, and neutral. With regular practice of the body scan, you expand your body's vocabulary, more readily identifying sensations, emotions, and feelings.

When you practice the body scan, the point is not to strive to feel calm or relaxed, for example, or to rid yourself of pain or discomfort. This may happen as a fruit of the practice, but the point is not to set a goal and strive after it, and then beat yourself up or feel like a failure if you don't succeed. In teaching the body scan to school leaders and others, we acknowledge the tension from trying to make something happen even if that something is feeling relaxed. Instead, with the body scan, you listen and learn from the body. You are cultivating a sense of acceptance—of openness to what is, a quality of allowing things to be as they are—and of connecting deeply with yourself. The body scan can be practiced in an abbreviated form for 3 to 5 minutes, or in an extended form for 30 to 45 minutes. The challenge with this practice is to remain awake and aware. But again, if you do fall asleep, don't make yourself into a failure. Be gentle and forgiving with yourself, as this is time set aside just for you. Try this practice of the body scan in the lying-down or seated posture:

- Find a quiet, safe place where you will not be disturbed.
- Lie or sit down in a way that is comfortable.
- Allow the head, neck, and torso to be in alignment.
- Close your eyes, if that is comfortable.
- Allow your arms to rest by your sides, or if you are seated in a chair, allow your arms to rest comfortably in your lap.
- Allow your feet to turn outward naturally, or if seated in a chair, allow the soles of the feet to be in contact with the floor.
- Feel the breath, the rise and fall of the abdomen.
- Direct your attention to your left big toe.
- Notice sensations, or no sensation at all, at the toe.
- Expand your attention to all the other toes of the left foot.
- Feel the heel, the ball of the foot, the sides of the foot, and the top and bottom of the foot.
- Expand your attention from the left foot to the left ankle, allowing your awareness to circle the ankle, sensing all the bones there, noticing whatever sensation might be present, or no sensation at all.
- Shift your awareness from the left ankle to the left leg and left buttocks, noticing whether there is any holding or gripping, and then settle your awareness on the pelvis.
- Allow your attention to rest at the pelvis, feeling sensations: tingling, numbness, pressure, or again no sensation at all.
- Move your attention down the right thigh and right leg to the right ankle.
- Allow your awareness to take in whatever feelings are present in this part of the body.
- When your mind wanders, gently and yet firmly bring your awareness back to its focus.
- Shift your awareness gently from the right thigh, leg, and ankle to the right big toe and then all the other toes of the right foot.
- Feel the top, sides, and bottom of the right foot.
- Feel the heel, the ball of the right foot, and the right toes.
- Direct your attention from the right toes, foot, ankle, and leg to the right buttock.
- Expand your attention to all the internal organs of the body: liver, kidney, spleen, and so on.

- Gently rest your attention on each organ.
- Expand your attention from these internal organs to the chest.
- Allow your awareness to rest on the lungs, sensing the expanding and contracting of the lungs, the intercostal muscles.
- When your mind wanders, gently and yet firmly bring your awareness back to its focus.
- Sense into the heart cradled between the lobes of the lungs.
- Feel the beating heart muscle.
- Shift your focus gently to the collarbone and the shoulders.
- Allow the shoulders to rest on the floor or cushion, or to remain neutral.
- Take in the sides of the body with your awareness.
- Become aware of your arms, allowing your awareness to travel down the right arm and fingers, and then shift your attention to the left arm and fingers.
- Direct your attention, as you would direct the beam of a flashlight to your throat, feeling whatever sensations may be present.
- Become aware of your face, all the muscles of the face.
- Rest your attention on the chin, the tongue, the teeth, and the lower and upper lips.
- Become aware of your nose, eyes, eyebrows, eye sockets, and eyelashes.
- Again, when the mind wanders, gently yet firmly bring your awareness back to its focus.
- Feel the ears, sides of the head, front of the head, and back of the head.
- Become aware of the crown of the head.
- Feel the breath come in and go out.
- Continue feeling, sensing, and breathing, observing whatever sensation may be there, or the absence of any sensation at all.
- Feel the whole body, resting against the floor, cushion, or chair, if you are seated.
- Sense the pressure and weight of the body, noticing all the places where the body comes in contact with the floor, cushion, or chair.
- Feel the clothes as they lie against your skin.
- Feel the breath, breathing you.
- When you complete your practice, stretch gently, and if your eyes are closed, gently open them, and notice how you feel.

Mindfulness Practice Aid 2.4: The Beauty Bath

We recommend this five-minute, sensually engaging practice to reset one's mood, to appreciate and savor the goodness that is all around us, and to create a transformative pause. We, the authors of this book, use this practice every day and find the act of gazing at something intently and with concentration, taking in its details and appreciating its contours, colors, contrasts, and scents, a transformative act. We hope you will give it a try and report back on its results. As many poets have noted, to really see a thing, you must look at it long.

- When you are feeling the need to shift or a reset, pause what you are doing and go outside. If you need to put on your coat and shoes, and the weather is terrible, all the better. There is beauty everywhere. If you cannot go outside and are cut off from the natural world at the moment, you can still find something of beauty around you.
- Walk around and notice something your eye alights on, something you have perhaps not looked at closely before. This could be a very ordinary thing: a crack in the sidewalk where a few blades of grass poke through, the petals of a petunia blossom in a window box on a busy city street, the vine that curves around an abandoned fencepost. You might ask yourself, gently, why has my eye alighted here? You do not need to answer this question.
- Now take some deep breaths, which you've been practicing since you began reading this book, with a deep gentle inhale and a powerful emptying exhale. You are preparing to let the thing you are observing really come into your eye and your inner eye, a place that sees and appreciates things with a quiet contemplative alternative vision.
- Simply gaze, with appreciative, curious eyes, at the thing your eye has alighted on. What is extraordinary about what you see here? How is it a miracle that that leaf has saw-cut edges? What does the deep pink of that lily blossom evoke in you? What is the effect of simply observing this beautiful thing?
- Allow yourself to take in all the details, without a plan and without too much thinking. Simply be in the experience of observing. Do this for at least a minute. Let the details of your observation sit inside you, in the clear space you have opened with your breath.

- After a minute or more, thank the object or formation you have been observing, and exhale one last time. (You can say "thank you" silently or out loud.) Remind yourself to be grateful for your capacity to see anything (for vision!), for this sweet object you have just observed, and for the miracles of our planet that lie all around us.
- Back to work! Notice how you feel when you return to what you were doing previously. Allow yourself to imagine that this act of visioning can be refreshing and resetting, and then see how this is.
- Make this a daily habit! Enjoy.

We believe that a daily habit of the Beauty Bath will dramatically increase your capacity for observation, and also broaden and build your sense of appreciation and connection to the world around you. And we think that will be helpful as a leader.

Portraits of Practice

2.1: Larry Ward, Head of Organizational and Business Development

The American School of Bangkok, Bangkok, Thailand

"Mindfulness is not a religious category. It is rather a category of human potential and empowerment."

We spoke to Larry Ward via Skype from the United States to his office at The American School of Bangkok, an international pre-K–12 school that focuses on creating global leaders in an academically rigorous environment. In Bangkok, it was a day of antigovernment protests and two explosions that left two-dozen injured, according to media reports. The city, and the country of Thailand, are the scenes of escalating tensions as a result of antigovernment protests that began in October 2013. Despite the violence, Larry's calm and composure comes through on the call.

We began talking to Larry about how he came to mindfulness. "My mindfulness journey began in India in the late '70s. I was on assignment with the Institute of Cultural Affairs, an international nongovernmental organization. The focus of my work was to serve as faculty to train local people in leadership methods of social-economic development.

"During my assignment in Calcutta, I became acquainted with a Buddhist monk, who on occasion said, 'Do you know the Buddha taught near here? It would be a pity to be here and not learn about his teachings.' I began to practice with him and found myself drawn to the teaching and practice even though they were different from my Christian background. As I was a Christian minister in the Baptist tradition, these teachings and practices appeared quite different at first. But over time I came to appreciate both the differences and the similarities." Listening to Larry talk about his background as a Christian and now his experience as a Buddhist is deeply inspiring. It's clear that he has discovered the interconnections between these faith traditions.

Larry speaks with clarity and courage about his many years of mindfulness practice. He says, "I have found many benefits to my lifestyle as a practitioner. Since that time, I have made an effort to continue my learning and practice. During my journey, I have benefitted from study and practice in Hong Kong with Tibetan Buddhism, Soto Zen in the United States, and Chinese Buddhism in Taiwan and China. Most importantly, my teacher Thich Nhat Hanh taught me the value of embodying mindfulness daily. I experienced his quality of presence in his movement to be filled with stillness and joy. I have practiced with him since the early 1990s, was both married and ordained by him into the Order of Interbeing [founded by Nhat Hanh, the Order, Tiep Hien in Vietnamese, is a community of monastics and lay members who are committed to living in accordance with the Fourteen Mindfulness Trainings, a distillation of the Bodhisattva (Enlightened Being) teachings of Mahayana Buddhism] and subsequently was ordained as a Dharma Teacher in his lineage."

Turning to his work life, Larry notes, "In my role as head of organizational and business development at The American School, responding to the invitation of the directors, I have joined in a team effort to launch a mindfulness curriculum for our K–12 students. Our curriculum is research based, of course, benefiting from the pioneering efforts of other schools worldwide. My practice on a daily basis attempts to embody alertness, ardency, and clarity as key qualities of mindfulness practice. This helps me as a leader to be more mentally attuned and emotionally stable. As school leaders know, each day is a mystery unfolding in many ways, requiring real attention to the people and issues at hand. Entering the day with this practice in my bones really makes high-quality attention and decision making possible.

"I engage in a daily routine of meditative practices before work, during, and after. These all center on my breathing, my body, and of course my mental/emotional activities. I start each day with body-centered awareness and meditation practices. In the early morning before I get out of bed, the first thing I do is direct awareness to my body and mental states, focusing on deeply relaxing where I find tension. My aim in this practice is to develop a sense of ease and peace as I enter a new day. On some days, I add in a silent sitting meditation period of at least 20 minutes. On other days, I recite Buddhist prayers, which help me to embrace any fears of change that may lie deep in my consciousness."

Larry speaks with a kind of dignity that is born from years of dedicated practice and effort. He says, "Once at the school, I notice that my awareness of each encounter is heightened based on my mindfulness practice: The energy required for each task seems more available. I find myself better able to be present to each moment of interaction. I create small moments of practice throughout the day by slowing down my walking and eating. I have found too that taking a few moments to breathe is a helpful way to prepare for a meeting. Each workday, I take a motorcycle to school. When I arrive at school, I really try to feel my feet touching the ground. This helps reduce my mind-wandering tendencies and improves my capacity to pay attention to what is happening within me and around me. I look at the smiles on the faces of children and parents and take a moment to get in touch with the good feeling of experience.

"We start most executive team meetings with some type of brief mindfulness exercise. Most often, we focus on an exercise that gets us in touch with awareness of our breath and body states in the present moment with the aim of relaxing. Other times, we may do a guided meditation/visualization. We also have formalized norms to encourage one another to listen and speak with full attention to our words spoken and heard."

He speaks frankly about the challenges, and makes them clear, saying that "the current political strife is of course the experience of peripheral chaos and uncertainty. Primarily, the political protests can disrupt class schedules due to traffic problems. However, we have systems and protocols in place to deal with any serious emergencies. We have also held sessions with our staff to provide training in coping with stress that may be a result of these current conditions.

"I consider myself lucky living/working here in Thailand, which has over 1,000 years of Theravada Buddhist roots. Many people understand and value the importance of mindfulness practice. Our school set up voluntary practice groups for parents, staff, and students before my arrival. My challenge is to continue both my formal and my informal practice at home and work as all this occurs while I feel the time crunch to complete my dissertation on meditation as self-directed neuroplasticity."

We conclude the interview, with Larry's observations. He speaks with a steady calm. "Mindfulness," he says, "is an experience, a matter of practice, not an intellectual construct. I would encourage everyone to taste and see for themselves. As a result of my practice, study, and research, I would suggest that mindfulness practice is an important aspect of our continuing human development, especially in education.

"I should stress too that mindfulness is not a religious category. It is rather a category of human potential and empowerment—there is mounting evidence of the measurable positive impact of mindfulness on learning, emotional resilience, and professional performance. For me, the key is to embody the qualities of mindfulness."

Larry is head of organizational and business development at The American School of Bangkok. He is currently completing his dissertation on meditation and brain plasticity at University of the West in Rosemead, California. He was ordained as a Dharma Teacher by Thich Nhat Hanh in 2000 and leads mindfulness retreats worldwide.

2.2: Mary F. Spence, PhD, School Psychologist

Ann Arbor Public Schools, Ann Arbor, Michigan

"I had a yoga teacher who really impressed me . . . she was so lithe and radiated life. I wanted to be like her."

Mary F. Spence is a school psychologist in Ann Arbor, Michigan, and has worked in mental health and educational settings for nearly three decades. She works in three elementary and middle school–level buildings, as well as for a district-wide initiative to serve students on the autism spectrum. As a special educator, she works with other

educators to help children and their families create a positive school experience.

She uses and teaches mindfulness techniques in school settings. We caught Mary in her office late on a Friday afternoon completing paperwork. Setting that aside, Mary became expansive and reflective about her mindfulness practice over some 30 years. Mary began practicing yoga when she was 15, growing up in Minnesota where she attended an open school. "I had a yoga teacher who really impressed me . . . she was so lithe and radiated life. I wanted to be like her."

Always interested in the social and emotional dimensions of wellness, Mary studied play therapy and majored in psychology and theater as an undergraduate. She became interested in women's prison work, and started teaching relaxation techniques to female inmates, ultimately taking a doctorate in psychology and working with behaviorally diverse special needs populations in schools.

In the late 1990s, Mary became interested in Buddhism and began to follow the work of the Mind and Life Institute (www.mindandlife .org), an organization in Hadley, Massachusetts, that coordinates and funds research at the intersection of contemplative practice, neuroscience, and psychology. Mary was working in a school district that provided services for children with significant disabilities, and she wondered how to apply what she was learning about contemplative practice with the children who were a part of her work every day. As she discussed the work of the Mind and Life Institute with colleagues, a Mind and Life group evolved, with six or eight regular members of the staff getting together during lunch to discuss emerging research on mindfulness and talk about the applications of this work in their professional lives. Mary was particularly intrigued with the work of Dr. Jonathan Cohen, a Princeton University psychologist who studies attention and cognitive control, and she wondered how she might incorporate his insights on attention training into her work with children.

As this wondering evolved, one incident, she says, really hooked her on the power of mindfulness and pushed her to become a mindfulness researcher, trainer, and practitioner. She was working with a middle school boy who had severe emotional dysregulation, and in order to find quiet time with him, she cleared out a closet in the boy's classroom. They went into the closet, where Mary provided the student with progressive relaxation instruction. They did deep-breathing practices together. "Back then, I was using neurolinguistic programming techniques, and we had identified a special word for calming: It was *chill*. The staff thought it was a bit crazy, but then an amazing thing happened. He was a large young man, and sometimes when he became activated, the teacher needed to clear the classroom. But the teacher noticed that he was beginning to be able to calm himself. The teacher saw him seated back at his desk, clearly breathing deeply and saying the word *chill* to himself. This really moved me and made me realize how powerful this work was for kids. You could help kids learn to be still, to get control of their bodies and then get control of their emotions, just by teaching them how to breathe, giving them centering words, and practicing with them." Mary was convinced. Building on her own evolving personal practice, she expanded her work to other students.

"Then I moved to Ann Arbor and began working with more neurotypical kids. In 2010, we obtained district support to collaborate with the faculty at the University of Michigan on mindfulness training for parents and educators of children with special needs. Using a previously researched curriculum, and with just five weeks of training, we realized we could make a difference in parents' and educators' lives. After that, I realized the incredible value such training could provide for parents and staff in my district." And like so many other practitioners and school leaders, Mary says she was very aware: "The main thing is that the training is secular in content and that it not be perceived as religious or as Buddhism."

Mary says the research study had a real impact on her. "I was a little bit arrogant going into the research study training; I didn't really think I needed it because I'd been studying these things and thinking about them for years. I had been doing yoga for 35 years and used numerous behavioral-change techniques that worked with the relaxation response to help me relax myself. But I found the consistent training in the research study really helpful to me in my own life. I notice I am much more able to meet the needs of parents, students, and staff now that I practice every day with great regularity.

"Personally, I meditate twice a day. I do a morning meditation and an evening meditation—perhaps a loving-kindness meditation in the evening and a calming-my-breath practice in the morning. I spend about 20 minutes doing each meditation, but I don't set an alarm anymore; I can just manage it. I have found that in my own life, through multiple life challenges, I've been able to stay much more calm. I'm not as reactive, and I do much less ruminating. I'm more resilient. Colleagues sometimes say to me, 'You really help us stay grounded,' and I attribute that to my practice. I see this work as critical to our needs to do the work of nurturing children and growing their minds. I am extremely grateful for this opportunity in both my professional and my personal life."

Mary is also a member of the advisory board for the Social Foundations of Education program at Eastern Michigan University.

She served as the training liaison for Ann Arbor Public Schools for a large study with the University of Michigan faculty in 2010, which examined the effectiveness of a five-week mindfulness training for parents and educators of children with special needs. This randomized clinical study[32] found that after five weeks of intensive mindfulness training, using the SMART curriculum (Stress Management and Relaxation Techniques), parents and educators showed significant self-reported reductions in perceived stress and anxiety, and increases in empathy, forgiveness, and personal growth.

"Professionally, I'm especially interested in play-based mindfulness, a technique I use a lot in my work. I find that mindfulness training helps kids be more in touch with their bodies, be engaged in school, and trust themselves. It changes everything. I think mindfulness training changes the world. It changed my world."

2.3: Pilar Aguilera, Associate Lecturer at Faculty of Education, Department of Research Methods and Diagnostic in Education (MIDE)

University of Barcelona, Spain

"Mindfulness has helped me greatly to understand the importance of giving time for myself—not in a selfish way—but to be the best leader I can be begins with caring for myself, to be calm and centered in myself before I can help others. A calm and centered educator creates a calm and centered classroom. The best way to lead is to be the leader I want others to be."

We interviewed Pilar Aguilera while attending an international retreat and conference on mindfulness and education for Wake Up Schools led by Thich Nhat Hanh. Wake Up Schools, an initiative launched by Nhat Hanh and the international Plum Village community, provides educators, students, parents, and the entire school community with mindfulness programs to promote and support a happy and healthy school environment. We talked to Pilar, a dynamo and major force in organizing this event, which was sold out within 48 hours, for a three-day retreat for 600 educators led by Nhat Hanh and a five-day course for 200 educators on the Wake Up Schools approach to mindfulness in education at the seaside city of Barcelona, Spain.

We caught up to Pilar after breakfast during a quiet lull before the start of the afternoon mindfulness course offering. Pilar began the conversation, talking about how she came to practice mindfulness and to organize this major event in Spain, Nhat Hanh's first visit.

Here's what she said: "I wanted to have a spiritual path. Something happened within me. I guess it was a crisis. I was looking for something, and I wasn't sure what. Spirituality was always very important to me from the time I was a small child. I was 27 when I went to Edinburgh, Scotland, to study in graduate school and found a Thich Nhat Hanh group, a *sangha*. I started practicing mindfulness: mindful walking, mindful eating, mindful speaking, mindful listening. I noticed how all this made me feel, and I just knew it was the right path for me. That was 12 years ago, and I am still on the same path.

"My practice is not perfect, but I have a deep aspiration to practice in a wholehearted way to transform myself and to help others. In organizing this retreat and conference to bring Thich Nhat Hanh to Spain, I worked with many people who also shared a similar aspiration. This has been a two- to three-year effort, and I have put my heart and soul into this project. There has been a lot of doing, and now I want to turn to a lot more being." Listening attentively to Pilar in the cafeteria of the University of Barcelona's busy Mundet Campus, we get the sense that she has carried the weight of this tremendous effort with grace and dignity. Despite the buzz of students coming and going, she glances off into the distance, and we can sense her strength and dedication. She turns back to us and continues.

"As a school leader, a researcher on mindfulness and education here in Barcelona in the field of higher education, I could get lost easily in the data of my research. Organizing this mindfulness retreat and conference has greatly enhanced my social skills, my ability to apply the skills of mindfulness to an actual leadership role. Mindfulness has helped me to be a more empathic leader. For example, with mindfulness, I am aware when I need to delegate and when I should not. I notice when people are overworked and when it is time to work together. I am aware of how I speak to others and how I listen, how I inspire and motive others, and how I make requests of others. These are very important leadership skills. I am a visionary leader—good at the big picture and not so good at the small details. I learned this about myself by stopping, pausing, breathing, and looking really deeply into myself, my aspirations."

Spending time with Pilar we sense her vibrancy, her wellspring of energy and passion for mindfulness that shines brightly through her expressive gestures. She concludes with these words: "Mindfulness has helped me greatly to understand the importance of giving time for myself—not in a selfish way—but to be the best leader I can be begins with caring for myself, to be calm and centered in myself before I can help others. A calm and centered educator creates a calm and centered classroom. The best way to lead is to be the leader I want others to be."

Pilar is an associate lecturer in the faculty of education of the University of Barcelona. She has an MAEd in institutional leadership and management in education, and teaches mindfulness and social and emotional learning courses for educators. She has practiced mindfulness in the tradition of Thich Nhat Hanh for several years and loves sharing and creating community with other mindful practitioners.

Please visit us on Facebook at https://www.facebook.com/TheMindfulSchoolLeader.

3

The Well-Focused School Leader

"Try looking at your mind as a wayward puppy that you are trying to paper train. You don't drop kick a puppy into the neighbor's yard every time it piddles on the floor. You just keep bringing it back to the newspaper. So I keep trying gently to bring my mind back to what is really there to be seen, maybe to be seen and noted with a kind of reverence."

—Anne Lamott, from *Bird by Bird*[1]

A Sleepless Night for Jason

It's another sleepless night for Jason, the chief financial officer of a prominent charter preparatory school in Chicago, Illinois. He's up at 3 a.m., his mind darting like a fish in tall reeds. He walks over to his bedside table and rests his hand on his dad's dog tags, Jason's reminder of commitment and courage. As he showers and dresses quickly, his mind races as he anticipates a tense departmental meeting with senior instructional staff. He turns his head while shaving to glance at the TV news, and inadvertently nicks himself. Hurriedly, he wipes his face and gulps down a handful of vitamins.

It's now 4 a.m. and Jason is at his computer, scanning the latest news feed and checking email. He sips strong coffee, which he says helps "kick start" his day, but he barely tastes it. Still dark outside, Jason begins emailing his staff, checking on the status of projects, confirming appointments, and skimming a district accountability report. "I can get these little details out the way early in my day, and get more done at school," he says.

He's heard about the benefits of mindfulness meditation, yoga, and just sitting quietly, but says he has no time. He thinks about more physical exercise, and really enjoys swimming, and says to himself that he will start next week. He turns to the pile of unopened mail on his desk and begins sorting through it, discarding envelopes, stacking new piles. Suddenly, he remembers today's his sister's birthday. He turns back to his computer, searching the Web for a gift. He gets sidetracked by an advertisement for a trip to Costa Rica, a place he has longed to visit. With his attention momentarily captured by images of Costa Rican beaches, he forgets completely about the gift for his sister.

It's now 5:15 a.m., and Jason is hunched over the computer while the first light of the day rises over the small yard behind his home. The birds outside—cardinals, wrens, and sparrows—begin their morning ritual, vying for a dominant place at the bird feeder he installed a few weeks ago. He is unaware of the morning light, the birdsong, not to mention the pain in his low back, shoulders, and face from tensing his muscles and gripping his jaw. Later that day, he will wonder why he feels exhausted and tense. Sound familiar?

Mindfulness and Attention Training

As we alluded to in Chapter 2, mindfulness strengthens attention, focus, and clarity. When you begin training in mindfulness, you recognize that your attention is flexible and that much like a beam of light, it can be focused anywhere from a narrow attention to a more open kind of awareness. Within the literature on mindfulness meditation, there are many ways of describing the flexibility of attention and focus. For the purposes of this chapter, we describe narrow-focused and open-focused attention, or what some researchers call "task-positive" and "task-negative" networks.[2]

Both networks are useful and important ("the crowning achievement of human brain"[3]; the task-positive network is the one we use when we are deeply focused on a single task, and the task-negative network is the one that's engaged when we are moving from one thought to another in the usual mash-up of our wandering minds (lots of creative thinking can occur here). Daniel Goleman in his book *Focus: The Hidden Driver of Excellence* describes the range of attention from narrow to open as well. Narrow-focused attention is often described as one-pointed, just as you might shine a laser beam of light in a dark room. You may begin a period of mindfulness meditation practice by starting with narrowly focused attention: becoming aware of the breath at the tip of the nose, for example. Open-focused attention is the ability to expand your awareness in a flexible, wide, and generous manner, fully taking in whatever is in your peripheral vision, much like sitting on a beach and taking in the fullness of the landscape: the waves, the sand, objects far out on the horizon, other people, and more. An example of open attention would be moving awareness from feeling sensation at the tip of the nose to feeling sensations in the body as a whole. This type of "open awareness" or "panoramic awareness" reduces impulsivity and decreases mind wandering.[4]

Both open- and narrow-focused attention require a balance of effort and ease: not too tight and not too loose. In focusing on the breath at the tip of the nose—narrowly focused attention, for example—you are not striving to get somewhere, to change the breath, to strengthen the breath, or to control the breath; you are not exerting brute force or willpower. Nor are you lying back with disinterest. As you become adept at shifting from narrow- to open-focused attention, you recognize another type of attention: meta-attention, or the attention of attention. You recognize the movement of attention from the object of attention (the breath, for example) to something else and back again. This noticing of the shifting away of attention from the intended objects of attention (i.e., noticing that the mind has wandered from attention on the breath to what you are going to have to eat in an hour), and subsequently bringing the mind back to the focus of attention, is like a bench press for the mind. You are training the mind, strengthening your capacity to focus the mind.

The third part of our attention system—the attention filter—helps us aim our attention and make choices about what we notice and attend to—and we believe that this is an increasingly important set of cognitive muscles and awarenesses for the contemporary leader. As we've described throughout, we live in an unprecedented era of information availability. As recently described in a *New York Times* piece on the importance of resting the brain, "on a typical day, we take in the equivalent of about 174 newspapers' worth of information, five times as much as we did in 1986. As the world's 21,274 television stations produce some 85,000 hours of original programming every day (by 2003 figures), we watch an average of five hours of television per day. For every hour of YouTube video you watch, there are 5,999 hours of new video just posted!"[5]

Your attention also filters all this incoming information—and learning how to notice what you are paying attention to, and to make choices about this, is part of the emerging skills of mindfulness. Without development, your evolutionary biology distinguishes the important from the unimportant, what to pay attention to and what to ignore, and as you engage in constantly switching between these two networks of the brain, you get fatigued, dizzy—there may be too much seesawing. This switching back and forth is competing for your finite attention capacity and makes you tired. Levitin and others[6] recommend for workday activity that instead of switching back and forth, you work in blocks, focusing on bundles of work projects, and then moving on to the next thing. For example, work on just emails, or just social media. Avoid interrupting composing an email by checking your Twitter feed.[7] One of the central outcomes of a developing mindfulness practice is the capacity to observe where (and how) one is attending, and to gradually, with practice, make decisions about whether these attention modes are serving us as leaders.

In our work with Jason and many other school leaders in mindfulness training—who made a commitment to beginning a mindfulness practice after really tracking how frantic their lives had become—we're convinced of the importance of focus and attention training to leadership effectiveness. Rather than sitting in a meeting, texting under the table, or excusing himself to take a call, after some commitment to beginning a mindfulness practice, Jason began to train himself to be more present to what was happening in front of him. Instead of giving advice, fixing others, or spacing out, Jason worked at truly listening to his colleagues, friends, and family. In conversations with his staff, Jason practiced speaking mindfully, sticking to the point without getting sidelined or interrupting others in midsentence. He found his interactions at work became easier and sensed a greater clarity in his own thinking, as well as a greater cooperation with his staff. Jason was learning to direct and sustain his attention for small tasks, using narrow-focused attention (like completing an email without jumping to a Twitter feed) and to expand his attention for larger tasks, like strategic planning and visioning. His attention filter was becoming more sophisticated, and he was gradually becoming more able to be choiceful about attention, which brought him a sense of accomplishment and emotional calm. All this, and he eventually remembered his sister's birthday gift too!

Two Ways to Practice: Formal and Informal

Formal Practice of Mindfulness

We find it helpful to distinguish between two ways of practicing mindfulness: formal and informal. More formal ways of practicing mindfulness often involve adoption of a regular schedule of silent meditation, like Sophia Isako Wong and Philip Altmann, who meditate formally every morning before beginning their day. This formal practice can be done not only while sitting, but also while standing or walking (see Mindfulness Practice Aid 3.2, "Mindful Walking," page 97). We have even experienced formal mindfulness meditation while eating (see Mindfulness Practice Aid 5.1, "Eating Mindfully," in Chapter 5, page 151). A more informal way to practice mindfulness is to bring mindful attention to the activities of everyday life; we consider this as important and effective as the formal practice. Both kinds of practices are life enhancing, and the two support one another like the wings of a bird. Both are meaningful to us as leaders because they scaffold and nurture self-awareness, concentration, insight,[8] and attention, which are central to effective leadership.

In some traditions, the word *insight* or *vipassana* may have a different and/or nuanced meaning. With greater self-awareness, you begin to know yourself in new and more conscious ways, which supports your self-confidence as a leader. For school leaders, we develop the capacity to understand the school environment as it is, seeing it clearly.

In formal meditation practice you intentionally set aside some time daily to pause, stop, be still, and unplug from the near-constant stream of incoming data and stimulus, which is your regular life. You take time to be with the experience of living: breathing, feeling the breath in your body, noticing the condition of your body as a whole. Jon Kabat-Zinn and other mindfulness teachers speak of this time as *being* rather than *doing*. Megan Cowan of Mindful Schools describes this practice as a laboratory for learning to watch your thoughts come across the sky of your mind. This is a moment, too, to be aware of the sensory experience of being: observing sounds all around you, observing thoughts and feelings as they come and go in the stream of awareness, observing your reactions without immediately jumping to change anything, observing bodily sensations—pleasant, unpleasant, and neutral. In our in-the-fast-lane lifestyle, most of us aren't used to slowing down long enough to observe ourselves in this way. As mindfulness meditation practitioners and in our work with school leaders, we know just how hard it is to move from doing to being, and that is why formal meditation practice can be important in growing these noticing muscles.

Breathing, Posture, and Practice

Mindful breathing is the foundation of mindfulness. We are always breathing, and our in- and out-breath is very often used as a way of anchoring attention to the "now." The breath is so simple, so essential, and so automatic that we often forget that it's there. Yet, of course, without the breath, there is no life. The breath is a good barometer of your emotions and the state of your body. The mind follows the breath, and when the breath and the mind unite, there is a sense of wholeness, centeredness, and integration. One way we experience this unity of mind and body is in our daily yoga practice. On the mat, standing, bending, lunging, or lying down, we've trained ourselves to bring conscious awareness to the breath as we move from posture to posture. This marrying of the breath with the movement really enlivens even super simple actions, like inhaling fully as the arms are raised up and exhaling completely as the arms are released down. You don't have to be an expert at yoga to see the benefits of breathing with awareness. It's important to take this body and breath awareness off the yoga mat and into our daily lives. A great place to start developing self-awareness is to begin with awareness of your breath. Too many leaders we work with tell us about feeling disconnected from their bodies, living largely in their heads. Some are hard pressed to locate where they feel the breath in the body. Mindfulness of the breath is largely about befriending the breath, becoming familiar with it, maybe for the first time.

Practice Pause—Breath Inquiry

We invite you to pause and breathe and to try this breath inquiry practice, allowing your eyes to be closed or open as is comfortable for you. The purpose of this breath inquiry is to gather information about how you breathe, to check in with yourself, not to judge yourself or set an ambitious goal for yourself. As you breathe through the nose, feel the full length of the natural in-breath and feel the full length of the natural out-breath. You may notice whether the breath is shallow or full, constricted or expansive. Allow the breath to anchor your attention. Place your attention on your breath for a few cycles. Feel the breath come in and go out through the nose. This is not the same as thinking about the breath or analyzing the breath. Instead simply allow yourself to feel the breath and to be with the direct, sensory experience of breathing. After a few cycles, stretch gently and open your eyes if they are closed, and notice how you feel. In what areas of the body do you most feel the breath? Can you describe the quality of your breathing—short, choppy, smooth? Now that you have some information about your physical state, do you have a sense about your psychological and emotional state? Do you notice a connection between how you are breathing and this state of mind?

Many of us, in the strain and rush of our lives, engage in unconscious inadequate breathing practices: breath holding, shallow breathing, and chronically holding in the abdomen to look trim and fit. As you breathe in, the abdomen expands like a balloon taking in air, and as you breathe out, the abdomen contracts. When you engage in diaphragmatic breathing, you bathe the heart, lungs, and other organs with oxygen-rich blood. While abdominal breathing is the way you naturally breathe, when you're under stress, this natural way of breathing can become compromised and shallow. During meditation, as with some complementary practices, like some forms of yoga or Qigong, you are not trying to manipulate the breath or control the breath. Instead, locate where you feel the breath, whether it is high in the chest or deep in the belly, and place your attention there. Stay present, to the best of your ability, to the wave-like quality of the breath. This takes practice and patience, and know too that wherever you are is just right.

Practice Pause—Diaphragmatic Breathing: A Snapshot

The diaphragm, a dome-shaped sheet of muscle and tendon that separates the chest from the abdomen, plays a vital role in respiration and breathing. Other muscles (and organs) are, of course, at work in the complex process of breathing and respiration, such as the intercostals between the ribs, the abdominal muscles in the front of the belly, and the sternum and upper trapezius, among many others.

Very simply, with healthy diaphragmatic breathing, as you inhale, the diaphragm lowers and the belly and chest expand to take in air; as you exhale, the diaphragm relaxes and compresses air in the chest, allowing for air to be released. This movement is multidirectional in healthy diaphragmatic breathing.

(Continued)

(Continued)

Please pause for a moment and try a few practice rounds of diaphragmatic breathing. Please put the book down and sit in a comfortable, upright position with the spine straight but not rigid. Close your eyes if that is comfortable for you. If you are wearing a tight belt or waistband, please loosen it. Breathe in through the nose and feel the belly expand and the chest rise. To help enhance feeling these physical sensations, place your hands at the belly. Breathe out through the nose and feel the chest gently relax down and the belly move in toward the spine. Breathe in this way for a few cycles, and when you are finished, stretch gently and open your eyes if they are closed and notice how you feel.

To continue the formal meditation practice preparation, after you've practiced breathing, it is useful to begin by sitting in a comfortable posture with your spine straight but not rigid. Sitting in a chair is just fine. You may also like to try sitting on a meditation cushion *(zafu)* with your legs crossed and your knees lower than your hips, resting on the floor, which helps to support a stable posture. This helps with good diaphragmatic breathing, which supports alertness and increases your energy level. If it is comfortable, allow the eyes to be closed as this helps reduce distractions especially when you first start practicing meditation. (However, many meditation teachers we know rightly say that the so-called distractions are part of the meditation.) Bring your attention to your breathing, focusing on where you feel the breath in the body. Notice how you are breathing, without judging it. When you notice that your mind has wandered, whether to your inner critic about how you are practicing, about a meeting later in the day, or anything else, gently yet firmly bring your attention and focus back to the breath. Mind wandering is universal and an essential part of the meditation process. Don't try to get rid of thoughts. Don't try to repress feelings. Don't try to ignore painful thoughts or sensations. As we have described in Chapter 2, the struggle and tension to try to control your experience sets you up for more struggle. Instead, though at first it may seem counterintuitive, allow yourself to be with all this, and notice how all this changes moment to moment. A formal meditation practice that cultivates the awareness of thoughts and feelings is described in more detail at the end of this chapter (see Mindfulness Practice Aid 3.1, "Mindful Sitting With Awareness of Thoughts and Feelings," page 83).

We've heard well-known meditation teacher Joseph Goldstein, the cofounder of the Insight Meditation Society, liken meditating to eating a meal: You don't get nourished by looking at the menu or having the waiter describe the meal. You have to actually eat the food to be nourished. Similarly, with mindfulness, it is not enough to intellectually know about mindfulness: to have read a few books about mindfulness, watched a video, or listened to a podcast. You have to practice, which requires a certain degree of discipline that can be difficult to attain. Too often, when you have a little free time, you think of ways to fill the void: watching TV, shopping, eating, whatever. In fact, a recently published study in *Science* found that individuals will go to great lengths, including administering electric shocks to themselves, to avoid being left alone with their thoughts.[9]

Committing to a formal practice of mindfulness creates the space and time for nonjudgmental awareness in the present moment to emerge. When you do this, you are learning new leadership skills and building cognitive management muscles. These take courage and commitment.

Later in this chapter, we describe important mind states—or "attitudes" of mind—that can be hugely supportive in your practice of mindfulness. School leaders, like many others, are a high-achieving group. Sometimes we hold ourselves to punishingly high standards and then get down on ourselves if we don't live up to unrealistic goals. Mindfulness invites leaders to explore mind states that can sometimes be undervalued in the school context. These include the capacity for self-acceptance, self-love, and self-compassion. We'll discuss these states below, as well as others such as nonstriving, nonjudgment, and equanimity.

We invite you to begin the formal practice of meditation now by trying this practice of mindful sitting with awareness of thoughts and feelings.

Mindfulness Practice Aids

Mindfulness Practice Aid 3.1: Mindful Sitting With Awareness of Thoughts and Feelings

As a way to calm a hyperactive mind and body, we recommend the practice of observing, without immediately reacting to, thoughts ("I'm not good enough") and feelings (anxiety, fear, worry) as they arise in the moment. While this sounds easy, it's not because of the mind's tendency to jump from thought to thought and feeling to feeling. For this meditation, as with the other practices, we invite you to visit our Facebook page at www.facebook.com/TheMindfulSchoolLeader for a free downloadable recording of this mindfulness practice, or record this yourself. It may also be useful to use a timer feature in a mindfulness app listed in Appendix C, online, page 17, to keep track of time and focus on the meditation.

- Sit in a comfortable, dignified posture, with the spine straight but not rigid, in a quiet place, and bring your attention and focus to your breathing.
- Allow your eyes to be open or closed—notice what feels most comfortable.
- Feel the breath come in and go out of your nose and mouth.
- Locate the breath in the body.
- Observe the full sensation of breathing from the beginning of breathing in to the very ending of breathing out, noticing the pause between the in- and out-breaths.
- When you notice that you are lost in thought, become aware of the nature and the quality of your thinking and your emotions. A thought ("I'm not good at this. He/she always . . .") is not a concrete fact; and yet, at times, you may feel it is.
- Notice any emotions associated with the thought (frustration, boredom, anticipation, etc.).
- Notice how fleeting thoughts are, and see them come and go like leaves floating by on a gentle current of water.
- Let feelings be; don't try to get rid of them. Instead, label the feelings—excitement, boredom, calm, irritability—and watch how they change, the ebb and flow like the waves of the ocean, and return attention to the breath.
- Do the same with thoughts. Notice how the thoughts come and go, a passing show.
- Do not reject the thought or emotion; do not resist the thought or emotion; do not attach to the thought or emotion. Instead, notice the thought or emotion, and return to awareness of the breath. Don't lean forward into the next thing, the next moment, and don't lean back into the past.
- Acknowledge and allow whatever thoughts and emotions may be present in this moment, and notice how they change.
- Practice in this way for two to five minutes, several times daily.
- When you have finished, stretch in any way that is comfortable, and open your eyes if they are closed and notice how you feel.

Informal Practice of Mindfulness

Mindfulness can be cultivated informally by focusing your attention on your moment-to-moment sensations during everyday, routine activities like brushing your teeth, walking the dog, or taking a shower. With informal mindfulness, you practice being fully present for the activity and using all of our senses. Informal mindfulness is a way of weaving mindfulness in everything you do in your daily life: sitting, standing, walking, lying down, eating, speaking, and listening. In other words, mindfulness is portable and can be practiced at any time throughout the day. Ordinary, everyday tasks like ironing clothes or washing dishes, a lengthy conference call with colleagues, or writing a performance review, when done with mindful awareness, can take on a quality of robust "aliveness." Everything we have just said about the formal practice of mindfulness can be said about the informal practice of mindfulness.

Many school leaders drive themselves at a pace that ultimately is burnout level and nonsustainable. You may feel you have a few options, and may be wondering whether mindfulness requires that you move at an unnaturally slow pace. Mindfulness does not require that you move slowly, though slowing down may support really being present moment to moment. We recall an interview with Zen Master Thich Nhat Hanh on National Public Radio many years ago. Nhat Hanh was asked by interviewer Terry Gross about how he stayed mindful in the midst of the Vietnam War, with bombs dropping around him. Nhat Hanh replied that he could "run mindfully." In other words, mindfulness is not about whether you move fast or slow. Instead, it is about the quality of your awareness in the moment. Can you find moments during your crazy busy school day to insert mindful pauses, to notice what is happening in the moment?

Daily practice of informal mindfulness helps you stop, pause, observe, and breathe. You are engaged in life fully to the best of your ability. You are not a bystander to your own life. We recall the very touching words spoken at the end of a weeklong retreat for school executives. A diminutive woman who was struggling with issues of self-esteem spoke up at the closing session: "I don't want to be late for my own life."

Living each moment of the day with this level of awakened concentration takes energy. As with the formal practice of meditation, your mind may wander as you engage in the informal practice of mindfulness. The practice is the same as with formal meditation: acknowledge the thoughts or feelings and accept them as they are without trying to push them away, without condemning yourself. Acknowledge that you are no longer focused on the object of your awareness and then gently yet firmly return your attention to its focus. The object of your focus in informal practice could be any number of things: placing the key into the ignition switch of your car, weeding the garden, baking bread, composing the next email you send. In the informal practice of mindfulness, many practitioners use ordinary everyday objects, like a stop sign or stop light while driving or the phone ringing, as tools to bring back the wandering mind to what is happening here and now, and to remember to stop to pause and breathe.

Formal and informal mindfulness practices are commonly used to cultivate both concentration and insight. When you are mindful, you are attentive and concentrated in what you are doing and in your environment; you are present. Your body and mind align. Your words and action align, and there is a quality of congruence and integrity of values and actions. With this focus and integrity, you are in a better position to choose wisely, and exhibit insight.

Think About It

Risa, a third-year principal at a rapidly growing charter school in Oakland, California, is a dedicated, deeply thoughtful school leader committed to improving the conditions of teaching and learning and to intensifying professionalism among her teachers. She works 12- to 14-hour days and has said, "This is what the job requires." While she has quickly gained the admiration of her staff and the school community, a constant refrain from central office staff and teachers concerns Risa's frequent habit of jumping from one thing to the next, leading to confusion, frustration, and anxiety among staff and an ever-growing mass of unfinished projects.

She schedules a meeting with us to talk about her leadership and leadership development, including the job's many structural and interpersonal challenges. But the meeting is cut short by another meeting that runs late. Risa says she must stuff ballot envelopes while she talks, so that students can vote on who is most professionally dressed in an upcoming advisory meeting. She stands up behind her desk so that she can stuff envelopes faster. She interrupts the stuffing to take a call from the executive director, then says she has to run to the front of the building to speak to a student who is out of dress code. Could we talk while walking through the hallway?

Can you relate? What kind of neurobiological conditioning is Risa's mind engaged in during her busy work life? What is she "teaching" her brain to do?

Many misconceptions about mindfulness abound. When things finally settled down and we talked with Risa, she asked: "Isn't mindfulness about not thinking, about having a clear mind, no thoughts?" We recognized that was an important moment to clarify a frequent misunderstanding about the practice of mindfulness. It's important to recognize that you can meditate and be in a contemplative state even when there are thoughts in the mind. The mind need not be completely still like a clear, still lake to experience a meditative state. Thoughts drift across the mind, much like clouds drifting in a blue sky. We may have an underlying current of mental activity even while we are settling down. The goal is not to get rid of thoughts altogether, but to learn to work *with* one's mind instead of against it. Next time you become frustrated, try allowing your thoughts to float by, like driftwood on a gentle ocean current.

Jason, our chief financial officer at the beginning of this chapter, started his practice slowly, setting realistic goals for himself: three minutes of sitting meditation, using his mindfulness app to sound once each hour to practice stopping, pausing, and breathing for 30 seconds. As he became more comfortable with these practices, he gradually broadened his practice to include listening to mindfulness CDs on his morning drive into work, as well as viewing online videos and listening to podcasts. He committed to eating mindfully for one minute during lunch. Eventually, he learned about a local meditation group and began attending monthly meditation sessions. Months later, Jason has noticed a difference in his ability to think clearly. He also feels more resilient, even during the most intense budget crunch cycles!

Throughout this book, we will introduce and share with you a variety of informal mindfulness practices: eating, walking, speaking, listening, and lying down. But now let's turn to helpful mind states or mindful attitudes that support your practice of mindfulness.

Mindful Attitudes

Contemplative Mind States

STRIVING VERSUS DILIGENCE

"When we meditate for a purpose—to be calm, to gain insight—we are striving, not meditating."

—John Tarrant, Director and Senior Faculty,
Pacific Zen Institute, from A Beautiful Wish *(2013)*[10]

(Continued)

(Continued)

Striving, in the context of mindfulness practice, means forcing or strong-arming yourself to achieve a goal, even if the goal is salutary. Mindfulness is about accepting things as they are in this moment, even if the present moment is difficult, fearful, or anxiety producing. This kind of welcoming mind-set is called nonstriving. With it, there is a quality of acceptance and ease in the body and mind, even if there are specific goals you seek to accomplish, and even if the circumstances are stressful. It does not mean that you lack goals, purpose, and direction, or that things are the way you want them to be. For school leaders, this is a radical shift; it represents a new paradigm, given the heavy emphasis on getting someplace "else" better than now. Please note that we are not also saying that leaders can or should give up purposeful action, direction, commitment, and planning altogether, but suggesting that having a nonstriving attitude toward some things is helpful and calming, and the sign of increasing leader maturity.

Diligence implies persistence and steadfastness but, from the perspective of mindfulness practice, also represents an added dimension of practice. While mindfulness practice should be done with sincerity, to the best of your ability, there is also an important quality of acceptance and tolerance for yourself and others. Diligence is not perfectionism, which the writer Anne Lamott called "the voice of the oppressor, the enemy of the people."[11]

Many mindfulness teachers, including Bob Stahl and Wendy Millstine in their book *Calming the Rush of Panic,* describe several attitudes of mindfulness that are essential to training in mindfulness. These mind states are important to be aware of because, as we discussed in Chapter 2, pages 48–49, your thoughts influence how you feel, and they change the very structure of your brain. We believe it is important for educational leaders to experiment with an assortment of meditative approaches in order to engage and strengthen contemplative mind states or attitudes. The capacity for greater openness, as an example of a contemplative mind state, when used in the appropriate context, supports trust building within groups. It does not mean passivity or indifference. Instead, it represents the capacity to maintain balance in the face of shifting and competing demands, accepting what cannot be changed for the moment, and calling on one's inner resources to stay poised under pressure.

While developing these contemplative mind states is important, we think self-compassion and compassion toward others are at the heart of mindfulness, and there is extensive research on compassion and self-compassion. Kristin Neff, associate professor of human development and culture at the University of Texas at Austin, a noted expert on self-compassion and one of the first people to operationally define and study it in the academic literature, and author of *Self-Compassion: The Proven Power of Being Kind to Yourself,*[12] says there isn't much difference between compassion and self-compassion. Neff distinguishes three features of compassion:

1. You notice that someone is suffering, and you feel moved by someone's suffering so that your heart responds to his or her pain;

2. You respond to another's pain with care, warmth, and understanding; and

3. You realize that another person's suffering is part of the shared human experience.

In self-compassion, you extend the same care and understanding to yourself. Neff says that self-criticism, the opposite of self-compassion, triggers the fight-flight-or-freeze response. Obstacles to self-compassion include the belief that self-compassion is self-indulgent, or that it might undermine your motivation to achieve professional goals. However, the ability to understand and connect with others, and to understand and care for yourself, is at the heart of outstanding leadership.

Practice Pointer—Mind States:
Developing Attitudes of Mindfulness

- **Create an Intention.** Intentions have power. An intention helps you define your goals, plans, actions, and vision. Intention also nurtures your internal capacity and resources in service of your deepest calling.
- **Embrace a "Beginner's Mind."** Have a mental posture that is filled with curiosity and wonder.
- **Practice Nonjudgment.** Cultivate impartial observation regarding your experience, not judging or interpreting thoughts and feelings as good or bad, right or wrong, and not showing indifference, either. Instead, notice thoughts, feelings, or sensations in the moment.
- **Practice Allowing and Opening.** Validate things as they are: the good, the not so good. Soften around mental states that feel particularly rigid. Ask yourself: Am I sure?
- **Practice Nonstriving.** Don't try to get to something else, other than where you are now; don't grasp or exhibit aversion to change.

(Continued)

(Continued)

- **Embrace Equanimity.** Practice feeling a sense of balance and centeredness, which promotes understanding and insight, supporting wisdom.
- **Practice Letting Be.** Allow emotions and feelings to "run their course"; don't try to change your experience. Let painful emotions be; don't try to get rid of them. Often the struggle to control or otherwise get rid of what is unpleasant backfires, causing you more anxiety and stress.
- **Practice Self-reliance.** Trust in your own direct experience. Your own life is your best teacher. This doesn't mean going it alone. Cultivate and cherish meaningful relationships.
- **Practice Balance.** Show steadiness or evenness of mind in the face of change.
- **Practice Self-compassion.** Show kindness toward yourself.[13]

We invite you to select one or more of these mindful mind states and throughout your day and your week practice with it. For example, you may choose to practice allowing and opening. How would that look in your school and home life? How might allowing and opening help you to be a more effective leader?

How Much Practice Time?

"If you have a daily regimen—exercise, meditation, prayer, sports, music, writing—you've learned to do the same thing day after day. You don't abandon it when it gets boring. You don't avoid the repetition. You learn to just do it, because you know that the repetition and boredom eventually serve your goal."

—Margaret Wheatley, from *Perseverance* (2010)[14]

When you first start establishing a mindfulness practice, you may set ambitious goals and quickly become discouraged if you don't meet them. One of our colleagues began a "formal" practice by lying under her desk twice a day with the door shut, listening to an audio meditation program that arrived from a teacher in New York City every day. The practice took 10 minutes. It is not so important how much time you set aside to practice, whether it is 5, 10, 15, or 20 minutes daily. What is important is to practice faithfully for whatever time you decide to set aside. As you begin to develop your practice, the length of time may organically lengthen as you begin to see and feel positive results. Even in moments when you find the practice challenging, you may notice that sticking with the practice is helpful. With a formal practice of mindfulness—whether sitting, standing, walking, eating, lying down, speaking, or listening, and so on—it is useful to set aside a special time and place where you can give your wholehearted attention. This can be indoors or outdoors.

Especially when first beginning to explore mindfulness, it is important to establish the conditions for your meditation practice to remain constant: same time, same place, same quiet spot. This consistency supports the body and mind in adopting new habits and experiencing a rhythm of practice; the same time and same place allow you to respond to positive cues, such as having a special space dedicated for the purpose of relaxation, or enjoying a special chair. But, even if this is not possible, please begin anyway. Give up the need to have all the right conditions and begin wherever you are.

> **Practice Pointer**
>
> "It is important to know that meditation has little to do with clock time. Five minutes of formal practice can be profound or more so than forty-five minutes. The sincerity of your effort matters far more than elapsed time, since we are really talking about stepping out of minutes and hours and into moments."
>
> —Jon Kabat-Zinn, from *Wherever You Go There You Are* (1994)[15]

Practices That Complement Mindfulness

While mindfulness is a foundational practice for school leaders, it's not the only practice we recommend to our clients. The Tree of Contemplative Practices in Figure 3.1 represents an array of contemplative practices compiled by the Center for Contemplative Mind in Society, whose mission is to transform and to support higher education through the use of contemplative practices. These practices are deeply supportive and complementary to mindfulness in that they support greater mind-body connection, focus, and reflection. They promote a contemplative mind state—mental, emotional, and spiritual qualities of openness, equanimity, acceptance, and gratitude. For the visual learner, practicing visualization from among these practices may be most useful. For the leader who learns best by reading, an approach to calming the mind and balancing the body may be the use of *lectio divina*, or meditative reading. Risa, our principal from Oakland, wanted to become more aware of her physical impulses and not just her mental and emotional impulses. To address this, we recommended that she develop greater body awareness through yoga and Qigong. Over time, with greater awareness, Risa recognized her habit of self-criticism about her weight and her impulse to reach for comfort food when she was feeling badly about herself.

Figure 3.1   The Tree of Contemplative Practices

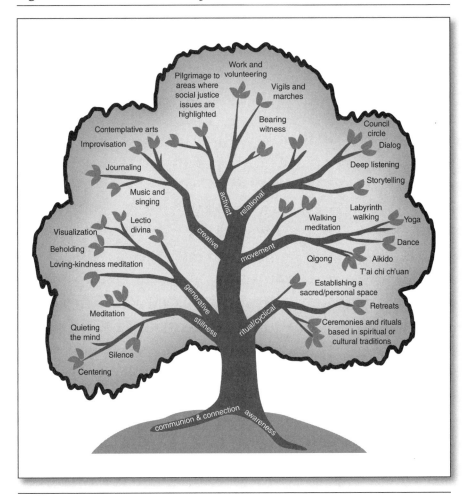

Source: Concept and design by Duerr, M.; illustration by Bergman, C. (n.d.). "The Tree of Contemplative Practices." Northampton, MA: The Center for Contemplative Mind in Society. Reprinted with permission. Retrieved from http://www.contemplative mind.org/practices/tree

Distraction: The New Normal and the School Leader's Dilemma

Distraction, multitasking, "continuous partial attention," cognitive overload: The educational sector is addicted to multitasking, and not just because our educational leaders are experiencing more conflicting accountability pressures than at any other time in American history. "Occupations shape people," wrote Dan C. Lortie in his classic study of the teaching profession, *Schoolteacher: A Sociological Study*,[16] and most educators today have almost no day-to-day socialization or support for sustained attention to their own learning and focus. This fracturing of focus is now coupled with intense performance demands based on the introduction of the Common Core, standards-based grading, and new teacher evaluation systems. It is a blunting brew. "I came into the superintendency wanting to bring reflection and focus to every aspect of my job," a school leader recently told us. "I feel like I've lost that right now."

Some of the most productive meetings in schools we have observed were held in a school district in New York City in the late 1990s. School leaders had drastically pared down agendas—only one or two topics were allowed per meeting, with unrelenting focus on teaching and learning: no announcements, no facilities talk, no discussions of budgets or schedules. These meetings were a revelation to us. Yet we've almost never seen them replicated, because they require so much focus and discipline.

"Attention is the most powerful tool of the human spirit," observes Linda Stone, who coined the terms *continuous partial attention* and *email apnea* (see Chapter 1, pages 22, 58).[17] Teachers and administrators dislike and feel disrespected by the continuous partial attention they receive from students, yet this is very frequently the attitude they bring to their own learning and thinking about their work. "You need time . . . to find solutions to the dilemmas that face you," writes Adrian W. Savage in his blog *Slow Leadership*.[18] His book with the same title advocates slowing down to regain work-family balance and because thoughtful decision making should not be rushed. Again, while slowing down may be useful, especially given our overbooked, overworked, and overextended lifestyle, the key is the quality of your attention and awareness. To make real change requires deep, devoted, unconstrained attention.

Distraction is the enemy of change, and multitasking is a roadblock to the satisfaction of focused, sustained attention. The late Clifford Nass, Stanford professor of communications and an expert on human-computer interactions, has said that half the time, we are sidetracked by distraction.[19] Our addiction to "doing" may make us feel engaged, active, and in control, when really we are spinning ever more out of control and moving farther from the real conditions that can change our work.

Negativity Bias: Part of the School Leader's Dilemma

"Employees are not emotional islands. Rather, they continuously spread their own moods and receive and are influenced by others' moods. When they work in groups, they literally can catch each others' emotions like viruses, a phenomenon known as emotional contagion."

—Wharton@Work, University of Pennsylvania[20]

Distraction and fractured attention isn't the only part of the school leader's dilemma. It has become common knowledge in the field of neuroleadership that our brains have a built-in negativity bias. We have a built-in bias toward the negative because our human ancestors once needed to focus on dangers and threats to stay safe and to pass on their genes. This meant being especially attentive to dangers and threats. Over hundreds of years, your brain has evolved to look for the bad and react to it intensely. This bias manifests itself in many ways in the present day. For example, say you have 10 great comments from colleagues about an important project you are working on and one negative comment about the project. Which do you remember at the end of the day, the 10 positive comments or the one negative comment? For most people, the negative comment stays with them. According to Rick Hanson, we overestimate threats and underestimate opportunities and resources. This Hanson says, sensitizes the brain to the negative, making it easier to have more negative experiences, a vicious cycle.[21] The effect of all this, according to Hanson, is that our brains are like Velcro for negative experiences and Teflon for positive ones.[22] What can you do about this? Hanson offers several suggestions in *Hardwiring Happiness,* which include making a conscious effort to pay attention to the many positive moments in your day: savoring a cup of tea or coffee, noticing the way the sunlight reflects off a windowpane, really noticing a smiling face. There are countless moments that pass us by unnoticed and unappreciated. Hanson's mantra is "Take in the good."[23] As school leaders, it is important to "take in the good" and to recognize and manage your mood to effectively lead others. This means recognizing when your mood has turned sour and how this might impact your school colleagues and your own effectiveness.

In his book *Primal Leadership,*[24] Daniel Goleman describes the "contagious" nature of a leader's mood, which can spread to others whether the leader is aware of that mood or not. He also explores the degree to which a leader's mood can influence the entire outlook of the workplace. Sigal Barsade, an associate professor of management at the Wharton School of the University of Pennsylvania, has conducted several studies of "emotional contagion"[25] in professional settings and found that a leader's mood does in fact have a dramatic effect on the team. Sour moods have what he describes as a "ripple effect" that affects everyone on the team explicitly and more subtly; even the most subtle emotional cues can affect everyone nearby. Luckily, school leaders can take advantage of emotional contagion in the workplace. School leaders who cultivate a broad repertoire of emotional intelligence skills, and frequently express positive emotions, will have more success at enhancing the performance of the individuals around them. The entire school or organization can benefit from a leader's subtle cues.

Think About It

Attitudes of Mindfulness to Address the Negativity Bias

How often is your negativity bias at work? How might it be affecting your leadership performance? How might the practice of mindfulness be useful in cultivating mindful mind states or mindful attitudes we described earlier in this chapter? Is there a particular mindful mind state that you might be willing to explore to address your negativity bias?

The Wandering Mind Is an Unhappy Mind

Mind wandering is a universal and inevitable occurrence during mindfulness meditation. Consider this: You're preparing for work, brushing your teeth. Your mind drifts from the sensation of holding the toothbrush and feeling the toothpaste to thoughts about an intensely difficult meeting planned for later that day. Unconsciously and reflexively, you begin to tense the muscles in your neck and upper back. Your thoughts speed up, cascading into one another, anticipating the worst. You finish quickly, feeling the pinch of time. It's no surprise that this diffused and unstable focus impairs an educational leader's performance throughout the day. What's surprising, once we become aware of it, is just how often our attention is drifting like a cork bobbing on a fast-running stream.

In *Focus* Goleman observes that while mind wandering occurs less often when people engage in pleasurable activity, they are still inclined to think negatively. When you're focused on a particular activity rather than thinking about something else, you're happier.[26] According to Goleman, a greater predictor of happiness is not the activity itself—external events and circumstances—but what you're thinking and whether you're engaging in mind wandering.[27] Goleman cites several commonsense ways of addressing "attention fatigue," such as spending time in nature, attending a retreat, and having quiet time, time when you unplug from your computers and devices.[28]

An important task for a leader is to bring the wandering mind back to the object of attention—often the breath is used, since it is always present—and to change one's relationship with the running mental commentary of judgments, criticisms, analysis, and planning. A leader should not try to suppress, grasp, or push away the thoughts and emotions. You are not striving to have a different experience. You accept things as they are: the pleasant, the unpleasant, and the neutral. This act in itself for many leaders is a huge step toward self-compassion and well-being.

To deliberately bring the wandering mind back is important for many reasons. The mind is a continuously engaged-in narration, like a TV set with the on switch continually engaged. When you notice that the mind has wandered, you are already back to the present moment, a critically important part of resetting one's focus. As you bring the mind back, you build focus and concentration. You notice where the mind is—in a distressing thought, for example, or noticing sensations in the body, stiffness in the lower back or pain in the upper neck, or whether your breathing has turned into panting, for instance. In this noticing, you'll find a lot of information about your stress level, the state of your well-being. Conversely, you may notice that in this moment, you are well, that you feel a sense of ease in your body and in your mind. You make the connection between what you think and how you feel—connecting the mind and the body. For leaders, this is a powerful form of integration and congruence: Your thoughts and body language align. This signals to others that you are trustworthy and authentic, comfortable in your own skin.

The Myth of Multitasking

"Multitasking is a myth—what we actually do is task-switching. . . . Out of all the things our mind does, that switching function is the most depleting."

—Amishi P. Jha, associate professor of psychology, University of Miami (2014)[29]

We have increasing scientific evidence that multitasking is a myth—our brains cannot actually handle multiple tasks simultaneously—and it is an untruth that multitaskers have an edge and are more productive. Multitasking is a poor way to manage your time. Multitaskers find it hard to ignore irrelevant information, so they have greater difficulty in remembering things according to the late Clifford Nass and his colleagues at Stanford. Multitaskers do things that they are not supposed to do, which interferes with what they should be doing.[30]

As most of us know, an essential leadership skill is the ability to focus and stay on task, to capture and direct attention for one's self and others. Daniel Goleman notes in *Focus* that continually splitting your attention diminishes concentration and focus.[31]

In Chapter 2 and throughout this book, we discuss the extraordinary demands facing school leaders today, which have contributed to the urgency to multitask. In her book *Real Happiness at Work*, Sharon Salzberg, cofounder of the Insight Meditation Society and a well-known meditation teacher and author, describes attention deficit trait (ADT), a workplace problem caused by constant input from high-tech devices in which workers find that they are not working to their potential, putting in more hours at work and yet being less productive.[32]

Think About It

Consider your workday. How often do you engage in multitasking? How does this contribute to your work productivity? How might you reduce workplace distractions?

Share your suggestions on our Facebook page at www.facebook.com/ TheMindfulSchoolLeader.

Mindfulness Practice Aid 3.2: Mindful Walking

Meditating While Walking Around

Even if you are like many school leaders and do not have time each day to practice formal mindfulness meditation, you probably do spend time walking around the school building. Here is a practice that you can do while walking to restore a sense of calm and focus.

How to Do Mindful Walking

In mindful walking, you bring your awareness and focus to the entire process of walking. Notice body sensations, shifting weight, balance, and the micromovements of the body as you take a step, noting your breathing and focusing on each step and your environment. Walking mindfully can be practiced in many different occasions: when you are taking a leisurely stroll on a beautiful Sunday afternoon, or when you are walking from your car to the office or walking from one meeting to the next. Even if the purpose of your walking is to get somewhere for an important event, you can enjoy walking in this way. With each step, remind yourself that you are here now. With each step, you feel your breath. With each step, you recognize how you are feeling in the moment. With each step, you connect with the environment—really see the sky, the trees, a chair, or a desk. When you walk in this way, each step becomes a meditation.

Begin with this practice for two to three minutes, and expand the time if you like.

- Calm your body and mind by breathing deeply, in and out of the nose three or four times.
- Become aware of standing, and feel your feet on the ground.
- Even before you move, become aware of the impulse to move.
- As you take a step, become aware of moving your body.
- Feel the heels, balls of the feet, and toes, and observe the contact between the soles of your shoes and the floor.
- Become aware of sensations that you might not ordinarily notice—feel how your body moves, and feel your feet, arms, legs, torso, and facial muscles. Feel the clothes against your skin.
- Be aware of balance and weight shift of the body.
- Stay with the sensory experience of moving, allowing for full attention of each movement to the best of your ability.
- When you notice that your mind has wandered away from awareness of walking, gently and firmly bring your attention back to the sensations of walking and breathing.
- Notice the sounds around you, without getting attached to any one sound.
- Become aware of scents around you, without getting attached to any one scent.
- When you have completed walking, be aware of stopping and standing still.

- Feel your breath.
- When you are finished, stretch gently and notice how you feel.

Mindful Leader Practice Connection—Tips for School Leaders

1. **Focus your attention on this step.** Notice when you are drawn into thinking about "what comes next." This focus brings you out of your head and away from being continually projected into the future, striving, and goal setting. Know that life can be lived only in the present moment. (Again, we are not saying that leaders should not act purposefully and with direction.)

2. **Change your perspective.** If you tend to walk fast, try walking slowly. When you change your mind, you change your body chemistry. Notice the thoughts and feelings that arise. This practice cultivates self-acceptance.

3. **Take mini-mindfulness moments.** Remember to notice that you are breathing. Pay attention to your surroundings. Notice sights, sounds, and scents. This brings you back to the present moment.

4. **Pause in your walk to say something positive about another person, and then notice how you feel.** It is easy to be kind to people you know and like. Extending kindness to strangers cultivates an open heart and mind, which promotes positive emotions and well-being. Kindness can be as simple as a smile, a simple hello. Kindness is contagious and builds a positive school environment.

5. **Allow yourself to be bored.** As we've said previously, often, we are human "doings" rather than human "beings." Instead of checking your smartphone, texting, or eating the next time you walk around the school building or to and from a meeting, do nothing else. Just walk. Breathe and enjoy this moment of being alive.

6. **Notice your thoughts and then let them be.** Most of our thinking is repetitive and, as we've mentioned, tends to be negative, which robs us of our capacity for peace. Instead of trying to get rid of thoughts, resist thoughts, or avoid thoughts, allow the thoughts to be as they are. Name the thought ("I am bored"), and watch it change. Naming the thought objectifies it, diminishing its charge.

7. **Focus your eyes softly.** Even if you have walked the same path a thousand times, look with a beginner's mind, like a child full of awe, curiosity, openness, and wonder. An element of creativity is curiosity and wonder. Openness promotes positive well-being in the mind and body.

8. **Feel and express gratitude.** The feeling and expression of gratitude is linked with positive states of mind and with overall well-being.

MINDFUL WALKING ON CITY STREETS

While at a mindfulness retreat and course for educators led by Thich Nhat Hanh in Barcelona, Spain, we enjoyed walking mindfully with 600 educators through the city streets!

Mindful walking city streets of Barcelona, Spain, with Thich Nhat Hanh. Photo by Valerie Brown.

Portraits of Practice

3.1 Sophia Isako Wong, (Self-Described) Disabled Writer, Musician, Spiritual Seeker, and Assistant Professor (2003–2009) and Tenured Associate Professor of Philosophy (2010–2013)

Long Island University–Brooklyn

> "Mindfulness helped me to accept my disabilities, the severe and chronic pain, the depression. I began to see that I was too burned out to remain effective as a school leader."

We met Sophia Isako Wong at a mindfulness retreat for people of color at Blue Cliff Monastery in Pine Bush, New York. We were touched by her openness and willingness to speak about her struggle with depression and how mindfulness has made an important contribution to bringing greater happiness in her life.

"Recently, I resigned my tenured teaching position at Long Island University's Brooklyn campus in New York City. In addition to my teaching responsibilities, I founded and led a campus-wide network for peer mentoring and was a member of the college's Teaching and Learning Initiative, which strategizes on ways to improve classroom teaching. Many of my students were women and people of color, and first in their families to attend college. As a woman of both Japanese and Chinese heritage, I really related to them, to their struggles and frustrations.

"I suffer from severe pain and chronic fatigue, and have a physical disability that limits my use of both hands and forearms. I can no longer type on a computer keyboard, write with a pen on paper, or lift more than a half-cup of tea. Before I started practicing mindfulness, I viewed myself as a person without disabilities. I saw my chronic pain and fatigue as something to overcome. My role was to help other people. Also, I lived with clinical depression, which I was aware of since my early 20s.

"I was raised to be very discreet about all of this, keeping this all hidden away. In my family background as an East Asian, there is such a strong emphasis on overworking, on being the 'model minority,' on making things look perfect. The message from my Japanese and Chinese heritages was 'Do what is best for the entire community. Put yourself last; others first.' I felt a lot of shame about the depression, believing that I could avoid the stigma of depression. I thought I could avoid being labeled with a mental illness if I didn't think about it and did not talk about it.

"Mindfulness helped me to accept my disabilities, the severe and chronic pain, the depression. I began to see that I was too burned out to remain effective as a school leader. Mindfulness helped me discern where to put my energy—what to hold on to and what to let go of. I realized that my particular job—working in this particular environment—was not the best place for me. I came to accept myself and my illness and then to disclose more of myself to others.

"I have seen many people in similar circumstances seemingly function perfectly and then one day disappear without explanation from the pressures of their work and their life. They resign quietly. Through mindfulness, I became more aware of my feelings, not just physically but mentally and emotionally. I did not want to just walk away, to disappear, to give up on my life.

"Today, my practice informs much of my day, from the time I wake up to the time I settle for bed at night. For example, every morning at home, I begin the day with a little ritual of sitting mindfully and quietly. I listen to a guided meditation, the same one I used to use in the classroom to begin class with my students. It's interesting. My husband has no formal mindfulness training or practice. However, since I have been doing this little ritual, he now starts his day sitting quietly, drinking a cup of tea. Before, in the morning, he would check his email and read online magazines. I love watching him sipping his tea. When I have time, I prepare and eat a mindful breakfast, mainly in silence.

"I have built many opportunities to practice mindfulness and meditation in my life. For example, I am a member of a local mindfulness meditation community in Queens, New York, and attend weekly sitting meditation practice periods. Also, I go out of town for a three-day silent retreat every two to three months.

"All these practices are grounding in my body and mind. It was through being more aware and having a sense of self-compassion that I was able to be gentle with myself, to be curious about the stiffness and pain in my body, to feel the tension and then to slowly learn to pause and relax.

"When my pain levels skyrocketed, I started using Tibetan bowls in my classroom with students. When I found that the room was too noisy, frenetic, and unfocused, and to soothe myself, I stopped what I was doing. I stopped trying to force things, trying to make the students listen. Even though they were taking college courses, I found that many of them were underprepared to do college-level reading and writing, partly because of the university's open enrollment policy. I also noticed some of my students behaving in ways that suggested they might have learning disabilities, ADHD [attention deficit/hyperactivity disorder], eating disorders, anxiety, OCD [obsessive-compulsive disorder], and other conditions they chose not to disclose.

"To soothe myself and calm the atmosphere, I stopped whatever I was doing in the classroom and then started softly playing the Tibetan bowl. This was an audio and visual cue to the students to settle down, relax, and reset their focus. I found that this really helped me to settle down and helped them to refocus and calm down. In fact, I didn't use any mindfulness practice in the classroom that I had not used regularly at home.

"I taught Intro to Philosophy for first- and second-year students, also two courses I designed, Health Care Ethics and Justice in the Family. My classes were about two-thirds African American and two-thirds female, and many of them were the first generation in their families to attend college. Many of these students worked two to three jobs to make ends meet while going to school. Many of them were also looking after children, grandchildren, or family members with disabilities.

"I asked the students to put the desks in a circle before we listened to a three-minute guided meditation to bring calm and focus into the classroom. I even carried a small wind chime with me around my wrist as I walked through the campus as a way of offering mindfulness to the entire campus. I found the sound healing, and so did many others.

"Today, I feel grounded in my body and my mind. I am speaking out and speaking up for myself. I trust and care for myself. I am very grateful to my mindfulness practice for having created deeper healing and openness in my life."

Sophia Isako Wong, PhD (Columbia), is a freelance writer, musician, and spiritual seeker. She taught Western European philosophy for 2 years at Columbia University and for 10 years at the Brooklyn campus of Long Island University in New York. She maintains a list of mindfulness resources for educators at www. sophiawong.info/mindfulness.

3.2 Philip Altmann, Former Fourth-Grade Teacher-Leader

Recently retired from Ardtornish Primary School, Adelaide, South Australia

We spoke to Philip Altmann on Skype late one school night. Modestly and haltingly,

Philip described the birth of his meditation practice, his own "awakening," and the ways in which his practice has influenced him as a teacher, school leader, and person.

Philip, recently retired, was a fourth-grade teacher and teacher-leader at Ardtornish Primary School in Adelaide, South Australia, and had taught for 37 years, mostly in the Australian public school system. He now teaches mindfulness classes at Lake Windemere School in South Australia.

Someone who knew early in his life that he wanted to be a teacher, Philip graduated from the Salisbury College of Advanced Education and took a bachelor of education. Later, he gained a graduate diploma of education in educational counseling from the University of South Australia. Along with studying pedagogy and classroom management, he became interested in "psychosynthesis," a school of psychological thinking that focuses on the direct experience of self. While studying psychosynthesis, Philip began "breathing meditative exercises," which he says helped him clear his mind, focus, and relax. He discovered this form of breathing and centering was pleasurable, and says "I found I really enjoyed it."

QUOTES FROM "RATE MY TEACHERS [WORLDWIDE]"

FOURTH GRADERS WRITE ABOUT MR. ALTMANN

[We pulled these off the Web before talking with Philip Altmann.]

"He is a great teacher and teaches us mindfullness and is very helpful and helps me with my work"

"Mr. Altmann is the best."

"Mr. Altmann is the best teacher I have every had, he is strict but fair, i lern a lot"

Then, in the mid 1990s, one of Philip's friends became a Zen meditation teacher and began offering meditation retreats. Later, Philip discovered the work of Eckhart Tolle and the idea of living vividly in the present moment, from Tolle's *The Power of Now*.[33]

Philip pursued his contemplative practice largely on his own, and for his own benefit for about a decade, until he took a course on mindfulness and mindfulness-based stress reduction (MBSR) through the Openground center in Sydney, Australia (www.openground.com.au). During that MBSR course, it became clear to Philip that mindfulness practices would be very useful to his students and in his classroom. As he said thoughtfully, "A door opened, and I took the plunge." He later attended a Mindful Schools training course in Los Angeles because, as he put it, "I thought it would be helpful to get some formal training in mindful classroom practice techniques.

"I began teaching breathing techniques and meditation techniques to my 10-year-old students, and they were quite receptive to it. I've begun to add on some other pieces, things from Martin Seligman's positive psychology work,[34] and I know students, parents, and my school colleagues have all begun to be influenced.

"Last week, we had our parent-teacher interview night, and I explained some of the curriculum, the research, and the things I am teaching in the classroom regarding mindfulness to my parents. A few said it was the best parent-teacher night they'd ever had, and one parent reported, 'I don't know what you're doing, but yesterday my 10-year-old daughter was stressed out, and I found her sitting on the kitchen floor meditating.'"

Philip says he noticed that his students, the ones he's taught over the last three years, are "the calmest group of kids we've ever had in the school. Teachers and staff really notice that." He also observed that given Australia's strict separation of church and state, similar to the United States, it was important to introduce mindfulness as a completely secular activity, "not religious in any way, which it truly isn't. This is about a way of managing oneself and one's thoughts."

Philip continued to describe the effects on his students, and himself, from his evolving mindfulness practice. "What I teach my fourth graders is consciousness of their own bodies, through breathing. We do breathing exercises once or twice a day, depending on how restless they are, how focused they are. 'Are their minds untidy?' I ask myself," and then Philip makes a determination based on this.

"Teaching is a job that requires you to constantly improve. My mindfulness practice has been a huge piece of my improvement and my evolution as a professional. Mindfulness is the water on which the boat floats; it keeps the water of my class calm. I've learned to notice my own breath, notice my mind, and this helps me be the teacher and the teacher-leader I wish to be." Although intensely modest, Philip believes what he teaches has a "ripple effect through the school." The kids say, "Thank you for teaching us mindfulness." A student who moved schools, to another state, emailed him to say that learning mindfulness was the best thing they had ever done.

"This is a way for me to be a better person, perform my role in a more effective way. I have learned how to be a happier person, in an informal way. I listen more, I don't talk as much, and people frequently ask me how I can be so calm."

When I ask Philip if he is interested in teaching mindfulness to larger groups of teachers and school leaders, he says, "I don't know. I'm about to finish my teaching career. I might rather go fishing. But I suspect I might be drawn to it, to training other teachers and leaders. There is a need for other practitioners to learn about how to teach mindfulness to their students to have calmer, more focused classrooms."

Philip Altmann was formerly a primary classroom teacher in Adelaide, South Australia. He has a bachelor of education (BEd) and a Graduate Diploma of Educational Counselling. He practices and teaches mindfulness to students as well as leading workshops for staff in the personal application and teaching of mindfulness in the classroom. He has completed a mindfulness-based stress-reduction (MBSR) course and trained with Mindful Schools in the United States.

Please visit us on Facebook at https://www.facebook.com/TheMindfulSchoolLeader.

4

Communication and Connection

Powerful Skills of the Mindful School Leader

"Our work, our relationships, and, in fact, our very lives succeed or fail gradually, then suddenly, *one conversation at a time*."

—Susan Scott, *Fierce Conversations* (2004)[1]

Donna S.T.O.P.s

Donna is an educational testing specialist executive from the Midwest who works at a private company that designs and administers a variety of standardized tests. She came to us through her supervisor, who wanted her to address concerns with her communication style that a recent performance review had revealed. Donna's way of relating to her colleagues had become a liability at work. Donna grew up in a large, boisterous family of six, and her earliest memories are of sitting at the dinner table trying to "get a word in edgewise." According to Donna, "Dinnertime was a free-for-all. If you didn't jump into the fray, you simply didn't exist; you were ignored. So I grew up believing that I had to fight my way into every conversation. I did this through college and graduate school, and on one level, it helped me get good grades. People paid attention and took me seriously."

A straight-A student, Donna pushed herself to excel and had little patience or empathy for others who didn't live up to her high standards. Always feeling the press of time, she routinely interrupted or finished other people's sentences. She prided herself on being "cerebral" and inclined toward research and analysis, yet her years of study and sedentary lifestyle left her with little physical energy and a tentative, almost abstract connection with her body.

"When I joined this company, things began to fall apart," she says. "I found myself just telling it like it is, and that got me in trouble. I guess I just wasn't comfortable with finesse and basically spoke before I thought. Plus, with my focus on growing my career, I was feeling lots of stress and pressure to get on with it, and saw social relationships as an add-on at work. The real work was my technical skill."

Donna's husband Gary, a bankruptcy lawyer, was very different. More than lawyering, he said his work involved counseling others at times of crisis. Donna admired Gary's ability to listen with complete attention and his way of communicating that seemed to give people permission to speak with greater honesty. While Gary and Donna's relationship was loving and supportive, Gary felt "pushed to the edge" at times because of Donna's cut-to-the-chase style. Things came to a head at work about year ago when Donna "exploded" in a staff meeting on a new test project, storming out of the room in a rage. This was her wake-up call; she knew it was time to change.

A friend mentioned mindfulness as a stress-reduction approach, and she began doing some online research about the effects of stress on the body. She ordered a book by Thich Nhat Hanh from Amazon (and read it!), and then watched a TED talk by Jill Bolte Taylor about living in new ways after her stroke, and she decided she might be open to making some changes in her life. Without actually realizing it, she slowly changed her morning routines. She began starting most days by lying in bed a few extra minutes to sense and feel her body, something she had almost never done before. This was her way of detecting tension in her body; she often found herself holding a sense of strain in various parts of her body. After listening to a Sounds True podcast on gratitude, instead of the morning talk shows, she started taking moments while showering and dressing to reflect and to feel grateful. This practice seemed to help her mood, too. We began working with Donna on her speaking and listening style.

Donna practiced S.T.O.P. (see Mindfulness Practice Aid 1.1, "Stopping, Pausing, and Observing," page 35), noticing the impulse to interrupt others. When the urge arose, she trained herself to S.T.O.P.: to concentrate and to listen, and then ask at least one open-ended question—a question that she could not possibly know the answer to—and to show sincere and genuine interest in the other person. She used a mindfulness app (see Appendix C, online, page 17) to stop, pause, and breathe several times a day, and even started doing Qigong as a way of reducing stress, getting physical exercise, and learning to slow down.

"Before practicing some of these things, I guess you would call me mindless. I would lecture, interrupt, try to fix people, solve their problems, or not listen at all, thinking about what I was going to say when they stopped talking. In providing feedback to a work colleague, the conversation was very one-sided. It was all about me, pointing out how my colleague could improve. I was not present for myself or for others. Today, my listening is much deeper. Even in typing emails, before I hit Send, I stop and check my posture. I notice: Am I hunched over the keyboard? I've trained myself to stop and take three good deep breaths before I go on to the next email. I'm not an expert; I'm new to all this, but I see the benefits."

In contrast to Donna, consider Allison, a new assistant principal from a rural K–8 school in the Southwest and a mindfulness practitioner for two years. She says she learned about communicating mindfully from a mentor, a college professor who, she says, "changed [her] life." We met with Allison during a brief lunchtime break at school in the early spring. Even before our arrival, she had arranged her day to set aside uninterrupted time to talk. During our 20-minute meeting, she took no outside calls or emails. She didn't check her phone or scan her computer for incoming messages. The door to her office was closed. She focused on just one thing: our conversation. Her energy was attentive, open, and warm, and as she spoke she allowed for natural pauses in the conversation. We had the feeling that she really listened and reflected, and we felt that we had her focused attention. We spoke about her communication style and how mindfulness supports good communication. She said, "More than anything, I take each conversation as a mini-mindfulness moment. I focus, listen, breathe, and pause before I reply—not every day or always, but a lot. I check in with my body. This only takes a few seconds, and the beauty is that no one except me knows my stealth mindfulness move. At first, this was challenging. Now it's a habit, and a good one. It's made a huge difference in my relationships. When I ask open questions and really listen for the reply, it's a fuller, richer conversation that causes me and others to reflect. I slow down these conversations, and I've learned that pausing can be powerful."

Mindful Communication: Mindful Speaking, Mindful Listening

"After all we go through, we are asked to lead a life of honest expression, which always starts with listening as a way to remember what matters, to name what matters, and to voice what matters. These are the practices that keep us authentic."

—Mark Nepo, *Seven Thousand Ways to Listen* (2012)[2]

Mindful communication, speaking and listening mindfully, is an "informal" practice of mindfulness. It is mindfulness in action. Speaking mindfully is communicating in a truthful, authentic way, aware of your thoughts, feelings, and emotions, and being sensitive to the same in others. It means noticing when you are triggered and using the mindfulness practices we describe in this book to regain a sense of emotional and physical equilibrium. It means choosing words that inspire and promote confidence. It requires paying attention to the small signals in others and watching for signs in yourself. It requires recognizing when you are no longer present, when you have tuned out of the conversation. In other words, communicating mindfully is about showing up as fully as possible, with the dignity of your presence, your attention, and your compassion. This all goes back to an important element of mindfulness: being where you are in the moment. If you aren't, you can't really listen for meaning, for connection and understanding. It's much like a very, very soft drizzle that doesn't penetrate bone-dry soil.

There are many approaches to communicating mindfully. And, we appreciate and admire the work of Marshall Rosenberg and the Center for Nonviolent Communication,[3] Gregory Kramer's Insight Dialogue,[4] and the Center for Mindfulness in Medicine, Health Care, and Society's work in interpersonal mindfulness, to name a few.[5] Communicating mindfully is a "live encounter" that sometimes doesn't fit into a rigid step-by-step approach, although they provide useful guidelines. The essence of communicating mindfully is about cultivating understanding and love. We practice pausing; noticing breathing; identifying and expressing feelings, needs, and expectations with care and respect; and listening for the same in others, asking open questions, and engaging in active listening, with all our senses.

As leadership coaches, we practice the art of asking open questions, which is a skill that develops over time. These questions share several key characteristics. An open question is one in which you could not possibly know the answer. It invites the speaker into a new perspective, a new possibility. Open questions are short and often go not just to the aspects of who, what, when, where, and why, but to the deeper question of meaning, values, and beliefs. Open questions invite the speaker to become accountable to him- or herself and to make the connection between beliefs, values, actions, and outcomes.

Recently, we led a Courage & Renewal retreat, focusing on listening and asking open questions at Ghost Ranch, a 21,000-acre wilderness ranch in northern New Mexico, a place that is sacred and special to us. During the retreat we had the opportunity to practice mindful communication with Sandra, a near-retirement Unitarian Universalist minister from the Midwest. Sandra attended the retreat partly seeking inner guidance about her approaching retirement and partly for rest and renewal. During the retreat, Sandra sat in a ball with her legs crossed and her knees pulled into her chest. She yawned frequently and seldom made eye contact. During meals, she rarely ate with anyone. Our conversation about our concerns about Sandra's body language went something like this:

Us: Hi Sandra. We want to talk with you early on in the retreat because we're curious and concerned about your body language and want to check out our observations with you. Is now a good time to talk?

Sandra: Yes, sure.

Us: What we notice is that while you attend nearly all the sessions, you sit with your eyes closed, your legs and arms crossed, and your knees pulled up into your chest, sending a mixed message. During mealtimes, you rarely join the group. So we are wondering whether you are getting your needs and expectations met at this retreat. We are feeling concerned and somewhat confused because your body language says one thing and yet you do show up to the sessions. Our goal is to ensure, as best we can, that everyone, including us, feels safe and welcome. Can you help us understand what might be happening for you?

Sandra: Wow. I had no idea that my body language conveyed that message. I sometimes get a bit sleepy and maybe I'm not getting enough sleep. I'm here partly because I'm exhausted and really need rest. I'm really loving the retreat, and being here at Ghost Ranch is a real gift to me. I guess I didn't realize just how tired I really am.

Us: We're glad to have this conversation now. Would you be willing to check in with us in a couple of days to see how you are feeling, and whether you are getting rest?

Sandra: That's a deal. Sure!

Communicating mindfully through both speaking and listening is a way of building understanding and connection with kindness and compassion. Adopting a mindful approach or mindful attitude (discussed in Chapter 3, page 83), like acceptance, nonjudgment, and self-compassion, strengthens and supports mindful speaking and listening. Listening in this way deepens connection. We have all had the experience of talking with people who "live in their head," cut off from the wisdom of their gut, their heart, and their breath. We have all had the experience of speaking about a difficult or troubling topic and feeling unheard, unseen, or unvalidated, and we know what that does for connection. To speak authentically is to practice self-awareness: Knowing your strengths and challenges, assessing yourself realistically, knowing your mood, knowing your energy level—all of these are drivers of the mindful school leader.

Think About It

Bring to mind a school leader you know who exemplifies excellence. Reflect on his or her communication style. What are the qualities of this leader? Is this person open, responsive, clear, present, and empathetic? Is he or she a ready listener, present, and attentive? What can you learn from this person about your own communication style? What do you wish to emulate?

Keys to Mindful Speaking

Let's turn to two key elements of mindful speaking: being present and speaking with clarity.

Being Present

The touchstone of mindful communication is being present. Time after time, we hear school leaders say that being present is one of the most important aspects of their work. In Chapter 3, pages 92–95, we discussed the forces that take you out of being present: Mind wandering, distractions, and multitasking are prime examples. As a school leader, you are called to be fully engaged—whether that is with a colleague, a student, or a parent—and not thinking ahead about your next commitment or what is going to happen at the next meeting. How practiced are you at being fully present in the day-to-day moments of your leadership life? What is the effect of presence when it is available to you?

Consider this: *At a public board meeting, you're dealing with a funding crisis and the financial concerns of parents, staff, and teachers. You're feeling anxious, overwhelmed, and fearful, and have a hard time focusing; but, in the moment, you are unaware of all these feelings of overwhelm. Your worry turns to mental rumination. You find it difficult to know how to respond, yet you don't know why.*

If you have been using some of the exercises in this book, and approaching them with an open mind and heart, however, you may experience a difference. Even with all of these stressors and distractors, you are able to "find" yourself. This is mindful presence—when you really need it. You are able to hear what is being said, to observe body language, and are also aware of what is not being said, thereby gaining a fuller perspective. You pause, breathe, and sense your arms at your sides and your feet underneath you, feeling more centered in your body. When you speak, you feel calmer and are able to stay on message, noticing whether your voice has an edge, and speak with clarity. With awareness of how you are feeling, you can make a better choice of how to respond.

Speaking With Clarity, Speaking From the Heart

Recently, we trained in the Ojai Foundation's Way of Council,[6] a spiritual practice of sitting in circle, engaging in the art of speaking and listening. Council is inspired by many traditions, including Native American and Quaker meeting for worship. Council has four primary guidelines: speak from the heart, listen from the heart, be lean of expression, and be spontaneous.[7]

While sitting in circle with a group of 40 teachers, students, faculty, and staff at an elite boarding school in the Northeast, we witnessed real transformation as those in the circle listened attentively and spoke with honesty and courage. A hallmark of speaking with clarity that supports real connection is speaking from the heart. Jack Zimmerman and Virginia Coyle, in their book *The Way of Council*, recommend an exercise to reinforce this heart connection by imagining words emerging from the mid-chest instead of the mouth.[8] They note too that speaking and listening in this way engenders greater connectedness among those in the circle and reduces personal positioning, reactivity, and defensiveness, supporting the circle as a whole.[9] When you speak from the heart, you talk about what *really* matters with passion and simplicity, avoiding long-winded theoretical or philosophical statements, and instead speak about your own personal transformation, observations, or insights.[10] Speaking from the heart is about being honest about your feelings, even when those feelings are painful, as is appropriate under the circumstances. It does not mean masking feelings to "make nice." Here is an example of speaking from the heart and the effect it can have, especially in very charged, difficult situations.

As director of athletics, your school was recently defeated at a crucial boys' varsity swim meet, and emotions are running high among parents, students, and teachers. You have been directed by the superintendent to reassign the head swim coach, an old swimming buddy from your college days, to a different role within the department and have called a meeting with him. You are dreading the conversation and put it off until the end of the day, having developed a habit of postponing difficult conversations.

But turning over a new leaf, because you've been practicing some of the exercises in this book, you have set aside uninterrupted time for this conversation and have checked in with your feelings (shame, guilt, and a little bit of anger) and your thoughts ("This loss will bring everyone down, and may make it harder for me to plead my case for an increase in my budget. This guy has been a close friend. How can I deliver this hard message?"). Without trying to repress your thinking, you turn your focus to your body and your breath, and notice how you are feeling. As your mind wanders off to ruminating, you gently bring it back to how you are feeling in this moment and feel your breath. After a few moments like this, you regain composure. You meet the swim coach. You speak without blame and express your regrets about the defeat. Though you are unaccustomed to talking freely about yourself and your feelings, you talk about a time in your life when you were defeated, fortunately a time your friend remembers because he witnessed this part of your life. Your attention is fully with the swim coach and what is happening in this moment as you speak. You deliver the message about the reassignment, about your expectations and needs, and then pause and listen before responding, reflecting on what to say before you say it. To ensure understanding between the two of you, you check in with the swim coach and then pause and listen again. Finally, you talk a little bit about the future and express hope for growth and continued relationship between the two of you. The coach leaves this encounter still disappointed by the defeat and the reassignment, but clear about where he stands, and feels heard. You exhale with a deep breath.

Sharing your feelings, expectations and needs, and self-disclosure in the appropriate context builds trust, understanding, connection, and a mutual relationship that bridges distance between people. Powerful leaders bring their rich life experience to their work. They don't fake being right when they are wrong. They demonstrate that they learn from challenges, and they exemplify coherence between what they do and what they say.

Speaking mindfully is grounded in body awareness. With enhanced body awareness, you become aware of where you might be holding tension, sensing rigidity in the body, as was the case for our director of athletics. Do you notice the pitch and tone of your voice? Are you mindful of the pace of your speech? Are you aware of the internal mental narrative, the assumptions, half-truths, and self-talk that influence what you say and how you say it? Mindful awareness offers clues about your thinking and your physical body, allowing you to notice, pause, breathe, and choose wisely.

Think About It

What is the quality of your speaking with work colleagues, family, and friends? Are you aware of unexamined assumptions that might influence your thinking and speaking? Consider a conversation in which you paused, listened deeply and openly. What happened, and what did you learn about your leadership from this experience?

In your last challenging conversation, were you aware of nonverbal cues? How present were you to intonation and facial expression? How present were you to your own internal cues: heart racing, sweaty palms? Challenge yourself in your next conversation to be fully present, and notice how that changes the relationship.

Keys to Mindful Listening

"The ability and willingness to listen with empathy is often what sets a leader apart. Hearing words is not adequate; the leader truly needs to work at understanding the position and perspective of the others involved in the conversation."

—Christine Riordan (2014)[11]

Listening is a core competency of outstanding school leadership. Mindful listening, like mindful speaking, is a body-centered practice that involves present-moment awareness. It engages all aspects of the body: our eyes to see, our ears to hear, our heart to feel. We listen with engagement for what is expressed and what is unexpressed. In our work with school leaders and in leading retreats, we have found that mindful listening transforms relationships and builds a deep connection, even among strangers, and even when words are not expressed. Paraphrasing Susan Scott, your listening *is* the relationship. Those who are listened to in this engaged way hear themselves differently and often find fresh insights just by the act of listening.

How to Listen Mindfully

Mindful listening is listening for understanding as opposed to waiting your turn to speak. Conscious awareness of your own hidden biases, assumptions, energy level, mind wandering, and more can affect how you listen. Jack Zimmerman and Virginia Coyle in *The Way of Council* suggest that listening heartfully, as in speaking heartfully, is to imagine the speaker's words entering your mid-chest rather than your ears, holding this image in your mind's eye while you take a few deep breaths, and notice any shift in perception. In your next conversation, we invite you to practice this way of shifting your listening. Notice what happens.

Too often we listen attentively when we are interested, excited, or in some way connected with the speaker. However, attentive listening flowers into kindness and compassion especially when you stretch yourself to listen mindfully to a speaker with whom you disagree, or where your immediate instinct is to tune out in irritation, or to judge, or when the speaker's voice is deadly monotone. Practicing listening mindfully under these challenging circumstances might surprise you by making you feel a sudden closeness because of the way you listened, even without saying a word, even when your impulse wanted to reject or turn away from the speaker. Remember, you don't have to agree to listen.

Practice Pause—Attentive Listening

As you consider your leadership listening skills, try these behavioral practices, which support attentive listening.

To prepare, take three deep cleansing breaths, allowing your exhale to be especially long—releasing tension and concerns. Do a short body scan (see Mindfulness Practice Aid 2.3, "The Body Scan," page 62), directing gentle attention to any parts of your body that may be holding tension or feeling especially tangled. Tune into yourself and ground yourself, feeling your feet underneath you. Become open to the act of listening. Imagine the front of your body (chest and heart) open, allowing the speaker's energy to come into your field (and in much the same way as in speaking mindfully, imagining the words emanating from the mid-chest and not the mouth). Turn toward the speaker and pause, noting the moment of beginning. Let the listener know you are attending by gazing at him or her with soft eyes, and occasionally affirming with a quiet "hum" or "un huh" or head shake. Don't overdo it. Before you ask a question, pause and "be with" what the speaker has just said. Then ask "open and honest" questions—questions you could not possibly know the answer to. Occasionally restate, "What I heard you say is . . ." and ask, "Did I get that right?" Genuine curiosity and nonjudgmental attention are your best tools. Be curious about what you don't know, and humble in how you ask. Attend to the rhythms of the conversation. Help move the conversation along if the pace has quickened, and also allow for periods of quietness and reflection. Don't be afraid of silence. Let silence do its work. Be grateful for your opportunity to listen to another human being, and let this person know you feel this way.

Listening to Your "Inner Leader"

"[T]he most practical thing we can achieve in any kind of work is insight into what is happening inside us as we do it. The more familiar we are with our inner terrain, the more sure-footed our teaching—and living—becomes."

—Parker J. Palmer, *The Courage to Teach Guide for Reflection and Renewal* (2007)[12]

Mindful listening is multidirectional: outward and inward, listening between and underneath the words. As we come to understand ourselves through greater self-awareness, we learn to listen, to befriend, and to trust our own internal compass. Wise school leaders don't sidestep this inward reflection; they acknowledge and value its importance in their leadership life.[13] As school leaders, we find it's really hard to encourage others to think creatively and innovatively if we are unwilling to look inwardly at what is unsettled and ambiguous in our own lives.

Becoming aware of your inner landscape is a continuing process of waking up to your thoughts, emotions, internal bodily cues, recognizing triggers, competencies, and challenges, which strengthens self-empathy, knowing "what we bring into the room." Try this practice to expand your self-empathy skills and ability to listen to your inner leader.

∽🙢🙢∽

Practice Pause—Self-Empathy:
How to Listen to Your "Inner Leader"

To prepare, take three deep cleansing breaths, allowing your eyes to close gently and your exhale to be especially long—releasing tension and concerns. Do a short body scan (see Mindfulness Practice Aid 2.3, "The Body Scan," page 62), directing gentle attention to any parts of your body that may be holding tension or feeling especially tangled. Tune into yourself and ground yourself, feeling your feet underneath you. Touch your face as an expression of gentleness and self-compassion. Stay present to your feelings whatever they may be as you breathe deeply and fully. Silently name feelings: irritated, rattled, perplexed, affectionate, hopeful, overjoyed. Touch your belly and soften, feeling the movement of the abdomen, rising and falling as you breath. Silently name thoughts: "I want to be right." "I'm really annoyed." "She is making my life miserable." Breathe deeply. Touch your heart, and silently ask yourself: "What would support me now?" Breathe deeply, and when you have finished, open your eyes and stretch gently. Jot down any new insights or observations.

Having Difficult Conversations

"Make no mistake: Rehumanizing work and education requires courageous leadership. Honest conversations about vulnerability and shame are disruptive. The reason that we're not having these conversations in our organizations is that they shine light in the dark corners. Once there is language, awareness, and understanding, turning back is almost impossible and carries severe consequences."

—Brené Brown (research professor, University of Houston),
Daring Greatly (2012)[14]

Consider the times you have reacted viscerally to a conversation. Did you find yourself boiling mad or feeling calm and collected? How did you feel physically? How you speak to another person, how you listen, how you send an email? The tone and pitch of your voice send a signal of your state of mind, your attitude, and the state of your body.

We want to become aware of these internal cues early on when they are an ember—before they become a forest fire. By touching and softening around these especially difficult emotions and feelings, we expand tolerance and acceptance for what is unsettled, uncomfortable, unfinished. Again, this does not mean that we agree or condone what has happened.

This reminds us of the ancient wisdom of *wabi sabi,* a perspective that infused Japanese art, architecture, and all manner of being for centuries. *Wabi sabi* roughly translates into a deep appreciation of things imperfect, impermanent, and

> *"As a leader, I am aware that all I've got is one conversation at a time. I'm acutely aware that with each conversation, I bring who I am in that moment—angry, agitated, calm—and that I can set the tone for the relationship, the interaction. This interaction sets the tone for how I want my team to interact with one another."*
>
> —Peter Godard, Chief Performance Officer, Illinois State Board of Education

incomplete. Too often when we are at an emotional low point, we feel isolated and separate from others. With mindful awareness, we begin to recognize that the human experience is a shared experience and is imperfect, and that we are not alone in our suffering and heartbreak.

We love the work of Susan Scott, author of *Fierce Conversations,* who provides a useful guide to speaking with greater clarity and authenticity. When conversations have the potential to turn confrontational, she recommends a three-part communications model, consisting first of an *Opening Statement* with a clear and specific example of the behavior you want to change, your emotions about the concern, what might be at stake, your contribution to the concern, an indication of your desire to resolve the concern, and an invitation for the other's response. The second stage Scott names is the *Interaction,* an opportunity to inquire into the other person's perspective; it includes paraphrasing and searching for deeper understanding. The final stage is *Resolution,* in which the speaker assesses lessons learned, next steps, and what might be needed now to move forward.[15]

Let's return to Donna, our educational testing specialist executive from the Midwest who opened this chapter. We worked with her to get more comfortable with having difficult conversations using the *Fierce Conversations* approach. In addition to practicing S.T.O.P., we coached Donna on the use of the body scan described in Chapter 2 (see Mindfulness Practice Aid 2.3, "The Body Scan," page 62) to give her a broader range of vocabulary of her body and to strengthen her self-confidence and poise under pressure. As an antidote to self-criticism, we encouraged her to practice acts of self-compassion, beginning with feeling care and kindness toward herself, and then extending those feelings toward others.

Managing "Negative" Emotions

Meditation teacher Tara Brach, author of *Radical Acceptance,* says there is no such thing as "negative" emotions.[16] We agree.

Emotions carry powerful information in them, and learning to accept and befriend anger, fear, or sadness is one of the benefits of a consistent mindfulness practice. As leaders, you have to work with difficult emotions. As we described in Chapter 2, page 52, you can sometimes become overwhelmed by your anger, your fear, or your regret, especially when the amygdala hijacks the brain. In mindfulness training, you take a step back to witness these emotions without immediately reacting. You recognize your inner critic's voice, perhaps like a familiar friend. You learn to extend acceptance of the full range of emotions—pleasant, unpleasant, and neutral—in much the same way that a school leader shared with us: "I look at my thoughts and notice the patterns. I'm aware of the big boundaries I set around myself, and now I am intentionally softening them." Meditation teacher Pema Chödrön offers similar guidance.[17] When experiencing emotional distress, she says, set aside the story you tell yourself and lean into the strong emotion. Stay with the emotion as it is without making it into more. Learn to be with what is distressing.[18]

Mindfulness offers another approach to addressing difficult emotions and having difficult conversations. Instead of denying or falsifying emotions, trying to manage situations intellectually to regulate emotions, or perpetually replaying the emotional event over and over again in your head, you cultivate a new approach: You allow the strong emotion to run its course and focus your awareness on your breathing. You avoid doing or saying anything that you might regret later, and take time to breathe or walk to calm and soothe yourself. You begin to recognize that your distress and your loss, though unique, is universal, and a shared human experience. Recognizing what is happening and accepting the universality of the human experience isn't simple and doesn't mean that your distress disappears instantly. It means changing your relationship to heartbreak and cultivating the ability in the moment to read and to understand yourself and others, and to ask: "What is here now?" Mindfulness helps you recognize negative self-talk that puts you in the downward spiral as we described in Chapter 3 in the section on negativity bias, page 94.

Accepting strong emotions, rather than struggling to get rid of them, is an important self-regulation tool. However, managing strong emotions is not enough. It is important to cultivate positive emotions. Rick Hanson's suggestions for "hardwiring happiness," which we discussed in Chapter 3, page 94, are useful. For example, Hanson recommends that you "produce good facts" that then generate good experiences.[19] Though this may be obvious, every day, you have countless opportunities to create good in your life, and these can be very simple, such as complimenting another person, giving someone a small gift, greeting another person, listening to wonderful music, or gazing at a flower. In other words, we consciously build moments of happiness in our daily lives. These actions get reinforced in the structure of the brain, making it easier to activate positive mental states, or "hardwire happiness."[20] (However, as we mentioned in the Introduction to this book, if you are experiencing consistent and extreme negative thoughts and feelings, consult an appropriate mental health professional.) Adopting the mental mode of allowing things to be as they are has a sort of softening quality to it. You begin to relax a little and to accept what is. Amrita, a school counselor and mother of three who put her career on hold for 12 years to raise her children and now, approaching her early forties, is finding the transition to full-time work daunting. Like many in her situation, she is deeply conflicted. She says, "I have no idea how to be a professional anymore. I've spent the last many years arranging play dates. I'm not prepared to negotiate the grownup world. I can't see my way clearly. I feel lost." Amrita was able to articulate these feelings and accept them, as painful as they were—at first for only a few seconds, and then for a few minutes. She placed her hand at her heart and felt her breath. Focusing on her breathing, she said, "As scary as they are, allow the feelings to be there."

Courageous Conversations

As facilitators with the Center for Courage & Renewal, we work with people across the country to engage in courageous, compassionate, and authentic conversations through the use of the center's *Touchstones*, developed from the work of educator and author Parker J. Palmer. The center's mission to assist people across the various professions, and especially educators, to live in a more authentic way, joining their soul with their role in the world. We especially rely on the *Touchstones* as a way of establishing emotional safety that allows for these types of conversations.

Our work in introducing these *Touchstones* in large- and small-group retreat settings is to encourage an emotionally safe environment that allows for honest, open conversation and support leaders to examine not just what they do and how they do it, but their deepest values. Sadly, very often we find that leaders attending these retreats have had little or no time to examine their own deep-seated values and how they align with their work. Participants in these retreats begin to let their guard down, getting real with themselves and creating a dynamic and trustworthy atmosphere. They become reacquainted with their deepest sources of wisdom: themselves—their bodies, mind, and heart. The *Touchstones* provide not only the basis for shared guidelines for how the group participants agree they will engage each other, but a standard of integrity that allows them to be refreshingly honest with themselves and with others. Under these conditions, real truth telling, vulnerability, and transformation happen. Below is an excerpt of these *Touchstones*.

- *Be present as fully as possible.* Be here with your doubts, fears, and failings as well as your convictions, joys, and successes, your listening as well as your speaking.
- *Speak your truth in ways that respect other people's truth.* Our views of reality may differ, but speaking one's truth in a circle of trust does not mean interpreting, correcting, or debating what others say. Speak from your center to the center of the circle, using "I" statements, trusting people to do their own sifting and winnowing.
- *No fixing, saving, advising, or correcting each other.* This is one of the hardest guidelines for those of us in the "helping professions." But it is vital to welcoming the soul, to making space for the inner teacher.
- *Learn to respond to others with honest, open questions* instead of counsel, corrections, and so on. With such questions, we help "hear each other into deeper speech."
- *When the going gets rough, turn to wonder.* If you feel judgmental or defensive, ask yourself, "I wonder what brought her to this belief?" "I wonder what he's feeling right now?" "I wonder what my reaction teaches me about myself?" Set aside judgment to listen to others—and to yourself—more deeply.[21]

Mindfulness Practice Aids

The practices in this chapter—half-breath, R.A.I.N., and speaking and listening mindfully—are meant to support you as a school leader and in life. As with all the practices, it is best to practice them when you are not emotionally triggered, to develop a habit of using these tools rather than waiting until the moment of distress. Start slowly and build gradually. Please try these practices over time and notice what happens.

Mindfulness Practice Aid 4.1: Half-Breath Practice

When experiencing extremely distracting thoughts and emotions, focus attention on a half-breath, an approach to quieting the mind we learned from meditation teacher Joseph Goldstein. When you are extremely triggered or overwhelmed, instead of focusing on the full in- and out-breath, bring your attention to just the in-breath or just the out-breath; trying to focus on both may be too much. Continue with this practice for one to two minutes, focusing on either just the in- or just the out-breath, until you feel calm.

Mindfulness Practice Aid 4.2: R.A.I.N.

We have all had occasions when we're really upset and reactive—say after getting a very upsetting email—and we've allowed our texting or typing to get ahead of our thinking. In Chapter 2 (page 58), we discussed email apnea, unconsciously holding your breath while in front of a screen. A practice we recommend to help you regain composure before you press the Send button, or before you begin shouting at a staff member, is R.A.I.N.

Meditation teacher Tara Brach and others have developed the acronym R.A.I.N. as a way of handling potentially explosive emotions. We like to think of it as a gentle spring rain, watering the soil of patience in us and helping us have more coherent and effective leadership reactions.

When you are triggered, take a moment to stop and pause and R.A.I.N.:

R—*recognize* what is happening

A—*allow* things to be as they are

I—*investigate inner experience* with kindness

N—[realize] *non-identification*[22]

Mindfulness Practice Aid 4.3: Mindful Speaking and Listening for Meaning and Connection

4.3a: Mindful Speaking

As facilitators trained at the Center for Courage & Renewal, we often use this approach to encourage mindful dialogue in large and small groups. During your next conversation, please try this practice of mindful speaking:

- Slow down your normal pace.
- Notice sensations in your body and your body posture. Are you leaning forward ready to pounce just waiting for the other person to stop talking?
- Notice your emotions: Are you anxious, impatient, excited, or crabby?
- Become aware of your thinking: "I can't wait for my turn to tell her . . ."
- Become aware of the fluctuation of these feelings, sensations, and thoughts; they come, stay awhile, and then go.
- Direct attention to the rise and fall of your abdomen.
- Feel your breath come in and go out.
- Breathe in and out of your nose, with awareness at your abdomen, or locate where you feel the breath and focus there.
- Visually take in the other person and give your full attention to him or her.
- Cultivate a sense of openness and curiosity about this person.
- Cultivate a sense of kindness toward this person, whether the person is someone you have a long-standing connection with or someone you don't know at all.
- Before you speak, ask yourself these questions: Will this contribute to a positive outcome in this interaction? Can I speak truthfully? What is my motivation?
- Allow silence to be a partner in this conversation; don't rush to fill the silence, or to fill the space with words, and if you do, notice this tendency.
- When you notice that your mind has wandered, gently and firmly return your attention to your body and to awareness of the other person, in this moment.
- Listen with interest and, again, notice when your mind has wandered from an open, curious, and interested mind-set to judgment, criticism, or another negative thought.
- Ask an open question as we described above—a question you could not possibly know the answer to—and wait to listen for the response. Notice any shift in the connection between you and the other person.
- After the conversation, take a few moments to jot a note to yourself about your observations, challenges, learning, and surprises.

4.3b: Mindful Listening

- Begin with the first several steps above.
- Notice the impulse to speak, and ask yourself: Is this necessary? Will my words support greater understanding? What is my motivation?
- Notice the impulse to correct, fix, counsel, or give advice, without acting on this impulse.
- While you engage in listening, observe your posture, feel your feet on the ground underneath you, and become aware of your state of mind.
- Bring your focus and concentration to the person speaking, giving him or her your full attention. Listen as an act of generosity.
- If you wish to ask a question, try asking an open question— one to which you could not possibly know the answer.
- Be fully present to the best of your ability to listen to the response.
- Suspend the impulse to interrupt with multiple questions.
- Observe feelings of judgment and criticism without trying to change them.
- Allow for silence to be a partner in the dialogue.
- When you notice that your mind has wandered, gently and firmly return your attention to your body and to an awareness of the other person, in this moment.
- Listen with interest and, again, notice when your mind has wandered from an open, curious, and interested mind-set to judgment, criticism, or another negative thoughts.
- After the conversation, take a few moments to jot a note to yourself about your observations, challenges, learning, and surprises.

Portraits of Practice

4.1 Robin Correll, Former School Nurse and Elementary School Mindfulness Teacher

Rural Pacific Northwest

"I found mindfulness after the death of my son."

Robin Correll, a retired school nurse in her local rural school system, began a systematic practice of mindfulness after her son, at age 21, was murdered in a tragic incident near home. "He was not a

blameless boy; he did a lot of drinking and was caught in the wrong place at the wrong time. Yet it is impossible to describe the intensity of that experience to someone who has not lost a child. All the beliefs you had about life, how things were supposed to be, were blown apart in millions of pieces in an instant. And you are left with those fragments, and the question, how can I put them back together? . . . or do I even want to put them back together?"

Finding herself lost in grief, she was introduced to the work of Pema Chödrön, the renowned Buddhist nun, teacher, and author of *When Things Fall Apart* and *The Places That Scare You: A Guide to Fearlessness in Difficult Times*,[23] among other best-selling texts. "Pema saved my life, taught me how to be in grief, how to sit with those very difficult feelings," Robin recalls. "A dear friend had given me the tapes on Pema's teachings of the Four Limitless Ones.[24] I took the loving-kindness and compassion teachings into my heart. This is where I learned the practice of *tonglen*, taking and sending. And in the early months of my grief, that was the only practice I could do: take in all my grief and breathe out space. When you breathe all of those difficult emotions into your heart, they are transformed into space, loving-kindness, or whatever you think might be helpful on the out-breath. *Tonglen* has a natural way of expanding itself outward to others, and so it became, not just for me but for other bereaved parents as well. I would walk and do *tonglen*. Sit and do *tonglen*. Breathe in the pain, breathe out space. It was very helpful."

Looking for more teachings and ways to practice in the wake of that terrible death, Robin bought more tapes of Pema Chödrön and Thich Nhat Hanh to listen to in her car on the way to work, and would find herself gradually bringing the practices into her life as a nurse at school. "Emotional pain is a great motivator," she wryly reflected. "In the early days, I would say to myself as I got out of my car, 'I am going to practice being more mindful today.'" And then at the end of the day, she would realize, "I had not practiced it at all. So, a daily sitting practice is really what helps the most. Practicing mindful breathing for a period of time every day, as a formal practice, helps bridge the gap between the teachings and integrating them into your daily life. That's why they call it practice! Becoming mindful is a very gradual process . . . a lifetime process. I have chunks of moments of nonmindfulness all the time!

"But at school, I realized that very often I could pause and breathe when I was getting reactive. I also began to think that if it helped me, it could help my students as well, and I began by having some quiet moments of just sitting and breathing with students. For example, for kids who were having an asthma episode, after taking their medication, doing some mindful breathing would help them settle down. Or for kids having an emotional time, mindful breathing often had a calming effect."

Feeling the powerful effects of this, Robin then joined a formal meditation group so she could practice with others, in addition to studying formally with a Buddhist teacher who visits a retreat center in her local area every summer. [It is a common practice with those who make a commitment to meditating—joining a formal group and engaging with a community and teacher to build mindfulness practice.]

Many years passed, and Robin noticed that she was beginning to be transformed by these practices. Learning the practices of mindfulness—and, in her case, the formal practices of Buddhism—"is like a red cloth being dyed many times. Many, many, a lifetime of immersions, are required for full coloration." Little by little, Robin recalled, "It seeps into you. You are sitting there, and you notice yourself being more patient. People who irritated you do so less often, and you find you are more compassionate and tolerant with the people you work with. Although, sometimes, you will still get caught up with anger, irritations, and so forth, you have the tools to work with those emotions. Work is a great practice arena for testing where you are. Actually, your whole life is a practice arena."

In 2011, Robin retired from district schoolwork and simultaneously began teaching a mindfulness program to first, second, and third graders in one of her local schools. She was able to have a voluntary teacher in-service at the beginning of the school year, using the Mindful Schools curriculum in Oakland (where Robin has trained as well). "Teaching mindfulness has been very successful. I see little kids on the street who ask me when I'm going to come back and teach 'that peace thing' again, and parents report that their own children are teaching them mindful breathing."

"I wanted to hit this kid," one child told Robin, "and instead, I took three mindful breaths." Although some people were initially a little skeptical of mindfulness classes, in her rural northern California school, "people have been asking for it now. You just have to get them through their initial skepticism or sense that they are so busy, and get them to try it. You have to be careful how you describe it, without religious language," and that is helpful, too, Robin cautioned, thinking of her own experiences.

Why are the practices of mindfulness important, we asked Robin? "Having more mindful schools is critically important. School is often a place where very powerful feelings come up. If we can teach kids at a young age about mindfulness—about creating a gap between what you feel and how you are going to act—that can change everything."

Mindfulness is a critical practice, Robin reflected, because it changes how we live our lives and understand the meaning of our lives. "Getting things done quickly is not always the best way," Robin observed. "We have the opportunity to create a kinder and gentler community, society, and world in which we live."

Robin is a retired school nurse who worked in that capacity for over 20 years in Northern California. She graduated from California Hospital School of Nursing, Los Angeles, and then received her BSN at Cal State University at Dominguez Hills and her MSN at Cal State Sacramento. She has practiced mindfulness meditation for the past 14 years. She currently teaches mindfulness in a local elementary school, using Mindful Schools curriculum, where she attended a workshop in Berkeley in 2011.

4.2 Peter Godard, Chief Performance Officer

Illinois State Board of Education

"The word *practice* is really important. Before I began with all this, I thought that unless I was a Tibetan monk or unless I looked like Deepak Chopra on *Oprah*, I would not be successful. Now I realize that I'm always learning, and even doing mindfulness imperfectly, I'm realizing a lot of benefits."

Peter Godard attended a Circle of Trust® retreat we facilitated several years ago at a log cabin retreat house on the Grand River in Michigan, and he has been a leadership coaching client. We talked to him on a wintery Friday morning in January.

"I am gay, and grew up in northern Vermont. My first mindfulness experience was, though I had no words for it at the time, with my grandparents at their farmhouse. In summer evenings, we would sit for hours in their screened-in front porch and listen to nature's night sounds and to the silence. Little did I know that I was learning to sit in stillness.

"As a leader, I am always curious about learning new things, and it took me a long time to discover the practice, but I did. My mindfulness practice began in earnest about two years ago and has three main components: yoga, seated meditation, and mini-pauses.

"For the past two years, I have participated in one weekly formal yoga class, and I incorporate some mindful movement in the morning before I leave for work. I started taking these classes to improve my physical health. About nine months ago, I started practicing seated meditation, which I do most days and especially when I know I have a really hard workday ahead, where things are really packed in. During this time, I practice open awareness and loving-kindness meditation, and sometimes I do a guided meditation from YouTube. The time spent with this can be anywhere from five minutes to a half-hour, and even just five minutes can calm me down. Finally, throughout the workday, I take a 30-second to two-minute mini-pause to insert a small moment of practice as I move from meeting to meeting or phone call to phone call. On really busy, packed days, I may not have time to eat lunch, but I can find one minute to take a few mindful bites of a sandwich; I can find time even on the busiest days to take a few mindful breaths before I go on to the next meeting.

"The word *practice* is really important. Before I began with all this, I thought that unless I was a Tibetan monk or unless I looked like Deepak Chopra on *Oprah*, I would not be successful. Now I realize that I'm always learning, and even doing mindfulness imperfectly, I'm realizing a lot of benefits.

"I notice that I have a greater sense of myself. Even when work is chaotic, I can sit quietly and become aware of my experience, my feelings, and my thoughts at that moment, and know that this is not the sum total of who I am. In others words, I have better perspective.

"As a leader, I am aware that all I've got is one conversation at a time. I'm acutely aware that with each conversation, I bring who I am in that moment—angry, agitated, calm—and that I can set the tone for the relationship, the interaction. This interaction sets the tone for how I want my team to interact with one another. It's so important to always practice, to always learn.

"I have learned, too, to be aware of my limitations, when I need rest and recharging, when I am hitting the wall. The enhanced awareness of my emotions helps me to notice what is happening with my team.

"Like many leaders, I carry a lot of internal dialogue: *You've got to get this done . . . You've got to reach your goal.* While I've never been inside another leader's mind, I suspect other leaders might be thinking something similar. I've learned to let go of a lot of the value judgments. On many days, I just sit with my busy mind chattering away, knowing that I will benefit from the practice nonetheless.

"To some extent, the crunch of time is a factor. It's true that 20 minutes of seated meditation may be better than 5 minutes, and that one minute of mindful eating is better than none. I've come to accept my time limitations and to work with them.

"I've had some great teachers and spent time sorting out all the mindfulness practices to find what works best for me. I've had lots of advice from many people who will tell you how. I have found that you have to figure this out for yourself, knowing yourself, knowing what works for you. I'm a researcher at heart. I work with data. I like facts. I like the great science behind mindfulness, the work of Richie Davidson and others.[25] I take seriously the real and tangible scientific mindfulness studies. I practice what works for me, for my brain."

Peter has devoted most of his career to education policy and research— serving most recently as a leader for Chicago Public Schools and then the Illinois State Board of Education. He is a graduate of the University of Chicago and is currently pursuing a degree from DePaul University focused on data-driven education leadership models. He is driven by his passions for learning, youth development, and social justice. He volunteers as a mentor for the Year Up program and is also energized by his hobbies of travel, gardening, and cooking. Peter's website is http://godardpeter.wix.com/internet-cv.

4.3 Todd D. Cantrell, House Principal

Central Bucks High School West, Pennsylvania

"As a school leader, being mindful, I can stay present to whatever is happening. I am a better parent at home and a better listener. Rather than formulating a response in my head, I've trained myself to stop and to refocus. I am really here for all the stakeholders: parents, students, staff, teachers, and all their different ideas. This is critically important for a school leader."

We were introduced to Todd D. Cantrell by Diane Reibel and the Mindfulness Institute at Jefferson University Hospital in Philadelphia. We visited Todd at his office at Central Bucks High School West on a rainy, chilly, early spring morning. He had set aside about 20 minutes to talk about his experience with mindfulness at his school and his efforts to bring mindfulness instruction to teachers and students. Todd's office was light filled, warm, and inviting, with large houseplants occupying the windowsill and a Russell Hobbs teakettle on a nearby table. In addition to family photos of his wife and kids, his office walls were decorated with a quote from the Dalai Lama and a serene image of a drop of water suspended in midair above a pool.

Todd had put everything on hold to carve out these 20 minutes of uninterrupted time from his busy day. He voice evoked a quality of both energy and passion that was contagious, and we felt that we had his undivided attention. He was a study in focus.

He began: "I became interested in mindfulness about four and a half years ago when my wife was experiencing anxiety and panic attacks that sent her to the emergency room a few times. I wanted to do something to help her. At school, I saw many students with pent-up anger. One student in particular comes to mind. She was a young woman who was carrying multiple AP courses and was a straight-A student. Things took a turn for the worse for her; the pressure was just too much, and she was admitted to a behavioral hospital, suffering from a breakdown. That was a real wake-up call for me." His voice trailed off as he looked out the window beyond the bare branches; in this moment of pause, we could sense the weight of these events on his shoulders. He continued: "We are an academic institution, but we also need to look at the well-being of these students. We began offering yoga as an experiential program, and then someone put a book on mindfulness on my desk, and I started doing research. I looked up Jon Kabat-Zinn and Jefferson's Mindfulness Institute. I applied for a $10,000 grant to bring mindfulness to the students and teachers at my school, and I got it, and we began offering a modified version of MBSR [mindfulness-based stress reduction] to students and teachers.

"My daily practice is 20–30 minutes of formal sitting meditation with awareness of the breath and the body scan at night when I come home. What I notice is that while the stress and pressures are the same, my reaction to them is different. Here at Central Bucks High School West, we have high affluence, high achievers, and high expectations. Before I started practicing mindfulness four and a half years ago, I really was not present to my own kids at home. I was physically at home, but I was thinking constantly about what was going to happen next at school. My kids would joke about all this, but it wasn't funny after a while." Todd turned around in his chair to look at the photo of his son and daughter, and we sensed his frustration and difficulty.

"As a school leader, being mindful, I can stay present to whatever is happening. I am a better parent at home and a better listener. Rather than formulating a response in my head, I've trained myself to stop and to refocus. I am really here for all the stakeholders: parents, students, staff, teachers, and all their different ideas. This is critically important for a school leader. I'm better at de-escalating situations, too. Before I send a potentially explosive email, I stop myself and breathe. I've trained myself to sit with uncomfortable, difficult emotions and not react out of anger or frustration, and this is huge. As a disciplinarian, I've learned, very slowly and with a lot of hard work, to notice my anxiety and fear and not to get hung up on it. Mainly, my communication skills have greatly improved, and my stress levels have been greatly reduced. I have been a migraine sufferer all my life, and these mindfulness practices have helped me to take my well-being a lot more seriously."

We asked Todd what was next for him. He didn't hesitate in his response. "Mindfulness is a lifelong practice, and I have no idea where it will take me. I need to steep myself more and more in mindfulness practices. I've seen the changes in me and the changes in others, and the potential for transformation is huge.

"I am a much better school leader because of my mindfulness practice. We've built a community of about 60 people here at the school who now practice mindfulness, which has created greater trust and compassion. I realize it's so important, as Thich Nhat Hanh says, not to lose myself in too many projects, to be pulled in too many directions, to forget myself in service of my work. Practicing mindfulness is an act of self-love and self-compassion. My advice to anyone: Start with yourself. If you want to sustain your leadership life, practice mindfulness."

Todd has been an educator for 15 years, spending the last 8 years as an assistant principal at Central Bucks High School West in Doylestown, Pennsylvania. He began a mindfulness practice four and a half years ago and trained under Diane Reibel and Trish Broderick to facilitate mindfulness-based intervention programs to teachers and students. He is the co-creator of a mindfulness curriculum for teachers at his school, titled "Breathing Across the Curriculum."

Please visit us on Facebook at https://www.facebook.com/TheMindfulSchoolLeader.

5

Reclaiming Our Wholeness

Four Educational Leaders Explore Mindfulness

"Some leaders recognize and hear wake-up calls—clear signs and messages that their lives have become something they do not want. These calls can be a first critical step to intentional change."

—Richard Boyatzis and Annie McKee, *Resonant Leadership* (2005)[1]

Mindful leadership practice involves engaging in enlightened self-care and self-management as a way of being a professional, in balanced service of oneself and others. Many of the individuals who have shaped the practices we describe in this book, and our understandings of them, are our associates and colleagues, individuals it is our privilege to work with. We want you to know that our clients—the people we work with every day—are actively reframing their leadership lives based on many of the practices we've outlined in the book here so far—just as we are.

Let's explore the real lives of four educational leaders, people just like you who are engaged in busy, demanding, intense professional lives and who manage complex professional cultures and are responsible for the emotional climate of their educational settings. Here, we describe in detail, and largely in the leaders' own words, the ways they've found to introduce mindfulness practices into their daily routines in ways that have helped them become more resilient, resonant individuals; how they work to be more inspiring, more courageous, and calm in the face of the many challenges of their work; and how their mindfulness practices evolved and the effect these practices have had on them as leaders, as well as the effects of all this on their communities and the wider world. We thank the four leaders here, Nicole, Cornelia, Dan, and Lucretia, for this candid and real look into their educational leadership lives.

Portraits of Practice: School Leaders Practicing Mindfulness

5.1 Nicole A. Falconer, Principal

(Formerly) Foundation Collegiate Academy, Trenton, New Jersey

"I see leadership as a 'Ministry of Encouragement.'"

Nicole Falconer, principal, formerly of Foundation Collegiate Academy in Trenton, New Jersey, has been up since 5 a.m. A dynamo

of energy, routinely described by her staff as "a huge presence" (although in a small physical package), Nicole is someone her colleagues and teachers say has "natural command." Dreadlocks bouncing, she sings in the hallways as she does a morning walk-through; she talks on the phone with parents, staff, and students as she helps run a morning gathering circle with ninth graders. Nicole checks in with a senior staff member, walks to the third floor to observe a drum circle in the gym, and answers a text about rescheduling a meeting—all the while strolling and observing instruction and culture in the hallways and classrooms of the school site she is responsible for.

Although barely out of her 20s, she is the founding principal of a "no excuses" high school designed to prepare young men and women of Trenton, New Jersey, to attend the most competitive colleges around the nation. Like so many formerly solidly middle- and working-class cities in the Northeast, Trenton is a city beset by chronic poverty and joblessness; its industrial base has collapsed over the last 50 years, and family-sustaining, living-wage jobs have disappeared. Growing up in urban Connecticut, and one of the first children in her own family to attend college (Yale University), Nicole's commitment to the school's mission and the no-excuses model are personal, deeply felt, and important to her on many levels. "The mission of this school reflects my own personal journey, and in every cell of my body I believe education is a civil right for the children and young adults we serve. Every day I see how we can, and must, succeed."

Nicole says she knew from a very early age that leadership was her destiny. Describing her as dynamic, professional, and "awe-inspiring" (sometimes even frightening, say some younger staff members), several young teachers and administrators say they explicitly came to work at the high school to be with Nicole or were drawn there "because of her"; the quality of her vision and her competence inspired them and made them feel sure that they would learn from her. "She impacts me every day," says one of her staff members.

Nicole's tireless work ethic, passion for the mission of her school, and dedication to the young men and women of Foundation Academies have led her to several major leadership transitions since becoming principal in 2011. She has become, as she puts it, less invested in "looking like I'm in charge," and more concerned about supporting and nurturing the competence of those around her. She has introduced innovations at her school like a summer camping trip and leadership retreats for the teachers and staff in the building, which include individual life mapping for new teachers, capped by a high ropes course challenge to help build trust and respect among colleagues. Nicole has instituted several administrative innovations in her short tenure also, like a revised teacher review and rating system. She has invested heavily in the learning lives of her staff (book groups in which teachers get to meet and have *real* intellectual lives) and worked hard on modeling vulnerability and respect herself so that "being connected" is more and more a part of how teachers and adults understand the mission of the school.

"Honest sharing about the difficulties of working in the high-intensity environment of Foundation Academies," she says, is critical. Very aware that as principal she is a role model for young African American men and women, Nicole observes that she's working on providing a balance between formidable and accessible, and showing what a young woman of color can do.[2] One staff member remembers seeing Nicole for the first time, interacting with middle school students. Nicole was a teacher then—a new teacher without a lot of credibility in the organization. Nicole "held up her fingers" in front of the children, and almost instantly a silence fell in the large cafeteria full of students eating lunch. She had that kind of power already, this person remembers, and the middle schoolers felt it. "Who is this?" this person wondered.

A Turning Point

Yet in her first years as a high school principal, Nicole noticed, and lived, "the downsides of my dynamism, work ethic, and dedication." She often felt overwhelmed and burned out. Even more important to her, she says, "I had insufficient time to reflect on my own leadership practice or to grow myself," and she felt herself "being cut off from the things I also love, like reading books for pleasure, listening to music, growing relationships outside of school, and learning just for the sake of learning." Nicole decided, with the help of her own senior staff and several important mentors and advisors, to introduce a modified mindfulness practice into her leadership life, to help focus herself throughout the day and build a sense of greater focus and satisfaction in her work life.

To accomplish this goal, first Nicole completed a comprehensive assessment of her life and work performance, and decided, among several important personal initiatives, to instantiate some daily mindfulness practices. The morning and night to-do practice is key for her, as is journaling.

Morning and Night To-Do Check-In

Here is what inspired Nicole's important to-do practice.

Nicole describes how throughout her busy day, before her mindfulness and pausing practices began, she would feel a cascading mountain of to-dos building up. "When you're a leader, you work from everyone else's to-do list, not your own. Why didn't I understand that in the first year?" she says with a chuckle. As a teacher, she says, "I worked from my to-do list like clockwork, and life was a little more contained." But when she became a school leader, "My mind was running all the time, racing. Sleep and concentration were interrupted by my thoughts, and I had to find a way to purge, relax, and rest."

Morning and Night To-Do: Breathe In, Breathe Out

To help with her sense of frenzy and pace, which she says made it difficult for her to sleep at night and "listen the way I wanted to" during the day, Nicole instituted a practice where she records a voicemail to-do list of everything that has collected in her brain—but she does this only twice a day. "I was waking up in the middle of the night obsessing, and I really needed a way to do a brain dump and train myself to let it all go—to get in the practice of this. So I started with the audio to-do, recording everything I needed to do or was thinking about, but telling myself afterward I was going to breathe and let it go. [Do deep belly breathing, hand on belly and hand on chest, as described in Chapter 2, page 61. See also Mindfulness Practice Aid 1.2, "Three-Minute Focused Breathing Practice," page 37.] The first couple of times I'd get up in the middle of the night and record, then I might have to get up again, turn the lights back on, and do some more because there was still more. But now I've really got myself trained. I do the complete 'dump' and then go right to the breath. At night, this helps me tremendously with sleeping, and in the morning, it helps me with focus and a sense of coming into the day unburdened." After the purge, Nicole makes a point to breathe (as described throughout this book) and then quiet her mind for several minutes. "Doing the mind dump practice has really become preparation for a little quiet pause for me, which has helped me so much as a leader. I know that I'm going to get a break from myself, at least for some part of the day. Also, the sense that I've got it all has helped with my capacity to delegate and trust. I know my staff is increasingly 'getting it all' because I've got it all."

Mindful Journaling Practice

On the advice of several mentors, Nicole also instituted a first-thing-at-her-desk mindful journaling practice[3] every morning when she gets into work. (Remember, the sun is not usually up.)

"I've trained myself now so that every morning, no matter what, I sit for a few minutes with one of my little journals and record my thoughts, good and bad, describing what's on my mind and what I'm feeling. I used to think that this was taking too much time for myself, but I've come to see that it actually sets up my whole day for being a better leader. I've already done some breathing, then I get to the office and I record my thoughts, and quickly I realize there is no difference between personal thoughts and leadership thoughts. They are one and the same. The journal helps me bring an awareness to me, about what I am feeling, what I'm embarrassed about, what I'm excited about. It's really a dialogue with myself."

Nicole has also used her journal to focus on specific mental habits, like narrating the positive. "At a certain point, I realized I was overly focused on the things that were going wrong, and having a hard time focusing on things that were going right. I'm also someone with incredibly high standards for myself, and very sensitive. So I realized that working on focusing on what I pay attention to—positive information rather than negative—could really change the way I felt day to day.

"The journal helps me take things outside myself, to challenge my own assumptions and look at things in new ways—to reflect. It's really become an invaluable part of my daily leadership practice, to the degree that I've bought Moleskine journals for all my teachers, and encouraged them to reflect every day, too. Their schedule is printed on one side, and a place to reflect is on the other. I thought they would think it was corny, but they don't. They like it."

Nicole says she sees the journaling practice as helping her, as a leader, "be a better version of myself" and move toward solutions. "When I'm working on a particular issue, I notice that by writing mindfully about it, and giving myself this time, I *notice* other people's practice around this so much more. The journal practically gives me a new set of eyes." She credits the journaling with big developmental jumps in her leadership growth, and for building her capacity to be a listener and a mentor. "I encourage myself there, I also cheerlead myself, and everyone can use encouragement, even me to me."

Getting Out of the Office and Walking, No-Work Saturdays, Committing to Reading by Taking the Train, and Drinking Water

Nicole has also developed a variety of mindful practices to support her in other ways, like mindful walking around her school (see Mindfulness Practice Aid 3.2, "Mindful Walking," in Chapter 3, page 97). "Walking and the rhythm of walking help me so much, putting boundaries around work that are inviolate, committing to a reading and prayer program, and drinking more water. All these things, in a variety of ways, help me calm my nervous system and empty out my brain, and that improves my ability to think," she reflects. Also for Nicole, prayer is a form of meditation, a kind of active imagining and being with God that for her provides direction, comfort, and focus.

Overall, the transformation in her leadership practice over the last year has been immense. "During my first year as a school leader, I truly was unhappy if I am being completely honest. I was frustrated and self-critical, and overmanaging others and overworking. And although I'm still working *a lot*—I'm not going to lie to you!" she says, laughing—"I am so much happier! And this makes me a better leader in every way. I have so many more ways of coping with myself and my anxieties and frustrations, and I think I'm more trusting and even more creative. These practices have changed my life."

With a high-stress leadership practice like Nicole's, we see nothing but upside benefit for the few moments Nicole takes every day to notice herself, notice her breathing, and pause. "I'm a different person now," she says. "I'm building a life of leadership that I can actually sustain."

Nicole A. Falconer recently accepted the position of Headmistress of Pine Forge Academy, in Pine Forge, Pennsylvania. She was formerly (until July 2014) principal of Foundation Collegiate Academy in Trenton, New Jersey. She also served as a history lead teacher and coordinator of students' affairs at Frederick Douglass Academy VII in Brooklyn, New York. She was a teacher selector for the New York City Teaching Fellowship prior to joining Foundation Academies. Nicole received an Excellence in Teaching Citation from the New York State Assembly in 2007 and again in 2010 for her students' achievement in the classroom and on standardized assessments. She holds a bachelor of arts in history from Yale University, a master's in the science of teaching from Pace University, and an advanced master's in education from the Teachers College at Columbia University. Nicole is currently working on a doctoral degree in organization and leadership.

5.2 Cornelia Cannon Holden, Director and Founder

Core Leadership Summer Program at The Hotchkiss School (Director) and Mindful Warrior (Founder)
Lakeville, Connecticut

"I came to mindfulness through athletics."

Even over the phone, Cornelia Cannon Holden's intensity and energy are palpable. A vivid and powerful presence, Cornelia recounts her childhood experiences growing up as an elite skiing athlete, competing throughout high school and in college, and dreaming of making the U.S. national ski team. "Competition shaped my early life, especially my teens and 20s," she says, until she had a life-changing accident that altered the course of her life and ushered in a "decade of healing" and an exploration of various modalities of connecting mind, body, and spirit to self-understanding.

"I didn't plan on sports performance and leadership coaching as a professional career; my career found me," Cornelia notes with humor. "My path has had so many twists and turns. I came to mindfulness through athletics. I was training and competing at a high level in college, and then I sustained a pretty serious head injury; that really began a decade of change and reevaluation," in which understanding how to take care of herself in new ways—and those around her—became the center of her life.

Cornelia has an unusual biography. She holds a master's degree from the Harvard Divinity School, and has also trained as a massage therapist, yoga instructor, and cranial-sacral body worker. She is the owner and founder of a sports and mindfulness coaching firm that works with Olympic-level athletes and other individuals and teams interested in elite-level performance. She is also a practicing meditator and retreat leader who enjoys long periods of silence, and serves as both consultant to and co-head of an elite private boarding school in one of the most competitive environments in the country. All of these seemingly conflicting pieces of personal story and career are held together with aplomb as Cornelia describes her world. "It's incredibly rich, full of opportunities to serve, and a tremendous privilege, even if it's not restful!"

We have connected with Cornelia through The Hotchkiss School's Core Leadership program, and Cornelia is describing the interwoven threads of her own mindfulness practice, a practice she teaches to young leaders and athletes at her school in northwestern Connecticut, as well as in her work with Olympic-level teams.

"Mindfulness, that moment-to-moment nonjudgmental aware-ness, is simultaneously simple and complex. Truly great athletic per-formance is mindfulness in motion even if the athlete doesn't realize it." Cornelia has come to this knowledge through her own experi-ence, and after training with several renowned meditation and sacred-tradition teachers.

A Turning Point

After the ski accident that altered her athletic life, Cornelia became interested in mindfulness and meditation. "I'd been a serious ski racer who previously tried unsuccessfully to make the U.S. national team. In 1996, I suffered a serious brain injury and was nearly paralyzed while training on a glacier in Austria. I landed on my head and neck going 60 miles per hour, stopping 10 feet away from an open crevasse. I woke up the next day in a hospital wondering if I was paralyzed. I was relieved when I could move my fingers and toes. I couldn't really walk properly for six weeks because the brain bruise was so severe, but once I recovered, I went back to ski racing, and everyone thought I was fine. The problem was that I had bilateral pain in the back of my neck and head when I would laugh. I suffered from headaches and from a kind of emotional malaise. I had all the signs and symptoms of mild traumatic brain injury, but I didn't know that."[4]

After the accident, Cornelia began a quest to understand better what was going on inside her body and brain, and also to discern a new life path now that it appeared that skiing might be over. "I was studying photography at Bowdoin and working on a documentary on 100-year-old businesses in Maine; I decided I wanted to be a docu-mentary filmmaker, but given the stories of trial and tribulation I was hearing as I traveled across Maine to interview craftspeople, I grew increasingly interested in questions related to vocation and spiritual discernment. I enrolled at the Harvard Divinity School. In 2000, I also went to the Upaya Zen Center in Santa Fe, New Mexico, which began my formal mindfulness training."

Since then, Cornelia has been a whirlwind of energy and innova-tion for at least two decades, combining sports psychology, mindful-ness, and the science of high performance. She has developed a curriculum for mindful performance, wellness, and healthy rites of passage for teenagers. She teaches a unique mindfulness and leader-ship program for high school and college students at Hotchkiss and to sports teams and athletes around the world.

Key Practice: Overcoming Limiting Beliefs

Cornelia sees mindfulness training as central to overcoming limiting beliefs. "The kind of mindfulness training my company offers helps coaches and athletes transform self-limiting beliefs like fear of failure and fear of success, burnout, selfishness, and perfection paralysis so they can succeed. Mindfulness is the art and practice of being fully engaged in the present moment. It's about being here, now. In a way, it is a form of mental training that allows us to witness, for example, our ego-based tendencies. The simple act of observing these habits—without judgment or attachment—can unsettle their power over us, and deny fuel to reactivity, addiction, anger, and egocentric behavior.

"Mindfulness is like having an internal video camera. I help elite athletes turn on this awareness—I help them become aware of their own internal observer so they can begin to experience the stability of this internal witness."

When we ask Cornelia about her own practice—what is happening with her at the moment in her practice and how she feels mindfulness has transformed her—she describes feelings that will be familiar to many of our readers. "Right now my sitting practice is not as regular as I would like due to so many demands . . . parenting and designing leadership programs, in addition to consulting and other professional responsibilities." Cornelia says she's managed to work mindfulness into her daily life through small moments, however, like the breathing practice (see Mindfulness Practice Aid 1.2, "Three-Minute Focused Breathing Practice" in Chapter 1, page 37, and Mindfulness Practice Aids 2.1, "One-Minute Focused Breathing Practice," page 60, and 2.2, "30-Second Focused Breathing Practice," in Chapter 2, page 61) and mindful walking (see Mindfulness Practice Aid 3.2, "Mindful Walking," in Chapter 3, page 97). She sits for 14–18 minutes with a group of 10 Hotchkiss students as part of a weekly 90-minute mentoring program open to the Hotchkiss students who have attended the summer Core Leadership portal.

"I practice mindfulness when I walk from my house to my office. I notice if I'm leaning forward or whether my whole being is centered over my body as I take a step. I return to my breath. And I open my eyes—we live in a stunningly beautiful part of the country. It's easy not to be present to this very place or this very moment, yet this is what mindfulness is about. And I do my best to notice that I have a body! To notice where my thoughts are and to bring my attention back to this moment, this beauty, this apple tree, that sound, this step." Right now for Cornelia, it's the small daily things that matter. "My husband and I light candles at breakfast and dinner; we pray with our daughter, Zuleika, who at age 2 knows to extend her hands to us and close her eyes for our pre-meal ritual; and we take deep breaths in a deliberate effort to bookend each day."

While speaking with us, Cornelia also has a revelation about her life right now as a parent to a young daughter. "There was a recent period when I didn't work out for a few months. Right now I'm pulled in a lot of directions. I'm tired as a new and working mom— but every time I nursed Zuleika I meditated." Cornelia nursed her daughter for 22 months and says, "Our time together nourished both of us in ways that extended well beyond nutrition. We breathed in and out as we sat together. I always took up a posture of meditation, and so nursing became an experience of just simply being. Being with the breath, with one another, and with that moment. Moment after moment. Now that we're done breastfeeding I realize what a treasure it was for both of us."

The effects of mindfulness on her "global personality," the big picture, Cornelia says, are incalculable. "I've come to realize more and more that the 'I' we tend to identify with is transient and not real . . . I am much more aware of the vicissitudes of emotions. I am less defensive around my insufficiencies, mistakes, and ego. I experience relationship—being in relationship—with greater ease. I am more willing to put the defenses down around my own ego and return to the beauty and benefits of beginner's mind.

"My career—and everything I do in my life—arises organically from my own trials, from listening from a place of not knowing, and from entering into groundlessness with people." In many ways, Cornelia's leadership practice arises out of her training in pastoral care and coaching. She is a nondenominational pastoral care provider with a keen eye for excellence and high-level performance. That combination of warmth and intensity informs her work with individuals and teams. Mindfulness practices have been at the center of her own journey to wholeness, and she is now a coach and consultant to others.

"My growing edge right now is how to live skillfully into the call of serving and being truly present with others—my husband, my family, The Hotchkiss School, my company, friends, extended family, professional opportunities—in an authentic and mindful way. And that doesn't mean I'm always serene! Some days are dark; hard stuff is inevitable. Or as my teacher, Roshi Joan Halifax, says, 'Pain is inevitable. Suffering is optional.' It's about finding the breath no matter what's in front of you and not adding pain on top of pain to create suffering. Leadership demands time and energy. As a parent, I've learned that my daughter needs me to be fully present to her, but not all the time. She just needs to know that I'm there—truly there and awake in a spiritual and energetic sense—and then she can go off more courageously into the broader world. She needs solid touchstones. I think leadership is similar. A mindful leader is one who serves as an empathic listener and has the courage and training to take skillful action. When that is true, the whole community begins to show up in a similar way.

"I'm still a little more frantic right now than I'd like to be. To get the reins on this situation, I bought a 4- by 8-inch calendar to mark the ebbs and flows of the year—boarding schools are notoriously intense places!—and for the past few weeks, I've been rigorously disciplined about exercise and quiet each day and each week. That discipline gives me the boundaries I need to maintain inner freedom. I love that I get to practice mindfulness—even if only moderately on some days—among teenagers who are eager to be known even if they don't yet know who they are."

Cornelia Cannon Holden has taught or implemented leadership and team-building programs at Bowdoin College, Boston College, Middlebury College, Georgetown University, and Yale University. She served as the sports psychology, team-building, and leadership consultant for four years to the U.S. Women's Ice Hockey Team and helped guide it to two consecutive World Championships (2008, 2009), gold medals at both the 2009 Four Nations Cup and 2009 Hockey Canada Cup, and its first-ever No. 1 world ranking entering the 2010 Winter Olympics in Vancouver, where it won the silver medal.

Cornelia graduated summa cum laude *from Bowdoin College, where she was a NCAA Division II giant slalom ski racing champion and a member of both the varsity tennis and crew teams. She also holds a master's of divinity from Harvard Divinity School, where her program of study included courses at Harvard Business School. She is the founder and CEO of Mindful Warrior (www.mindfulwarrior.com), and her approach has also been influenced by her tenure as a nonprofit consultant and a decade in private practice as a body-centered psychotherapist and complementary and alternative medicine consultant. Employing a spectrum of mindfulness practices and citizen-leadership models, Cornelia has spent her career helping individuals and teams achieve remarkable value-driven performances. Still an avid skier and outdoorswoman, Cornelia lives on Hotchkiss's campus with her husband, Kevin Hicks, headmaster, and their daughter, Zuleika Alice.*

5.3 Dan Huston, Professor

NHTI, Concord's Community College
Concord, New Hampshire

> "I am an awareness practitioner. I have trained myself to be more present in every moment."

Dan Huston is a professor of English and communication at NHTI, Concord's Community College in Concord, New Hampshire, and a one-man revolution for the practice of mindful communication. Early in his career, as an adjunct professor teaching a relatively conventional communication course, Dan discovered mindfulness while going through a painful divorce.

"The intensity of that situation, and the difficulties I was having in accepting what was happening and being present to emotions at that time, made me search for new ways to handle the experience productively." Serendipitously, Dan discovered John Welwood's *Journey of the Heart,* a text by a psychotherapist who explores intimate relationships in the context of psychology and spirituality.[5] "That book really saved my life," reflects Dan in our interview. "I need to be in touch with John Welwood and tell him that."

Key Practice: Awareness Notebook

What Dan found so compelling in Welwood's work was the author's instructions for and emphasis on becoming present in the moment, "a moment in which anything can happen, and a moment that will never happen again." From this, Dan has created an "Awareness Notebooks" assignment inspired by Welwood's instructions; it is an integral part of every communication course or workshop he offers. This awareness assignment helps students open themselves to the moment, and notice the beauty and insight that reveal themselves in a sunset, a baby's hand, or stones on the walkway, or conversely to notice a repetitive thought pattern, an unpleasant story, or the way in which one is becoming emotionally triggered. "Recognizing that each moment is new, unpredictable, and impermanent is a fundamental piece of mindfulness practice," Dan says.

"Allowing yourself to open to now without imposing expectations or judgments helps you be more present and productive."

That transformational life experience was 15 years ago. Now Dan is a full professor at his college, and his "Communicating Mindfully" course now combines classic material on intrapersonal communication, interpersonal communication, and public speaking with in-class mindfulness practices and out-of-class mindfulness work. Dan sees the two bodies of material, communications and mindfulness, as very much supporting each other, and teaches them as a fully integrated and interwoven unit. Each chapter of his textbook *Communicating Mindfully: Mindfulness-Based Communication and Emotional Intelligence* includes an "Application Journal" assignment that provides students an opportunity to integrate communication and mindfulness concepts covered in the chapter and apply them to their lives.[6]

Through this kind of work, students in Dan's classes become increasingly aware of their inner monologues, develop the ability to listen fully to themselves and others, and discover unproductive behavior and thought patterns and modify them using the skills they have learned throughout the course. In many cases, students emerge with a greater ability to pay attention; the willingness to practice acceptance, discipline, and patience; and the capacity to nurture loving-kindness. Many of Dan's students have told him the course also helps them manage underlying conditions like attention deficit/hyperactivity disorder (ADHD), obsessive-compulsive disorder (OCD), and panic attacks. Even those who were initially skeptical of the teaching methods—which include regular meditation practice in class—report that their relationships with nearly everyone—family, friends, coworkers, and teachers—have improved as a result of the course. Students are more focused, more productive, and happier.

The course has become so popular that Dan is now overseeing approximately eight sections each semester, some of which he teaches himself while the others are taught by professors he has trained. Dan is also working with other departments and faculty at the college to incorporate mindful communication practices into their courses, as well as their interactions with students and colleagues. He leads seminars for faculty, which others have reported have increased collaboration, reduced conflict in faculty meetings, boosted productivity, and reduced the number of grade complaints and appeals from students. "It's not that professors have stopped disagreeing with each other or lowered their teaching standards," Dan explains. "It's that they have learned to express themselves with respect, compassion, and clarity. People understand themselves and each other better, so there is less resentment or feeling of being mistreated."

Now Dan says he can't imagine teaching communication courses without mindfulness practices and material. "It's all so interwoven for me; there isn't a mindfulness part and a conventional curriculum part anymore. It's all connected. I'd be hard pressed to teach a mindfulness course without including communication concepts, and the reverse as well."

Gifts of Mindfulness

What changes does Dan notice in himself, his own patterns of thoughts, and his own ways of being as a longtime mindfulness practitioner? "I am able to accept unpleasant thoughts without grasping, and I am much less reactive and more empathetic. I'm more patient, and I enjoy my life more. Ironically, I'm very grateful for that divorce almost two decades ago because it changed the course of my life, adding more pleasure and more joy, and more courage at facing change and difficulty." Dan is now happily remarried, in a relationship where he gets to practice mindful relationship work. "I am truly a much happier man, and a much better teacher than I ever was before."

We ask Dan if he sees his version of mindful communication as a movement—whether he has a social movement model for mindfulness. "This work is definitely spreading across the college, and there is an increasing call for my workshops. To date, over half of NHTI's full-time faculty have received at least some training in communicating mindfully. Meanwhile, faculty at eight other colleges and universities have adopted my book. People from all over the United States and about 20 other countries have expressed interest in the book and curriculum. I'm working across disciplines now, in information technology, early childhood education, human services, dental hygiene, math, nursing, orthopedics, and radiology. We're also working to offer the course and training online to make it available to people who don't live close enough to Concord, New Hampshire, to attend the live versions. As we move forward, we are continuously conducting studies to measure outcomes and refine curricula if necessary.

"My vision is to build programs that frame students' college experience with training in mindful communication, and reinforce it in between, beginning with the 'Communicating Mindfully' course their first term, ending with an internship course that emphasizes mindful communication in the workplace their last semester, and infusing mindfulness in other core and general education classes students need to take in order to complete their degree. We're already offering the 'Communicating Mindfully' and internship courses, and some general education courses. I'm working with colleagues to develop the others, including literature, math, humanities, and human development classes. We're creating courses and programs that I hope other colleges will adopt. I have also brought this training to prison populations, and plans are under way to bring it to high schools and businesses as well.

"So, 'Is it a movement?' Maybe. It's certainly moving forward." For more information on Dan Huston's book, *Communicating Mindfully,* or his workshops, visit www.communicating-mindfully.com.

Dan Huston is a full professor in the English Department at NHTI, Concord's Community College. He teaches writing and communication and serves as assistant to the department head. He has been incorporating mindfulness meditation and emotional intelligence into his communication curriculum for over a decade, and he was awarded NHTI's 2008 Chancellor's Award for Teaching Excellence. His work at NHTI resulted in the college becoming a 2013 Bellwether Award Finalist. Dan has received training at the renowned Center for Mindfulness in Medicine, Health Care, and Society at the University of Massachusetts Medical School. His essay "How Mindfulness Can Help Us Become Better Communicators" was published in a 2006 Rowman and Littlefield anthology titled Teaching With Joy: Educational Practices for the Twenty-First Century, *and he is a contributing author to a Jossey-Bass Sourcebook titled* Contemplative Teaching and Learning. *His chapter is called "Waking Up to Ourselves: The Use of Mindfulness Meditation and Emotional Intelligence in the Teaching of Communication."*

His textbook, Communicating Mindfully: Mindfulness-Based Communication and Emotional Intelligence, *details the teaching methodologies he has developed, which have helped many people achieve personal and professional success through their improved communication skills. A recent controlled study conducted at his college suggests that students who study communication using Dan's "Communicating Mindfully" curriculum not only increase in mindfulness more than those using a more traditional curriculum, but develop positive reappraisal skills characterized by an ability to identify and express emotions without placing blame on others during stressful situations.[7] Dan presents at national and regional conferences, and provides training in communicating mindfully.*

5.4 Lucretia M. Wells, Head of School

Buckingham Friends School
Lahaska, Pennsylvania

> "When I first started working at Buckingham Friends School, one of the first things I did was attend the Headmaster's Bootcamp. They said there are three things that will kill your career: promiscuity, alcohol, and your health. This was a real wake-up call."

The Relationships Among Consumption, Food, and Mindfulness

We interview Lucretia "Lukie" Wells in her office, a gracious, modest space at the center of Buckingham Friends School (BFS), a thriving Quaker school north of Philadelphia. Filled with energy, enthusiasm, and a sense of quiet drive, Lukie opens our dialog by reflecting on the relationship between consumption, food, and mindfulness. "I am a tri-athlete and have raced and exercised my whole life. My dad was a world champion rower and is in great shape at age 86, so I guess I inherited good genes. I have been on the job at Buckingham Friends School as head of the school for two-and-a half years, and when I first came to the school, I ate every baked good that passed my desk. I ate out a lot, too, because I didn't have time to cook or just felt overwhelmed by work. Sometimes I would drink on the weekends also because I thought, 'I deserve to drink; I've been good all week.' When I first started working at BFS, however, one of the first things I did was attend the Headmaster's Bootcamp. They said there are three things that will kill your career: promiscuity, alcohol, and your health. This was a real wake-up call."

A Turning Point

Lukie continues to describe her journey to wellness as it relates to mindfulness. "About a year ago, I tore my meniscus, which meant I couldn't exercise; I couldn't run, and I began to have trouble sleeping. I had my knee operated on and gained weight. About this time my husband invited me to read *The Chemistry of Joy Workbook: Overcoming Depression Using the Best of Brain Science, Nutrition, and the Psychology of Mindfulness* by Henry Emmons, MD.[8] The book changed my life. After reading the book, I began to make changes. I reduced my consumption of coffee and red wine. I became more mindful of how much sleep I was getting, and I cut out processed foods and sugar. I didn't want to be hard on myself in doing all this, making these changes. So, I just started making changes slowly. I started pacing myself. I noticed that when I first began, I was feeling off-balance, not myself. But once I really thought about all of this, I began shifting toward more mindful, better eating and better care of myself.

"Looking back on all of this, I think the biggest thing that precipitated my shift in thinking and then taking action to support my health was that I began to feel happier in my work. Reading that book shifted my thinking, too. I began to partner with myself to feel good, to be well. Now I eat five times a day. I have a regular breakfast of two eggs and toast with coffee. In the late morning, I have a snack of yogurt and coffee. For lunch, I have a salad with chicken. In the late afternoon, I have yogurt, fruit, or cheese and crackers. And for dinner, I have a protein, veggies, and rice. Rather than eating out or grabbing something from the convenience store nearby, I bring snacks and my lunch from home, using leftovers. Eating like this, I have lost 20 pounds, and my race times have improved!

"If I had to give one piece of advice to a head of school or to anybody interested in practicing mindfulness, with eating at the center I would say, 'Don't be hard on yourself. Our bodies are engines, and our bodies run best on good, wholesome food. Give yourself the gift of healthy eating.'

"Eating like this, eating healthy, I have more energy, going from meeting to meeting. At home, too, with my husband (we don't have kids), we care about each other's well-being by having a weekly breakfast date and an evening date night.

"I have long believed that we are responsible for the hours we put in at work, and if we put in the hours—being at school from 7 a.m. to 9 p.m., shame on you—that isn't healthy and balanced. You need to take care of yourself!

"I have my health and my life partner, and I want to be here for the long haul!"

LUCRETIA M. WELLS'S SAMPLE DAILY MINDFUL EATING MENU

- Breakfast: Two eggs, toast, and coffee
- Late-morning snack: Yogurt and coffee
- Lunch: Green salad with chicken
- Late-afternoon snack: Choice of yogurt, fruit, or cheese and crackers
- Dinner: Protein, veggies, and rice

Lucretia "Lukie" Wells is in her third year as the Head of School at Buckingham Friends School (BFS). BFS is a kindergarten through eighth grade Quaker School in Bucks County, PA. She is originally from the Finger Lakes Region of Central New York where she and her six siblings grew up drinking whole milk and playing outside whenever possible. Lukie has worked in several independent schools for over 25 years in varying capacities from dorm parent to coach to English teacher, Learning Specialist and senior administrator. She has most enjoyed her work in schools' upper administration and loves the sense of community that schools have to offer. Having had the opportunity to attend boarding school and work in different regions of the country has offered a unique perspective on adjusting to cultural expectations and learning from others. It is through these lessons that Lukie enjoys getting to know a school, its culture and how a community can grow to be a safe and supportive experience for students and their families. By having a number of school roles, Lukie also has a sense of how to support faculty, staff and administrators to grow professionally. Addressing the needs of all the constituencies unifies the community as they work to embrace their mission and ethos. She can be reached at www.bfs.org.

We consume all day, every day. We consume not only food but books, newspapers and magazines, television, conversations, and the Internet, and in countless other ways. As busy school leaders, we may also have developed a habit of overconsumption of news, data, and policy information. Lukie's story, and her focus on mindful eating, makes plain that a critical aspect of the practice of mindfulness is learning how to stop ourselves, and then to notice what we are eating, how, and why. There is a larger message here about consumption in general. With mindful awareness, we are better able to make choices that support our well-being and our health.

Mindfulness Practice Aids

Mindfulness Practice Aid 5.1: Eating Mindfully

"Mindful eating is not a diet, or about giving up anything at all. It is about experiencing food more intensely—especially the pleasure of it."

—Jeff Gordinier, "Food for Thought" (2012)[9]

Overview

We need food to live. Yet for many of us, eating is an afterthought or an obsession, or may be filled with shame or guilt. More than a third of us in the United States are obese, and obesity is related to a host of other medical conditions. As we know in our educational leader roles, obesity also does not affect all equally, but is also related to the growing income inequality that plagues our country. Non-Hispanic blacks have the highest age-adjusted rates of obesity (49.5%), compared with Mexican Americans (40.4%), all Hispanics (39.1%), and non-Hispanic whites (34.3%).[10]

These sobering facts point to the need for taking mindful steps toward greater physical well-being. As with many things in life, the first step in mindful eating is becoming aware of our body and mind, becoming aware of our food choices, and noticing how we are eating.

As school leaders, we may be accustomed to using food to comfort ourselves after working too hard, or to ease anxiety, stress, sadness, and loneliness. We may long for foods from our childhood, especially when we are feeling down. Holidays, a time of celebration, can often turn into a time of eating to relieve stress. We may find ourselves struggling with weight issues and have grown accustomed to viewing mealtimes as a tiresome moment of counting calories. Mindful eating helps bring awareness to the choices we make, and awareness of our mood, our emotional state, can affect portion size and quality of food—all the choices involved in eating.

Educational leaders are squeezed for time, and often the casualty of this is planned mealtimes and well-cooked, nutritious food. By default, we may turn to fast foods and convenience foods that may be higher in salt, sugar, and fat—which keeps us craving them—and traps us in a cycle of desiring them.

Following the mindful eating practice outlined here is not about another diet. It is about developing awareness to support our nourishment and greater well-being. It's also about moving us toward habits that are aligned with the long-term sustainability of our planet.

Step 1: Notice How You Are Feeling

The first step in eating mindfully is to become aware of your body. Notice how you are feeling in the moment: anxious, nervous, tired, lonely, hungry, full, impatient? (You may want to try a body scan here, a practice described in Mindfulness Practice Aid 2.3, "The Body Scan: Mindful Awareness of the Body," in Chapter 2, page 62.) There is a lot of information available if you observe the state of your body and mind in the moment. In other words, become aware, conscious, of what is happening right now.

Many of us skip this stage. We eat impulsively. We binge on junk food. We snack without realizing that we are eating. We eat because others are eating, or we eat on autopilot, with no thought at all. In this step, we make the important connection between how we feel and what we eat.

Step 2: Notice What You Are About to Eat

Take a moment to become aware of what you are about to eat: What is it?

- Look at your food and become aware of your body posture as you are doing so. Are you standing at the fridge, sitting at your desk hunched over a burger and fries?
- Consider where this food came from. Is the food from the local farmers' market or from the fast-food restaurant nearby?
- Consider for a brief moment the people who prepared the food, and how the food was grown. Become aware of the connection you now have to those who grew the food, those who made the food, those who transported the food, and those who sold the food to you.
- Notice its colors, textures, and fragrance. Notice the portion size.

This does not have to be long, just a few brief seconds. In this step, the point is to bring attention and consciousness to the connection between you and the food production. We don't need to be hard on ourselves or feel shame or guilt. Instead, the point of this step is not only to recognize how our choice of eating affects us internally, but to make the connection between how we eat and our external environment.

Step 3: Pause and Be Quiet

Before you pick up a fork and start eating, pause and quiet yourself for a brief moment.

- Take in with your senses—your eyes, your nose, your body, your mind—what you are about to consume. Even the slightest pause is useful to bring mindfulness to the act of eating.
- Put down the fork between bites or put down the sandwich to train yourself to stop.

In this step, we slow down the process of eating, and become aware of feelings of fullness, which may help you avoid overeating. This is a key way to train yourself to really taste the food.

Step 4: Enjoy Eating

Enjoy what you're eating. Eating is one of the great pleasures of life, a source of happiness and contentment. However, often we are oblivious to it, or we overlook the joy of eating. This is squandering joy!

- Are you thinking about your projects, your worries? Ask yourself whether your attention is divided between the food you are consuming and your worries. Are you eating your worries, your anxiety, or your fear?

As we've said throughout this book, there is increasing neuroscientific evidence that how you use your mind changes the physical structures of your brain. Taking in positive events, pausing, really feeling good about the meal you are eating, and letting this really sink in even for a few moments can gradually change the shape of your brain, building neural pathways that promote greater calm and inner contentment. This may sound way out or corny, but it's true. This practice is about generating happiness from within, and sharing that with others.

Step 5: Just Eat

Unplug. Put aside your devices. Put down the newspaper. Turn off the television.

- As you chew, become aware of the food's taste, texture, and fragrance. Experience the array of sensations in your mouth.

Savor the taste: sweet, sour, bitter. Become aware of the texture: chewy, grainy, smooth. Become aware of the fragrance: savory, buttery, and so on.

- If you are standing, please sit down.
- Chew the food thoroughly. Many experts recommend that we chew 25 to 30 times for each mouthful. In other words: *Slow down.*
- Focus on the experience. For many, we have grown accustomed to eating and doing something else at the same time.

Step 6: Focus on How You Feel While You Are Eating and After You Are Finished

As you chew and swallow, notice how you feel. Are you full, nearly full? If you feel full, stop eating.

- When you are finished, notice how you feel. (Remember that it takes about 10–30 minutes to experience satiation physically.) Do you feel better or worse after eating? Do you feel sleepy or energized? Your choice of food greatly impacts your energy level and overall well-being. In this step, we begin to make the connection between the food we eat and how we feel.

If trying Steps 1–6 all at once seems like too much, begin slowly. Start with just one step.

Years ago, we led a retreat in Michigan at a lovely log cabin retreat center near the Grand River. We introduced the practice of mindful eating to a group of mixed professionals and will never forget the comment of a middle-aged African American woman. "This was the first time I have been gentle with my food." Mindful eating, as with mindful consuming, is about coming into a new relationship with our food. Enjoy.

Please visit us on Facebook at https://www.facebook.com/TheMindfulSchoolLeader.

6

Mindfulness and Emotional Intelligence

*Principles and Practices to
Transform Your Leadership Life*

"[T]here is a limit to the role of the intelligence in human affairs."

—James Baldwin, *Notes of a Native Son* (1955)[1]

A Leader Fails to Notice

Jonathan, a 52-year-old chief academic officer (CAO) of a large suburban district in California, is a scholar. Not only does he work tirelessly planning professional learning in his district; he also finds time to write several articles for professional trade publications and has authored a chapter in a well-received book on new forms of teacher evaluation from an administrator's point of view. Recently promoted, he has asked us to observe him during a senior staff meeting to help him with some "communication fine-tuning." We happily agree. After some preliminaries and a couple of agenda items are announced, we observe Jonathan talk for almost 12 minutes about his goals as a new CAO, the latest district strategic planning session, and the books he is reading. He appears not to observe the body language of others in the room, and sometimes seems only distantly aware of their presence. Finally, he turns to his executive staff to ask whether anyone has anything to contribute to the "discussion," yet before anyone can reply, he shifts into another discourse about the iPad policy at one of the district's schools. His colleagues begin to give each other side glances, adjust their clothing and hair, move about in their seats, and reach for their phones but Jonathan doesn't seem to notice. What skills and attributes does Jonathan need to help him become a more effective leader? How might he develop them? (And have you ever been like Jonathan, or worked for someone like him?)

Throughout this book, we have made the case for why and how mindfulness supports and nurtures your capacity to notice what is happening within yourself, and with others—or to develop emotional intelligence (EQ).[2] We think these are central leadership skills, and as most know, they are now considered the foundation of leadership development. Increasing your ability to notice what is happening both inside and outside yourself, and then make reasonable and wise judgments based on an evaluation of these awarenesses, is supported by mindfulness practice. These EQ components are like Russian nesting dolls, supporting each other as mindfulness based-practices nest within mindfulness.

Dan Goleman's groundbreaking work on EQ is the foundation for this chapter. Goleman notes that these competencies are twice as important as cognitive and technical skill.[3] EQ is a range of sensitivities that help you manage yourself and your relationships. EQ and mindfulness both center on a quality of awareness, and both promote prosocial behavior. The practice of mindfulness as with the development of EQ supports leadership that is grounded, centered, and effective, as well as awake to the wisdom of the heart, mind, and spirit. EQ makes for better leaders who bring a range of awareness to their school and to life. Mindfulness makes for leaders who are aware of the complexity of the school environment *and* aware of themselves and others. It is impossible to lead others when you are walking around mindlessly unaware of yourself, your emotions, and your values. Emotions affect your thinking, attitude, and mood, and these in turn affect your actions and behavior. You don't leave emotions behind when you show up at work. We think, feel, and act. The leader's capacity to hold tension and ambiguity without becoming reactive, to sense and understand the feeling of others and yet make tough decisions, to understand what motivates others toward change, and to build relationships across networks and with individuals is critical to transforming leadership through mindfulness. Mindful awareness supports EQ in that it builds the capacity to engage experiences—pleasant, unpleasant, or neutral experiences—without clinging or attaching to an outcome. With nonjudgmental awareness, mindful school leaders are able to engage multiple and sometimes competing perspectives, taking in the larger picture, fostering fair and reasonable decision making, supporting greater trust and openness.

EQ Component 1: Self-Awareness

To return to Jonathan, the CAO who opened the chapter, we sit with him and settle in to learn a little bit more about him. Raised in a family that he describes as "hyper-achievement oriented," Jonathan said that he was raised to "show what you know"; that's how you got attention and praise in his family of origin. Consequently, he read avidly and rarely left work before 7 p.m. He seldom ate lunch because of the "unrelenting demands" of the job. He observed about himself that he had a hard time delegating work to others and found it difficult to ask for help, and was also, in spite of his real intellectual gifts (appreciated by many!), too ready to take up space with others to lecture them about what he knew. These clear self-observations helped set him up to develop critical new emotional intelligence capacities, using many of the exercises in this book.

A self-described explorer by nature, Jonathan was open and willing to try mindfulness practices. To get more connected to himself, more grounded, he began to use the Body Scan (see Mindfulness Practice Aid 2.3, "The Body Scan," page 62) and, surprisingly, after only his first 45-minute practice session was able to identify that the pain at the back of his knee was related to the way he tightly gripped his shoulders. Within a few practice sessions, he looked more relaxed and "felt better in his skin." This led to a few more openings. He began to notice how tiring it was to "always be the expert," and to also question his familiar patterns of hyper-responsibility. Through more honest conversations, where he was able to open himself more, he made some connections between these beliefs and how hard he worked and how frequently he found himself impelled by the need to tell how much he knew. In a breakthrough moment of self-awareness, he said, "I don't have to do it all myself. I don't have to have all the right answers. I can ask for help and still be OK."

Self-awareness is multilayered. It includes the capacity to recognize how your feelings affect you and others, and, in turn, how your environment shapes you. Self-awareness is awareness of your thoughts and emotions, as well as how they sit in your physical body, in the moment. With this awareness, you can begin to recognize the impact of your behavior—your words and actions, what you say and do, how you say it, and physical sensations: a tightening in your stomach, clenching your right hip, difficulty fully inhaling (to name just a few common ones). As you become more attuned, you begin to understand that your actions and beliefs are not isolated, but rather are interconnected: Your school, your family, and your environment are all a part of a large universe connected by thinking and feeling. A self-aware leader begins to recognize in a conversation, or after a long day, when she is at an emotional or physical tipping point, and exercises self-regulation. You sense the physical cues, the physical sensations in your body—when your face is flushed, or when you feel exhausted or hijacked by emotions, or when you need to give yourself a break or adjourn a difficult meeting for the day.

Self-awareness carries with it a quality of accurate self-assessment and self-regulation—for instance, if you are delivering critical feedback to a contentious staffer. If you are unaware when the conversation turns heated and don't notice your heart beating faster, your palms getting sweaty, the rising tone of your voice, or the growing feelings of anger and defensiveness, before too long you are talking louder, cutting off the staffer in midsentence, and defending your position. With self-awareness, you engage in self-regulation and can:

- Avoid overreactions that may be potentially damaging.
- Be in a better position to think clearly and act in a way that fits your deepest values.
- Be in a better position to take in the fullness of the situation.
- Consider another's point of view.

Entertain the possibility that you may not have sufficient information to make a decision.

A self-aware leader is flexible in thinking and acting and demonstrates a willingness to consider others' views within reasonable limits, even when doing so might challenge one's beliefs, be contrary to one's beliefs and thinking, or conflict with one's agenda. We believe that the mindfulness exercises suggested throughout this book do begin to build the kind of flexibility and self-awareness that are the underpinnings of true emotional intelligence, which as we've described is now classically defined as having a range of sensitivity to one's self and to others.

EQ Component 2: Self-Regulation

A critical benefit of a regular mindfulness practice is the capacity to regulate ourselves emotionally: to notice when we are tired and jumping to conclusions, when all the world seems dark and stormy and threatening, or to observe that we may be a little too emotionally buoyant and not able to assess risk in the moment. When we are able to self-regulate, we are able to recognize what's happening to us emotionally or physically or spiritually, inwardly and outwardly, and have the capacity to control and redirect disruptive impulses and moods. The kind of cognitive control that is required to perform under pressure—composure, focus, and flexibility—is not something you can easily maintain when you're emotionally hijacked or your reserves are too low to show up as your better self.

Here's an example in Valerie's leadership life. Recently, I was working with a prominent Quaker high school to implement diversity within the curriculum. (I am also a Quaker.) My role was to facilitate discussion on diversity among members of the school's diversity committee, using the Courage & Renewal approach of individual and self-reflection, listening and asking open questions to build trust and authenticity for courageous conversations on diversity within the school. I was working directly with the school's diversity committee of faculty, administrators, and parents tasked with implementing diversity within the curriculum. We held a series of meetings which began with looking at diversity from the lens of our own biographies, and then examined some models as a way of uncovering our own hidden bias and implicit assumptions. At our last meeting, a math teacher and active member of the committee turned to me and in a visibly annoyed tone said: "If other people want me to get to know them, they have to come to me and tell me what I need to know. I can't read their minds." In that moment, I felt a flood of anger in my face, and my mind flashed back to the many indignities of living as a black woman in a racially polarized culture: feelings of being disgusted by belittling comments and the false projections. I recognized in the moment that if I said anything, I would likely regret it. Thankfully I regained enough emotional composure and internal balance to pause and then replied, "So let me stop you right there, John. Can you imagine another approach that might turn the tables, that might look more like you and the other person equally reaching out as opposed to the other person telling you what you need to know?" The math teacher hesitated, and then said, "Well I'm not sure what that would look like." I replied, "Well, I'm not sure either, but every bone in my body says that waiting for the other person to tell you what you need to know puts a lot of pressure on them." "You may be right," he said. Clearly this was a murky, unsettled, and emotionally charged exchange that could have gone down in flames. Since the encounter, I've thought about lots of other things that I could have or should have said, and second-guessed myself. The big learning for me, though was that in the moment, I noticed my anger and felt the rush of it flash up in my body. I knew what was happening and controlled the impulse to respond in anger or rage. I recognized my feelings—appalled, furious, and agitated—and allowed them to be there without acting on them. I allowed the mental flashbacks of other racially charged insensitivities to be there too (which was *really* hard), and I chose to respond without pretense.

As Daniel Goleman notes, "People who are in control of their feelings and impulses—that is, people who are reasonable—are able to create an environment of trust and fairness. . . . The signs of emotional self-regulation, therefore, are easy to see: a propensity for reflection and thoughtfulness; comfort with ambiguity and change; and integrity—an ability to say no to impulsive urges."[4]

EQ Component 3: Motivation

We are passionate about our work with the Center for Courage & Renewal, consulting with organizations and schools and facilitating retreats for educators and other professionals to strengthen one's inner capacity to lead a meaningful life and the clarity and courage to bring one's true self to one's work. As we mentioned in the Introduction to this book, when Valerie passed the bar exam, she had no intention of practicing mindfulness or leading retreats. Her focus and motivation was making money and getting out of Brooklyn, which was not the swanky place it is today. She spent years on the run—running from undergraduate to graduate school and then to law school and the bar exam, and then to the so-called job of her dreams. The only problem was that the job made her sick: physically, mentally, emotionally, and spiritually. For years, she trained herself not to question her "success" and believed that the good job and nice house (out of Brooklyn) meant that she was worthy. It wasn't until she came face-to-face with divorce and then her own infertility that she began to wonder about the "success." But by then, she was deeply invested in the job: the regular paycheck, the pension, and health care.

Slowly, very slowly, after a series of stops and starts, she left the dream job and regular paycheck to take the shaky step of creating a new and different life that she hardly had a way to describe to others and could barely understand herself. She was clueless about how her law school training would serve in this new work. Today, her strongest motivation is to be part of transformation in others and in herself because she believes your transformation affects her transformation, which then leads to societal transformation. (This wasn't what she had in mind when she went to law school!)

Recently, we co-led series of four seasonal retreats held for professionals in the fields of education, health care, and law. The participants met for one weekend each season at Pendle Hill, a beautiful and bucolic Quaker retreat center in suburban Philadelphia, in an environment that nurtures their needs and creates an opportunity for personal transformation. We often use tools for personal and group reflection that may be unfamiliar to school leaders, such as poetry, mindful movement, video, art-making, and small- and large-group dialogue within a structured setting. We also spend much time reflecting on the retreat design and rhythm, carefully selecting pieces that don't just enliven the retreat, but touch their own "inner leader" or "inner teacher," and also encompass various cultural traditions, allowing participants to interact on a deeper level with the material. Often, people are unsure about their motivation for attending the retreat. They show up with uncertainty and doubt, taking the first step toward trusting their "inner leader." We set the tone for the retreat on the first night with the *Touchstones*, guidelines designed to set boundaries and establish safety and group norms, mentioned in Chapter 4, pages 121–122. Many of our participants are school leaders and other educational professionals who say they don't know where to begin, feel intimated, or have little or no time to ask big questions about motivation, life passion, and purpose.

Participants are invited to speak about the intense yearlong practice of mindful self-inquiry: holding and asking open questions; staying open in the face of uncertainty, doubt, and resistance; living with paradox; practicing mindful listening; and valuing diversity. They report that what motivated them toward change was finding a deeper sense of purpose and meaning to their lives, to discovering themselves in ways that surprised even them. Awareness of thoughts and emotions, awareness of physical cues, and a sense of intuition support understanding motivation, which forms the basis for purposeful action.

Practice Pointer—Using a Poem to Build Emotional Intelligence

In our work with the Center for Courage & Renewal, leading retreats for school leaders and others, we often use poems or poem fragments as a way to understand one's motivation and direction. Judy Brown's poem "Fire" speaks to creating greater spaciousness in our lives. How might you use this poem in your own self-inquiry practice?

Fire

What makes a fire burn
is space between the logs,
a breathing space.
Too much of a good thing,
too many logs
packed in too tight
can douse the flames
almost as surely
as a pail of water would.
So building fires
requires attention
to the spaces in between,
as much as to the wood.
When we are able to build
open spaces
in the same way
we have learned
to pile on the logs,
then we can come to see how
it is fuel, and absence of the fuel
together, that make fire possible.
We only need to lay a log
lightly from time to time.
A fire
grows
simply because the space is there,
with openings

in which the flame
that knows just how it wants to burn
can find its way.

—Judy Brown[5]

Take a few moments to reflect on these questions. There is no right or wrong.

- How do you create "breathing space" in your life?
- What can you learn about yourself, your motivations from giving your attention more fully to those ordinary moments of life, to the "spaces in between" the wood?
- What insights, observations, and surprises, and what new learning about your own motivations, are there for you?

EQ Component 4: Empathy

Carlos is the head of an independent K–12 college preparatory school. He wants to increase the racial and ethnic diversity and engage administrators and faculty in discussions around this issue. In conversations with his staff who are white and middle class, Carlos hears the same thing over and over again. Individuals at his institution say, "I don't see color. It's just not an issue for me. Aren't we beyond that? Besides, we have several new Korean students, and they seem to be doing fine." He comes to understand that he must deliver a clear message about why diversity is critical to the school's mission.

Carlos calls a staff meeting and begins by talking about his own experience with diversity. He acknowledges that his perspective is subjective and limited. He says, "I'd like to know what you think would be meaningful and important for the school to accomplish, and for us together to consider ways that we might do that." And because he has been practicing many of the exercises in this book, although this is a very stressful moment, he is able to be aware of his body language, his tone of voice, and the pacing of his words. Reading the discomfort in the room, he says, "I understand this is new territory for us and that we may be moving outside of our comfort zone. We are all in a learning zone." Still unsettled, a longtime science teacher asks, "What if we simply can't recruit more diverse students given the demographics of our location?" Carlos takes a moment to check the physical sensations in his body and his posture. He replies, "I can sense the uncertainty in your question and maybe even some fear of failing. I have to admit, I have those feelings, too. I know this is not something that I can figure out alone, and I do know people who can help us. Would you be willing to explore that approach?"

Here Carlos is able to be empathic about the discomfort of the speaker, and of others in the room; his mindfulness practices support his capacity to imagine and feel their emotions. An empathetic response does not necessarily mean you agree with the other person or that you avoid tough decisions (recall the swim coach example in Chapter 4, page 144). Instead, an empathetic response, supported by mindfulness, has a quality of care and kindness. An empathetic response is nonjudgmental. The foundation of mindful action is understanding, kindness, peacefulness, appreciation, and happiness (recall the mindful mind states on pages 89–90). There is a sensitivity to your own and to another's condition. Empathy is the ability to recognize the emotions of others and to "feel into" them. Since the capacity to understand what someone else may be feeling and sensing is key to maintaining meaningful connection with them, mindfulness helps build our receptivity to this. We think this is an extraordinarily important leadership skill. Daniel Goleman suggests why empathy is particularly critical today for leaders: "The increasing use of teams; the rapid pace of globalization; and the growing need to retain talent. People who have empathy are attuned to the subtleties in body language; they can hear the message beneath the words being spoken. Beyond that, they have a deep understanding of both the existence and the importance of cultural and ethnic differences. . . . Leaders with empathy do more than sympathize with people around them. They use their knowledge to improve their companies in subtle but important ways."[6] Google engineer and author Chade-Meng Tan, in *Search Inside Yourself* , says that "empathy increases perceived similarity."[7] When you perceive that others share your views and beliefs, your response is measurably different on an unconscious and neurological level, and we believe mindful practice makes this possible.[8]

How might you use empathy, even when a tough decision is called for, to promote kindness in yourself and within your school or family? How might such a response support your leadership, your life?

Think About It

How might you in your next conversation create a more empathetic relationship? What would you say? What are the risks? How might this help you be a better school leader?

ॐ

Practice Pause

Loving-kindness or *metta* is an ancient meditation practice that supports empathy, kindness, and compassion for one's self and others. The word *metta* comes from the Pali language, meaning friendship. In this practice, we generate a quality of self-acceptance, friendliness, empathy, connection, understanding. and warmth in stages. Begin by setting aside quiet time and lie down comfortably with your eyes closed and take a few deep breaths. Gently and silently offer these words to yourself: "May I be safe. May I be happy. May I be healthy. May I be at peace." Repeat the phrase silently to yourself several times, and when you notice that you are distracted, that's OK; just begin again. Be gentle with yourself. Allow the breath to anchor your attention. Next bring to mind someone you appreciate or someone you feel kindness toward, and picture that person in your mind's eye and silently direct the verses to that person: "May you be safe. May you be happy. May you be healthy. May you be at peace." Bring to mind next the person you may have difficulty with, and if it is appropriate and you feel ready, direct the verses to even this person: "May you be safe. May you be happy. May you be healthy. May you be at peace." Notice emotions and sensations as you silently repeat the verses and again be gentle with yourself. Finally, expand your awareness to take all the people in you family, your friends, your neighborhood, your town, your country, all beings, and direct the verses to all beings: "May you be safe. May you be happy. May you be healthy. May you be at peace."

A Leader Grows EQ Through Mindfulness Practice

Allison, a new assistant principal in a large urban school district and an avid runner, had "an issue with trust." She described herself as a cautious person who seldom relied on others and preferred to offer help rather than to accept it. She had a nagging sense that this pattern was related to her childhood. Her mother died when she was 4, and she was raised by her paternal grandmother. She described herself as having little use for "touchy-feely stuff," keeping her emotions "under wraps." Allison's get-it-done-myself style had caused turmoil in her school because colleagues seldom were included in her decision making, making people feel disconnected from the life of the school, and creating underlying feelings of distrust among central office staff.

This pattern started changing after Allison began practicing mindfulness and supportive contemplative practices to "help with stress on the job." She journaled and patiently observed feelings as they arose in the moment. Much to her surprise, she noticed how her emotions changed without her realizing it. Sometimes, when her mind wandered to "feeling lost," instead of busying herself, going out for a run, or turning on the TV, she "allowed the feeling to be there, and just breathe." At first, she practiced for 10 minutes at night at home, and then she slowly began practicing during the school day, noticing her feelings and then jotting a note about how she felt. She realized that she had been avoiding feelings of fear, of "being lost" because it was easier to ignore than to "deal with it." Over time, she realized that the fear was "part of her unfinished business," and that to regain trust in herself and others, she needed to look at this.

This advice has been repeated in Jon Kabat-Zinn's numerous writings. In studies with chronic pain patients, he urges patients to turn toward their pain. Many of these patients report hating their pain, wanting it to just go away. Kabat-Zinn's clinical trials demonstrate that turning toward painful sensations, rather than distracting yourself or adopting a grin-and-bear-it, stoic approach, is a better way of reducing the level of pain experienced.[9] Instead of outwardly pretending that she wasn't feeling distress, while inwardly feeling tied in knots, she began to allow painful feelings to be and to acknowledge them, reacting less to them. As a way to soothe and comfort herself, she extended her journaling to the questions below. Less than searching for "answers," Allison said that asking these questions "was opening a door to her heart that had long been closed."

- What is the root of the feeling?
- Why am I feeling this way?
- Is there a pattern?
- How might I approach this differently?

Again, there are no right or wrong, good or bad, responses. Instead, these questions are prompts for self-reflection as a tool of self-awareness, self-understanding, and self-confidence.

Mindful Practices Develop Compassion and Self-Compassion

We love the work of Dr. Paul Gilbert, professor of clinical psychology at the University of Derby in the United Kingdom and international expert on compassion and self-compassion as applied to clinical populations. In his book *The Compassionate Mind,* he says that focusing on compassion for ourselves and others stimulates the brain and body to promote well-being.[10] Developing compassion, he says, helps with coping with strong emotions, resolving conflicts with others, and with our outlook generally.[11]

Nathan, a near-retirement superintendent from the Pacific Northwest, has lived his whole life with a strong inner critic. "If you could hear the way I speak to myself, you would be shocked," he says. And the inner critic has long had the upper hand. As Nathan begins a mindfulness sitting practice, he becomes acutely aware of the critical voice. At first, he has a hard time separating the voice of the inner critic from most of his thoughts and emotions. He says, "It's all one jumble." After weeks of sitting quietly, watching his breathing, and noticing his thinking and his emotions, and especially being aware of the internal voice of the inner critic, Nathan is able to feel his breath and notice when his heartbeat increases as his thoughts turn to the inner critic. He practices feeling a sense of warmth and kindness for himself, and even for the inner critic—something that feels totally foreign and strange at first, but over time, becomes easier. After several more weeks of practice, he says, "What am I choosing to listen to? I don't need to battle with myself. I know what is underneath all this; it's an old fear of not being 'good enough.' I can trust myself. I'm enough."

Kristin Neff often speaks on three fundamental guidelines of compassion:

1. Show kindness toward yourself.

2. Recognize that the human experience is not perfect, and that you are not alone in your suffering (frustrations, losses, disappointments, and tragedies). When you notice that something is amiss, this cuts you off from others. You feel isolated and disconnected.

3. Be mindful: Pay attention to your suffering without immediately trying to fix it, deny it, push it away, or ignore it. Pause and recognize what is happening now. (This step is a balance of getting help you need from the appropriate professional when you need it and accepting things as they are, knowing that things change.)[12]

As leaders, we at times hold ourselves to punishingly high, unrelenting standards. We cut others a break, but not ourselves. Neff identifies important roadblocks to self-compassion: the belief that self-compassion is self-indulgent, that being self-compassionate might undermine your motivation, that you might lose your competitive edge. The internalized message is that self-compassion is self-pity, and self-pity is egocentric—that it is good to be compassionate toward others, and it is bad to be compassionate toward oneself. Neff's research indicates the opposite, that persistent stress and your own inner critic not only compromise well-being, but also activate the body's threat defense system, triggering the release of cortisol and other stress hormones. (Add to this the dynamics of the negativity bias we mentioned in Chapter 3, page 94.) Self-compassion, on the other hand, supports your goals out of love, not fear; it encourages persistence, an important motivational mind-set. Self-compassion is not the same as self-esteem, which is thinking positive thoughts about yourself compared to others; rather, self-compassion is about relating to yourself with kindness. The pace and intensity of high-stress school and work environments and the unprecedented levels of exhaustion create a new urgency to adopt practices that not only restore balance but also address the emotional overwhelm experienced by many school leaders. Compassion training is particularly helpful for school leaders who may feel isolated and unable to share their emotions with colleagues, and who may train themselves to ignore warning signs of extreme emotional overload. Compassion is about connecting with yourself and others and that begins with paying kind attention.

Practice Pointers—Ways to Strengthen Self-Compassion

Self-compassion can be strengthened in many ways. Here are three suggestions from Paul Gilbert:

- Use your memory to create a compassionate feeling, recalling a kind, loving, joyful experience (either receiving or giving one) and allowing a sense of compassion to flow in and out of your heart and mind.[13]
- Try compassionate writing—writing down your thoughts, reactions, and feelings and your compassionate response to them.
- Focus on your heart. Make a physical gesture of kindness and compassion toward yourself, such as placing your hand on your heart and imagining compassion flowing into you and this area through your hand. We are programmed to respond to touch, and this simple gesture calms the body and mind, activating the parasympathetic nervous system.[14]

Embody Mindfulness—Belly Breath

Belle Linda Halpern and Kathy Lubar, in *Leadership Presence*, say that an important step in cultivating authentic leadership presence is to breathe, to find "your belly breath."[15] We use this tool extensively with our clients, and you have read about other school leaders in this book who practice noticing their breath. See Mindfulness Practice Aid 1.1, "Three-Minute Focused Breathing Practice," in Chapter 1, page 35, and the one-minute and 30-second breathing practice aids in Chapter 2, pages 60–61.

Practice Pause—Belly Breath

Try this belly breath practice:
- Come into a comfortable posture either seated or lying down where you will not be disturbed.
- If you are seated, allow your spine to be comfortably straight, but not rigid.
- Loosen any tight clothing around your waist, and please allow your head, neck, and spine to be aligned.
- Allow your eyes to be closed, if that is comfortable for you.
- Place your dominant hand on your belly and your nondominant hand on your chest.
- Observe, without judgment, the rise and fall of your belly.
- Notice the movement of your dominant hand at the belly and the movement of your nondominant hand at your chest as you breathe in and out of the nose for 10 breath cycles. If breathing in and out of the nose is not comfortable for you, breathe in and out of the mouth. There is no need to force or control the breath. Just be with the breath as it is.
- When you are finished, stretch gently and open your eyes if they are closed.

Jonathan, Carlos, Allison, and Nathan are models of school leaders who are extending themselves, embodying components of EQ.

Practice Pointer—Ways to Bring Mindfulness Into Your Day

Please try these ways of creating mindfulness in your day:

- Practice mindful walking from one meeting to the next.
- Practice one minute of diaphragmatic breathing or belly breathing before a stressful meeting.

(Continued)

(Continued)

- In your next conversation, notice your impulse to interrupt or finish some-one else's sentence, and practice being fully present.
- Practice noticing emotions and feelings without pushing them away.
- Use one of the mindfulness apps in Appendix C, online, page 17, to stop, pause, and breathe.

Now it's your turn. Please contact us at www.facebook.com/TheMindful SchoolLeader with your tips for creating mindfulness in your leadership life.

EQ Component 5: Social Skill

Let's return to Jonathan, our CAO from California. To help him gain greater self-awareness of his behavior and social skills, we suggested the Four-Minute Mindful Check-In (see Mindfulness Practice Aid 6.2, page 174) to strengthen emotional intelligence. Initially, Jonathan found it difficult to sit in silence, for even one minute. He found his mind racing, thinking of all his many projects. Over weeks, though, he trained himself to sit quietly, without the sound of TV or radio, and gradually increased the time of his Mindful Check-In to five minutes each morning. He found that he had more energy and focused better throughout the day.

As he began to examine his core values, he realized that he had a strong need to be recognized and appreciated. He recalled that growing up as kid and throughout school, he rarely felt appreciated. His family, he said, "had high expectations and were no-nonsense." With this new insight, Jonathan made the connection between his relentless push for excellence and how this affected his relationship with colleagues. His Mindful Check-In practice was a way of regaining balance and developing his social skills.

EQ and mindfulness are about developing leaders who are aware of the wisdom of the what is happening inside—body, mind, and spirit—and what is happening outside—the school environment, home, community, and relationships. Mindfulness practices, with their emphasis on present moment nonjudgmental awareness, support this wisdom. As we grow in mindful awareness, we gain a critical leadership ability to understand ourselves, to observe what is happening honestly, to respond intentionally as opposed to reactively, to allow for purposeful choice instead of autopilot and defensiveness. Mindfulness and EQ are about the capacity to connect with yourself and to others in meaningful ways: to give and receive honest feedback and to perceive the feelings of others, which is the basis for compassionate action.

Think About It

The Dark Side of Emotional Intelligence

In an article in the *Atlantic Monthly*, writer Adam Grant points to the "dark side of EI." He notes that in some jobs it is essential to be in touch with emotions and in others it may be detrimental, such as in certain roles in the military. The capacity "to read" others may be used for good or not-so-good purposes, such as manipulating others. It seems obvious, though worth stating, that EI skills should be used to promote well-being and prosocial behavior.[16]

Mindfulness Practice Aids

Mindfulness Practice Aid 6.1: Mindful Concentration Exercise

Build your capacity for connectedness and empathy with others by training yourself to pay attention and boosting your ability to focus. It's very difficult to empathize with another person when you are distracted or tuned out. Use one of the mindfulness apps we list in Appendix C, online, page 17, to set your mindfulness timer for this three-minute, sound-attention training exercise.

- Sit in a quiet place, with the spine comfortably straight but not rigid.
- Allow your eyes to be open or closed—notice what feels most comfortable.
- Notice how you are sitting without judging yourself.
- Feel your feet on the floor.
- Feel your legs, hips, torso, arms, chest, and face.
- Bring your attention to the physical sensation of breathing with a sense of curiosity and openness.
- Locate where you feel the breath in the body.
- Feel the breath come in and go out, accepting things as they are for the moment.
- Observe and feel the in-breath without judgment.
- Follow the breath as it comes into the body.
- Notice the slight pause between the in-breath and the out-breath.
- Follow and feel the out-breath, noticing that the out-breath turns into the in-breath.
- Be with the sensations of breathing.

- Shift your attention from the breath to the sensation of hearing.
- Listen for sound around you. There is no need to strain or to strive to hear. Allow the ears to receive whatever sound is present.
- Focus on sounds close by, such as the sound of your own breathing, and then, after a while, direct your focus to sounds in the distance: street sounds, the wind, birds, car horns, people talking.
- Notice if and when you are creating a narrative, a story about the sounds.
- Notice when you are no longer focused on sounds and when your mind has wandered away from its focus on sounds.
- When you find that your mind has wandered, gently and yet firmly escort your attention back to its focus on sound—sounds close by or sounds at a distance.
- Notice feelings of attraction or aversion to certain sounds without acting on these feelings, without trying to push away or cling to any one sound.
- Observe how the sounds come and go, like passing clouds in the sky.
- Return your focus to awareness of the breath, feeling the fullness of breathing in and out.
- When you are finished, stretch gently and open your eyes if they are closed.

Mindfulness Practice Aid 6.2: Four-Minute Mindful Check-In

At the beginning of each day, take two minutes of quiet time either before you leave home, in the car before you enter the office, or when you arrive in the office before you start your day. Ask yourself the following questions:

- What do I most value?
- How do I want others to perceive me today?

Jot a note to yourself or journal about any insights.

Again, at the end of the day, take two minutes of quiet time. Ask yourself the following questions:

- Did I live today in accordance with my most important values?
- What did I learn from my interactions with others today?

Jot a note or journal about any new insights for one minute.

This simple practice helps leaders gain clarity and strengthen emotional intelligence through greater self-awareness. Reflection on interactions with colleagues encourages better working relationships with others and empathy. Reflection on core values enhances direction and purposefulness.

What outcomes might you expect from this daily practice?

- Greater self-awareness and awareness of others. Change begins awareness.
- Greater calm and clarity by focusing the mind. A calm mind aids focus, concentration, and clarity.
- Greater awareness of values and priorities. This leads to a greater likelihood of acting in conformity with deeply held values.

Portraits of Practice

6.1 Irene McHenry, PhD, Recently Retired Executive Director

Friends Council on Education
Philadelphia, Pennsylvania
Co-author, *Tuning In: Mindfulness in Teaching and Learning* (2009)

"I teach my staff mindful breathing practices, and we begin each staff meeting with silence."

Irene McHenry, Quaker educator, researcher, retreat leader, and mindfulness teacher leader, exudes quiet groundedness and confidence in conversation. A mindfulness practitioner for over 30 years, and an early educator of mindfulness practices in schools long before there were many programs, and long before mindfulness was culturally popular, Irene says, "I'm an explorer!" Irene's early book (with Richard Brady) on mindfulness in teaching and learning[17] was one of the first to offer mindfulness instruction to classroom teachers, and it is grounded in the observation that "mindfulness practice develops a powerful

foundation for all teaching and learning—the core skills of concentration, observation, relaxation and empathy." Irene has also been a close observer of the neurobiological research linking mindfulness to improved cognitive function, helping to lead a research project in 2012 in Friends schools using the *Learning to Breathe* curriculum,[18] and was a senior investigator at the 2010 summer session of the Mind and Life Institute. She is especially interested in the promotion of human flourishing in classrooms and schools.

Convinced that mindful practice was uniquely suited to preparing the mind for learning, Irene began some of her mindfulness teaching through experimentation. As a longtime practitioner of meditation, she began using mindfulness practices with young children, teens, and adults in her psychotherapy practice and teaching seventh graders at the William Penn Charter School in Philadelphia. She began to use meditation techniques for centering and quiet focusing during weekly Meeting for Worship, as she noted children and young adults need scaffolding for preparing themselves for worship. "I noticed that even Quakers could benefit from learning how to use mindfulness tools to settle into silence." Often called "expectant waiting," silence is at the center of Quaker services, and many children had little practice calming their bodies for this kind of experience.

Irene speaks about her mindfulness practice as simply at the heart of how she lives her daily life: how she leads, how she conceives of instruction, how she grounds herself for her busy and varied days teaching, speaking, and serving as the executive director of Friends Council on Education, a national association of Friends schools. (Irene retired from this position in June 2014. We spoke to her just prior to her retirement.) "I came to Buddhist meditation almost by accident in 1969. I was traveling through Europe with my boyfriend, and we picked up a Dutch hitchhiker who was on his way to a Tibetan Buddhist monastery in Scotland, and we decided to go with him. I found so much there of value I began to get trained. Because I was also a Quaker, I began to see some of the similarities between Buddhism and Quakerism, and I realized that Quakers needed tools to get centered and settled for worship, and in schools people need help getting settled and centered for learning. Over the decades, many of my worlds have converged."

In the early 1980s, Irene began to participate in retreats with Thich Nhat Hanh, the Vietnamese monk whose "compassionate teachings, engaged social activism, and abundant creativity in making mindfulness accessible across many religions and cultures was tremendously appealing to me. He was my teacher in the 1980s, and was starting to develop a following in the United States. He was doing small retreats, and this was all very vivid and exciting." Then Irene discovered mindfulness-based stress reduction (Jon Kabat-Zinn) and trained with Diane Reibel in MBSR techniques. Finally, she speaks of her gratitude to Shinzen Young, an American meditation teacher, who "helped me see that the practice of mindfulness develops a powerful foundation for all teaching and learning."

As Irene retires from Friends Council on Education and contemplates the next stages of life, she thinks about the influence these mindful practices have had on her life. "I tend toward being a busy, optimistic perfectionist, a doer kind of person. While I believe I would have found mindfulness practices in some way, I'm glad that I discovered them early in my adult life. I have been tremendously shaped by them, and I am grateful for them. They have helped me move into greater relaxation, contentment, and nonjudgment." In terms of facing the challenges of practicing, Irene notes that people worry a lot about "whether they're doing it right and have trouble committing to regular practice. Most people need support, and support is now available everywhere, such as a group (*sangha* or ongoing classes), guided meditations (CDs or YouTube), and/or a meditation teacher, to build a practice. Since mindfulness is really an embodied practice, teachers cannot easily instruct children or adolescents on this without a grounding in it themselves.

"I have been practicing for a long time, many decades, so this is at the center of what I do, in an explicit and nonexplicit way. I tend to do a 15- to 20-minute sit each day, and a 10- to 15-minute movement practice daily. I also do a Body Scan (see Mindfulness Practice Aid 2.3, "The Body Scan," in Chapter 2, page 62) when I get into bed at night, and I attend a *sangha* once a week, as well as a Quaker meeting every Sunday. I also go on retreat every year, at least one or two long retreats yearly and several one-day retreats. These practices are incorporated into my daily life. I take three relaxing breaths, breathing in and breathing out and focusing on the elongation of the exhale, frequently throughout the day. I teach my staff mindful breathing practices, and we begin each staff meeting in silence."

Reflecting on the main effects of a long life of mindfulness practice, Irene offers very simple observations. "I notice more. I notice the flowers, the sky, the birds, the wind on my face. I have an attitude of gratitude about these simple things and moments, and a capacity to slow down." When asked whether mindfulness is the basis for a worldwide movement toward peace, Irene says, "What you can change is yourself. You can look at the reality of what is and work on what's going on inside of you, working toward inner peace. And how you practice peace and compassion in your everyday relationships has huge impact on others."

"My profession is a calling, and I am called more and more into mindfulness. That is what I want to continue doing in some of the next portions of my life."

Irene McHenry, PhD, was founding head of Delaware Valley Friends School, a founder of Greenwood Friends School, and a founding faculty member of Fielding Graduate University's doctoral program in educational leadership and change. She has taught students from second grade through graduate school, and worked with children and adults in her practice as a psychotherapist.

6.2 Anita Garcia Morales, Former Seattle Public School Teacher, Now a Half-Time Equity and Race Trainer

Seattle Public Schools, and Facilitator at the Center for Courage & Renewal
Seattle, Washington

"Being mindful helped me learn to listen to the brown girl inside me as I walk in the world of white."

We first met Anita Garcia Morales, a 30-year veteran teacher and equity and social justice trainer in the Seattle public school system, in our training as facilitators at the Center for Courage & Renewal in Seattle, Washington. Anita immediately stood out as someone of unusual depth, wisdom, and experience around issues of social justice and race in America. She has capacity to gently, and with great firmness and authority, bring a sense of quiet moral grounding and compassionate curiosity to intense, emotionally charged situations that led us to inquire about her contemplative practice and powerful biography, which she expanded on when we interviewed her for this book. To meet Anita is to feel oneself in the presence of a strong spiritual force. In our interview, she explained some of the roots of her experiences of "being a brown girl," the child of migrant farmworkers in America, and finding ways to hear her inner voices and inner teacher as she set out to become a teacher and social justice educator.

Anita was the sixth child of 11, "a migrant farm kid," in her own words. "I didn't grow up having anyone's special ear for the many questions that came up in our life as migrant farmworkers"—there were too many children to be attentive to. So life, for Anita, was often about learning to keep her own counsel and to observe the world around her with her own powerful set of eyes—and to learn to listen to those observations—"to learn to trust the brown girl inside me who is always talking to me. I had to learn to hear her voice, because she is me, even as I learned to walk in the world of white and navigate worlds of great privilege."

Anita tells us about a particularly searing memory of her childhood, one where the divisions of social class and race were particularly apparent to her. She and her family were driving in the Southwest on a long trip between jobs, the car packed full of children and belongings. The children were thirsty, and her father pulled over to buy drinks for them at a roadside store. On the door of the store a sign read, "No Mexicans or dogs." Anita recalls her father awkwardly coming back (she wasn't sure how well he could read English but believed he understood *No* and *Mexicans*) and saying to the children in the car, "I could tell they didn't have the kind of drinks you wanted." A deep silence hung in the car for the remainder of the trip, but loud voices with questions clamoring to be answered filled her head.

As Anita recalls, a keen sense of equity and social justice was being born in her, one that she has matured through the decades—supported, nurtured, and clarified by a powerful mindfulness and contemplative practice. Her official biography notes that as a classroom teacher (now retired after 30 years), Anita honored the gifts children brought and created a safe and nurturing environment that allowed them to take risks, make mistakes, and learn. As a migrant farmworker for the first 21 years of her life, Anita sought to include all that had been missing in the many classrooms and teachers she had experienced in her own school career. She is skilled at creating brave and hopeful spaces for people to reflect on why they came to do the work they do with children and families and how to tap their inner resources to continue to do what is needed for our children. Anita firmly believes that the growing ethnic and cultural diversity in our cities, our states, and the nation hold great promise and opportunities, and that people must not be encouraged/forced to shed their racial/ethnic identities to be successful and contributing members of our society. Indeed, the differences they embody are the gifts they bring.

Currently as a half-time equity and race relations specialist with the Seattle school district, and an independent consultant/trainer/ facilitator who works with various Puget Sound school districts on race and class issues, Anita describes several mindfulness and contemplative practices that undergird her work in the world and her work within herself. "I have many practices I engage in. The first perhaps is a practice of listening, listening to myself and listening to others." She describes preparing herself for a training by learning to sit quietly and understand the work that needs to be done, then planning carefully for the specific circle of folks she will be serving, and finally driving to a training in deep contemplation, gradually readying herself for the work. "All this undergirds my ability to listen, to take in someone's voice, and to hold the attitude of curiosity and wonder when difficulty or challenging things are coming up, when I sense I want to judge." A strong journaling practice also is a part of Anita's mindfulness practice, helping her explore what lies beneath and hold herself accountable to "the brown girl." "Sometimes I think of myself as being just quiet little brown Anita, and the questions that were alive in her head are still the ones I am seeking answers to. Journaling helps me understand the real importance of what is showing up inside me, and what I need to do about it."

Walking outside in silence, taking breaks from the busyness of her work, making sure to recharge, and "being in touch with my core values allows me to hold on to what I need to do. I always have a consciousness of race in the white worlds I travel in. I want to work with that in ways that help others, bring greater justice and peace to the world, to expand the world's understanding. I think I've always been contemplative—kept my own counsel—but my ever-growing mindfulness practices are growing these capacities for love and hope."

Anita Garcia Morales is a former Seattle public school teacher and now a half-time equity and race trainer. She is also a Certified Class Action Trainer, a Center for Courage & Renewal facilitator, and a Certified Positive Discipline Associate Parent and School Trainer. The common thread that runs through all that Anita does is her focus on social justice and equity.

Please visit us on Facebook at https://www.facebook.com/TheMindfulSchoolLeader.

7

Mindful Leadership
in Action

Putting It All Together

"Research clearly shows that no school improvement effort
can succeed without effective leadership, and such leadership is needed at all levels—federal, state, district, and
school—in our current systems and in the systems we will
create in the future."

—Christine DeVita, former president of the Wallace
Foundation (2009)[1]

"What if we could sit together in circles of honesty and trust,
sit in stillness, welcome silence, be patient, discover wonder
and mutual gratitude, learn together, and gradually build
new confidence in our ability to create spaces in which to hear
and speak our unique stories and find our common truths?
What if we could learn to listen and let our lives speak? What
kind of world could we create together on this earth if we

were able to speak to and hear one another from our deepest yearnings and our most heartfelt concerns and dreams?"

—Diana Chapman Walsh, president emerita of Wellesley College (February 2005)[2]

Walsh is also profiled at the end of this chapter.

Fundamental Principles: The Evolution of the Leader Evolves the Team

Some fundamental principles underlie the views of leadership presented in this book and the practices we encourage you to engage in. The first is born of long experience working with a variety of educational leaders—and ourselves, perhaps our most troublesome and difficult clients. "When your soul awakens, your destiny becomes urgent with creativity," to quote the great Irish poet John O'Donohue.[3] Powerful leadership practice is, in many ways, about awakening the soul and engaging with ourselves and our own deepest capacities and most powerful principles. Personal transformation underlies all deep change; sustained improvements in leadership practice, and renewal of organizations, is tied to the work we do internally to understand our own destinies and develop the courage to be present to ourselves. Put more prosaically, to truly transform the education sector and the settings in which we work, we must first nurture transformation in ourselves.

For us, this is captured in a variety of ways. Consider Whole Foods founder John Mackey reflecting very publically that "more than once in the history of Whole Foods Market, the company was unable to collectively evolve until I myself was able to evolve—in other words, I was holding the company back. My personal growth enabled the company to evolve."[4] Or consider Chade-Meng Tan's assertion in *Search Inside Yourself* about bringing mindfulness practices to Google: Self-awareness and the capacity to recognize and regulate emotions are the keys to great leadership and star performance.[5]

We notice again and again that the developmental growth and increased effectiveness of educational organizations and leadership teams is almost inevitably linked to the growth, evolution, and improved performance of their leaders. As leaders grow and become more aware of their ingrained defense strategies, their inaccurate self-assessments, their emotional triggers, and their leadership "stories" (see the stepping-stones exercise on page 185), the educational organizations they lead take on new buoyancy, zest, energy, capacity, and performance. This is why we frequently begin our work with educational leaders with self-reflective exercises and questions about what has shaped them as leaders, querying them about when they feel most connected to their core values as leaders and asking them to think about who has been most influential to them as role models when they imagine themselves as leaders. We want to create spaces where leaders can consider who they are and who they want to be—and how to lead with integrity. We want them to be able to access and connect to their deep-seated moral, spiritual, and professional goals and discern their particular gifts as leaders. We believe our sector desperately needs this kind of integrated, grounded leadership. We find that most educational leaders we work with have had far too little opportunity to do this kind of reflection—reflection that is considered essential in many other sectors.[6]

I Can't Change Anything, Really

> "Live your life like it really matters."
>
> —Jon Kabat-Zinn (Harvard Graduate
> School of Education, 2013)

One of the problems we confront in our sector, and in our leadership coaching practices, is the sense from many educational leaders that their actions *seem not to matter.* Highly bureaucratic educational systems, where positional authority, entrenched procedures, and hierarchical decision making often overwhelm attempts to create new leadership cultures—along with vast sectoral change[7]—have left some leaders feeling disempowered and ineffectual as they try to sustain new work in the schools, classrooms, school boards, or district offices they head.

A Downward Spiral

Many of us, those newly promoted to leadership roles, or founders of new and visionary kinds of educational organizations, begin with enthusiasm and boldness—a sense of clarity and vigor that allows us to negotiate many hurdles. We have ideas about broad systemic change and are eager to see our values enacted, only to be beaten down by factional politics, passive-aggressive communication patterns, self-interested negotiations, and skirmishes over power that drive leaders into a spiral of overexertion, overwork, and exhaustion. Many of us become disillusioned with ourselves, drawn away from what Parker J. Palmer calls our "inner teacher" and our sense of inner compass, as we feel less clear about our central values and most profound commitments. Eventually, and perhaps inevitably, this disillusionment leads to less-than-stellar results, subpar performance, and, frequently, movement to another job or withdrawal from the field.

You Matter

While we are keenly aware of the embedded nature of hierarchical culture in many of the systems in which educational leaders work, and the complex worldwide transformations in our work, we also believe—and everyday experience and research tells us—that the actions of the leader matter enormously. From whom you nod to on the way to the restroom, to where you sit at the table in every meeting, to the Common Core training program you choose to roll out in your district and how you announce the mandatory professional development sessions around it, to the reserved parking space you turn down at the district offices—*they all matter.*

Bold, politically savvy strategy matters; powerful instructional leadership matters; clear communication of values and ideals matter; and—most importantly—your daily actions matter. They are the fabric of the leadership culture you create. We see again and again that a powerful, compassionate, honest, values-driven leader has the capacity to change the environments in which everyone around the leader works. That is why in this book we emphasize contemplative practices that help leaders renew and recharge to stay fresh for the daily demands of leadership. That's also why we offer so many case studies of individuals who have found ways to practice contemplative, mindful leadership and self-awareness moves, even in the midst of immense sector change, whether that is a shift to the Common Core, or coping with budget shortfalls, staff cuts, student enrollment issues, or eroding support for public education. In a sector that often seems to suffer from a *sense of deficit* and *not enough* (not enough money, not enough respect, not enough competent staff, not enough time, not enough parental involvement), we believe it is still possible to shift to a leadership paradigm that highlights abundance: enough of what is required to do some important work. For us, the culture flows from you and your capacity for clear judgment, reflective practice, and decisive action and renewal of self. Self-renewal is linked, we believe, to the practices we outline here.

MOVING FROM THE MIND-SET OF SCARCITY

"We each have the choice in any setting to step back and let go of the mind-set of scarcity. Sufficiency resides inside of each of us, and we can call it forward. Sufficiency is an act of generating, distinguishing, making known to ourselves the power and presence of our existing resources, and our inner resources."

—Lynne Twist (2003)[8]

Stepping-Stones in Your Leadership Journey: Know Yourself

This is an exercise we use frequently when working with groups of school leaders, and it was developed out of our training with Parker J. Palmer at the Center for Courage & Renewal (CCR) in Seattle, Washington.[9] As we've described, CCR offers many programs for teachers and school leaders that are focused on connecting their inner contemplative lives with their external professional lives.

This exercise can also be used as an in-house professional development reflection for school leaders with their staffs. The exercise is done in pairs, with a large-group sharing session at the end, and takes about 40 minutes.

Reflecting on Yourself as a Leader

"Caminante, no hay camino. Se hace camino al andar."

"Traveler, there is no road. You build the road as you walk."

—Antonio Machado[10]

"Everything that happens to you is your teacher . . . the secret is to learn to sit at the feet of your own life and be taught by it."

—Polly Berends[11]

1. Take a few minutes to jot down three or four critical milestones

Photo © Volker Kreinacke/Thinkstock Photos.

(stepping-stones) in your leadership journey (5 minutes). These might be:

- An early moment when you noticed yourself "being a leader"
- When you first were promoted or assumed a leadership role
- A moment when you felt your core values especially connected with a public leadership move
- A challenging moment in your leadership life right now

2. Reflect to yourself (10 minutes): What do you notice about yourself as a leader from these stepping-stones? Do you see some themes or patterns? For instance:

- What has helped you grow as a leader?
- What has stood in your way, and created obstacles to your growth?
- What does leadership require from you?
- What helps you show up as a real leader in moments of challenge?

3. Find a partner. Take about 5 minutes (each) to "explain" your stepping-stones to your partner. Say what happened at each one, why it's important, and what feelings you associate with each one.

4. Finally, conclude with your partner (5 minutes each):

- What did you learn about yourself as a leader through this exercise?
- What is the "shape" of your leadership journey? Where are you now in the arc of your leadership life?
- In what ways are you satisfied with your leadership life so far? What are you proud of?
- What is your growing edge as a leader? How would you like to sharpen or focus your leadership practice?

What Mindfulness Practice Supports

We've provided dozens of examples throughout this book of how we think mindful leadership practices—those of even the simplest and least time-consuming nature—allow you to show up more wholeheartedly[12] in your role as leader.

But before we go farther, we want to clarify. We have worked in the education sector for many years, so we want to be clear about our values and commitments—our nonnegotiables—before proceeding to a last case study.

- We believe it is critical for leaders engaged in real transformation or improvement efforts in education to be committed and well-informed instructional leaders. Knowledge of the actual work of instruction and learning undergirds any really meaningful cultural and leadership shift, and the capacity to sustain it.
- We believe focus is critical, and we often work with teams and individual leaders on paring away their instructional and organizational plans to create greater clarity and more coherent institutional messaging. Much too often we observe organizations involved in dozens of individual improvement efforts and initiatives, none of which is receiving enough attention to make it effective. Yet these initiatives drag like an anchor on the ship of transformative change.
- We also believe the systematic use of student achievement data is central to individual leadership accountability. Yet we are also keenly concerned about what Rick Hess calls "the new stupid,"[13] the embrace of glib organizational solutions based on superficial framings of data and research, rather than on real understandings of complex problems or good judgment.

Most importantly, we believe leaders have to show up authentically to their leadership positions, with fierce energy, intense commitment, and a gracious willingness to admit their mistakes. Mindful practices are immensely helpful in cultivating the calmness and stillness, the resilience and self-compassion, that leadership requires. Our observations have convinced us that these kinds of resilient, creative, and core-value-connected leaders are the ones paving the path to our sector's future.

As the following case study demonstrates, a leader we worked with recently was in a crisis of leadership, when so many things he'd worked for all his life—the founding of an innovative charter school network, the promise of serving young men and women who were a lot like him, being the first in his family to go to college—seemed to hang in the balance. James was not personally inclined to be interested in mindful leadership practices, as slowing down for him wasn't fun and felt time wasting, and very few people in his leadership world were publically talking about these practices. James wasn't "into this stuff," he'd say, but he had come to a point in his leadership life where he needed to find new ways to cope with the events of his professional life, and in crisis, we often are opened to new learning in ways we are not when life appears more stable. The personal leadership practices this case study highlight the gifts of adversity: how educational leaders, during very intense moments, may help themselves do four critical things: reflect more, learn more, listen more, and lead more effectively.

A Mindful Leader in Action: A Last Case Study

James, the executive director and founder of a network of innovative charter schools that serve first-generation college students, brought an initiative to his board of directors with great enthusiasm. Frustrated with the pace of replication at his own school sites, James suggested his schools merge with a larger, more established charter school operation to achieve greater impact in its geographical area and to allow the schools to benefit from the resources of a long-established network. Instead of James's board being enthused by his entrepreneurial spirit and lack of self-interest in suggesting the merger (James considered it a point of pride that he did not put his own foundership ahead of the schools' interests), his board instead was deeply offended by the merger suggestion. Some board members regarded James's merger proposal as showing a lack of commitment to his founding organization, and others thought it was self-interested, assuming James desired to move to a bigger playing field and gain more national recognition for himself. James was astonished. How could a merger suggestion so obviously in the best interests of his organization, and one that he had openly and energetically brokered, have been perceived so inaccurately? Shocked and disheartened, James said, "I ran into the ring expecting cheers, and instead got showered with trash and rotten tomatoes."

Angry, humbled, and in search of some answers about how he could have been so misunderstood, and unclear about what he didn't see, as part of the leadership coaching he initiated, James began a daily journaling practice and a mindfulness S.T.O.P. habit (see Mindfulness Practice Aid 1.1, "Stopping, Pausing, and Observing," in Chapter 1, page 35) that allowed him to reflect more deeply on his leadership assumptions, reactions, and reflexive moves. (He began writing every morning about what he "noticed" about himself the day before—sometimes just some random jottings—and also, before any meeting, he would take 30 seconds or a minute to S.T.O.P. before going in.) James realized he often didn't know how or what he was feeling, and he "had been taught by the culture" to mask it over and ignore it: "Journaling helped me be more clear about what was actually going on inside me, which had previously been unknown."

To prepare for this journaling every day, James began to practice the mindful breathing practice described in Chapter 2 (see Mindfulness Practice Aids 2.1, "One-Minute Focused Breathing Practice," page 60, and 2.2, "30-Second Focused Breathing Practice," page 61, as well as Mindfulness Practice Aid 1.2, "Three-Minute Focused Breathing Practice," page 37). He said the stopping and the breathing, which he practiced at least three times a day, allowed him to pause and discover what he was experiencing—which frequently surprised him ("I am pissed off a lot!")—and to prepare to determine his next right courses of action. Reflective practice based on fundamental mindfulness techniques helped James learn from his daily leadership experiences, not by judging them or deciding what to do, but just by becoming aware of them.

Critical Action 1: Reflect More

Next, James decided to go on a listening tour with all of his board members, using techniques like the ones suggested in Mindfulness Practice Aid 4.3, "Mindful Speaking and Listening for Meaning and Connection," page 123. He described new practices he used to prepare himself before every conversation with a board member as "trying to empty the bucket of defensiveness—spit the blood out of my mouth"— and actually listening to and taking notes on what every board member said about the recent skirmishes and the emerging leadership crisis in his organization. (He had to commit to a practice of taking notes in conversations, which he said helped him focus on what was being said, rather than reacting to it. This alone was a significant shift.)

To support this new kind of listening, James decided that he would take notes on whatever he heard so he could reflect on it later and not react in the moment. (He often felt very defensive and misunderstood in these conversations, and wrote down his reactions rather than speaking them.) He was determined to learn more about how his actions and motivations were regarded, no matter how negative or defensive this process made him, because he had committed to learning and being truthful in his reactions. James reported frequently that it required a lot of self-control "to handle my reactions. Being very truthful, I wanted to just get up and storm out of that room. A lot of my feelings of being misunderstood and underestimated were getting triggered."

Critical Action 2: Develop Habits for Deeper Learning

After engaging in challenging and "fierce" conversations with many board members, James finally determined a course of action. Gathering up a lot of courage ("Wow, this is hard," he said), he decided to go to his senior staff and have a dialogue that was unusual in his organization's culture. First he apologized for "any pieces of the merger and the fallout" that had hurt them. (That took some guts.) Next James proposed that they together look honestly and clearly at where the organization stood based on what had happened during the last several months. He asked his staff to consider what the organization's future held, given the board's reluctance to grow in the ways James had envisioned. These meetings, and this kind of "listening with a sense of being OK with whatever I heard, no matter what it was," seemed to communicate something new to his senior leaders. Over the course of several weeks, they began speaking much more candidly to James about tensions they thought had been brewing in the organization for a couple of years, about some hiring practices and leadership moves they felt were inauthentic and not "mission focused," and about how they sometimes felt James was an unsupportive or insensitive boss, based on how he interacted with them in high-level, highly charged meetings. Again, James felt he was learning more and listening more than he had ever done, trying not to "judge the speaker" and discount what the speaker was saying but to hear the kernels of truth in the person's honest expressions of discontent and concern for the organization's future. "This is very challenging," he reflected. "Clarifying, and challenging."

Critical Action 3: Listen More

After several months of candid talk, strategic planning with senior board members, and some dawning new perceptions of his own behavior, James said, "I learned to say 'I'm sorry' in new ways and see that this wasn't demeaning. It tended to clear the air, even if it felt like it was taking a chip out of me at the time." James and the board managed to co-craft a plan for moving the network of schools forward, a plan that did not involve a "threat from the larger organization" but still served the purposes of creating more schools for those in critical need. James reflected: "I was so charged up by the prospect of creating this merger—it seemed like the answer to so many of our problems—I railroaded it through and stopped picking up on the signals that the organization really wasn't ready for this.

I cast aside any naysayers as those who didn't have the commitment to the mission of the organization that this work requires, and that commitment is incredibly important. But I also almost sank the organization. I realized that this crisis was a way for me to understand my own leadership at a deeper level, rather than go on to a new job and repeat the same mistakes. I really don't think I could have done this without building some new capacities for listening to others and listening to myself. It was painful, really hard, but I feel like some of the newer practices of observation and listening have now become hardwired."

Leadership in education is challenging work—we offer James's story as an example. But the practices here actually do help leaders become much more effective: To reflect more deeply, collaborate more, make more and better decisions, mentor and coach others with more skill and compassion, and create an organizational culture that is more trusting and candid allows everyone to become more effective and efficient.[14] For James, these practices led to a new self-understanding that he said "will take me farther wherever I go next."

Critical Action 4: Lead More Effectively, and Folks Want to Follow

SIX FOUNDATIONS OF TRUSTWORTHY LEADERSHIP

The Center for Courage & Renewal's Academy for Leaders offers cohort-based programs that provide leaders with opportunities to reflect on their leadership lives and to develop practices that support effective and courageous leadership. (See www.couragerenewal.org/academy for more information.) We offer the academy's Six Foundations of Trustworthy Leadership here, in relation to James's story and the practices outlined in this book, as powerful principles for leadership effectiveness. Do they resonate with how you are leading and learning?

The Courage & Renewal Academy for Leaders is centered on these six foundations of trustworthy leadership.

- **Clarify purpose and integrity through an ongoing inner journey.** Effective leadership hinges on your ability as a leader to know your own values, to remain present to your context and colleagues, and to resist the impulse to grow distant or disconnect. The Academy provides a hospitable yet

(Continued)

(Continued)

demanding space for disciplined reflection around core values and vocational and leadership aspirations.

- **Ask honest, open questions and apply deep listening.** All people yearn to be heard. Leaders and organizations benefit from practicing a disciplined approach to listening. Open and honest questions help surface human resourcefulness and foster a sense of community with colleagues in service of worthy goals. In the Academy, we emphasize the importance of speaking from each person's unique vantage point and the enduring power of listening.

- **Hold paradox and tensions in the face of complexity and uncertainty.** The daily life of a leader is accelerated, fragmented, and filled with unsettling tensions. Leading with integrity requires learning to manage these tensions by working creatively with paradox—the both/and nature of most profound challenges. The Academy helps leaders hold tensions as constructive forces for meaningful change and strengthens their capacities to help others discover creative potential hidden within daunting realities.

- **Build trustworthy relationships in communities/organizations.** When work gets heated, positions polarize and people feel vulnerable. Leaders must read the emotional currents and help others contribute constructively. Good leaders create cultures in which conflict and anxiety are honestly acknowledged on the path toward meaningful change. Circle of Trust® principles and practices are at the heart of the Academy. You'll participate in a learning community that fosters honest conversations and develops trustworthy relationships.

- **Appreciate the value of "otherness."** Each person we work with brings unique gifts, perspectives, and life experience. This diversity can be a source of strength, richness, and wisdom for our organizations and communities. The capacity to welcome and make space for diverse voices and perspectives is integral to organizational learning and trust building.

- **Grow through seasons/cycles of personal, professional, organizational change.** Over time, stress, pressure, and uncertainties can grind leaders down. Leaders must develop intentional processes to discover opportunities for change and renewal that lie hidden within the inevitable challenges that fill the arc of a career. The Academy is built on the understanding that leadership is a very human journey with natural seasons and cycles of discovery, challenge, and growth.

Source: Center for Courage & Renewal. "Six Foundations of Trustworthy Leadership." Seattle, WA: author. Used with permission. Retrieved from www.couragerenewal.org/wpccr/wp-content/uploads/CourageRenewal-SixLeadershipFoundations.pdf

Well-Being and Compassion at the Center of a New Educational Vision

"The basic ingredients of well-being and compassionate social living are, in fact, teachable. Reflection is the common pathway by which our brains support such abilities."

—Dan Siegel (2007)[15]

We have great hopes for the ways in which mindful leadership practices might transform our sector, and ultimately help create a more sustainable and just world. We regularly see transformations of self that mindfulness practice brings, offering leaders new kinds of vision, humility, openness, realness, interest in growing and serving others, and capacity to work with rapid change. As Chade-Meng Tan says in *Search Inside Yourself* (2012), "Like many others wiser than me, I believe world peace can and must be created from the inside out." And Tan's long-term wish for leaders and anyone who practices is that with mindful meditation and enhanced emotional intelligence, world peace can be achieved! ("Give them the tools," says this Google engineer, "and let's make it happen!") Tan continues, "If we can find a way for everybody to develop peace and happiness within themselves, their inner peace and happiness will naturally manifest into compassion. And if we can create a world where most people are happy, at peace, and compassionate, we can create the foundation for world peace."[16] We are convinced that for educational leaders, the path to sustained transformational practice is by embracing mindfulness—to inspire those around them; to see clearly what is necessary and next in their organizations, no matter the costs; and to continually renew themselves for the challenges of the work.

We look forward to hearing from you about your growing mindfulness practice and its influence on your team, your organization, and the world. Please visit our Facebook page at www.facebook.com/TheMindfulSchoolLeader, and share your leadership story with us.

Where the World Is Going

"Leaders all over the planet are beginning to understand the benefits of purposefully learning to be more attentive and focused, non-reactive, and clear."

—Saki Santorelli, EdD, executive director, Center for Mindfulness in Medicine, Health Care, and Society[17]

In the last decade and a half, several major initiatives specifically linking educational leadership to contemplative practice have been initiated. Many of them share the hope of helping educational leaders understand themselves better so that they might be more resilient, feel more ethically grounded, and become more creative, initiating leaders in their educational settings. We outline a few here with which we are most familiar, and with which we feel most allied. We hope you will explore them and also keep in touch with us to let us know what we've missed or what's emerging.

Courage in Schools, Courage to Teach, and the Courage & Renewal Academy for Leaders, based out of the national Center for Courage & Renewal headquarters in Seattle, offer programs around the nation (and internationally) for teachers, educators, and educational administrators, that are based on the work of the author and educator Parker J. Palmer. Courage in Schools and other programs, retreats, and workshops are designed to help educational leaders renew themselves and translate personal transformation into the renewal and strengthening of their schools and institutions. CCR offers educators opportunities to reflect on the inner dimensions of teaching and leading and to increase their capacity to listen to themselves and others more deeply. In a cohort model, participants join with fellow educators to engage in honest self-reflection and explore questions about purpose, values, and commitment to their challenging work and, in particular, to focus on building relational trust in the adult school community. Courage in Schools program *Leading Together: Building Adult Community in Schools*[18] is a yearlong professional development program specifically designed to build school leadership teams' capacity to facilitate the strengthening of the adult community in their institutions and develop relationships that are critical to creating the trust and social capital essential for common purpose in effective schools. CCR is the sponsor of these programs and has a 20-year history of offering workshops, retreats, and programs grounded in the idea that to make the world a better place, it's vital to align one's daily work life with core values. The center's website (www.cour agerenewal.org/programs) offers more complete information on programs. The authors of this book met each other while being trained as CCR facilitators, and have been profoundly influenced by the center's work and the life and thinking of Palmer and the many visionary individuals who loosely gather around these programs.

The **Mind and Life Institute** in Hadley, Massachusetts, is a not-for-profit organization committed to a multidisciplinary investigation of the mind, leading to greater emotional balance, kindness, and compassion. It recently announced an initiative in ethics, education, and human development (EEHD). The initiative has three goals: (1) the development of a curriculum and pedagogy to help schools and school communities become "central sites of care and compassion"; (2) the creation of an online set of modular courses to help offer program opportunities worldwide; and (3) the creation of an academy for contemplative and ethical leadership. To support these goals, the EEHD initiative will investigate how the field of education can apply research at the intersection of evolutionary psychology, moral philosophy, developmental science, and contemplative scholarship to better nurture compassion in education and other social institutions. This initiative will take a multipronged approach, including the development of a survey of existing contemplative practice programs relevant to compassion training, a critical review of the existing literature on compassion and compassion training, and funding for the development of more sophisticated methods and measures for investigating qualities such as compassion, kindness, and empathy. These research objectives will be accompanied by an extensive public outreach campaign that will include grassroots organizing for contemplative practice program developers, with the goal that the training of compassion at all levels of society be developmentally appropriate, systematic, rigorous, and evidence based.

Most recently, the Mind and Life Institute's EEHD initiative has designed a platform for a comprehensive, pre-K–12 curriculum and pedagogy for students and teachers titled *A Call to Care* after in-depth consideration of the best ways to support children and young adults in the development of prosocial skills and ethical sensitivity.[19] The program integrates social and emotional learning (SEL) with developmentally sensitive care and compassion-based skills training and contemplative practices. For more information about the institute's initiatives and current research and thinking, please see its account of its research.[20] The work of this committee and its research report (soon to be released) is also a very useful and up-to-date survey of the state of caring and contemplative pedagogy in education at the present moment.

The **Mindfulness in Education Network** (MiEN) was established in 2001 by a group of educators deeply influenced by the work of Thich Nhat Hanh. MiEN sees "mindfulness as an antidote to the growing stress, conflict and confusion in educational settings as well as an invaluable gift to give students."[21] The network has defined its purpose as facilitating communication among all educators, parents, and students interested in promoting contemplative practice in educational settings. It currently has about 1,100 member participants. Anyone can join this network; simply Google the organization and send its leaders an email. MiEN also holds an annual meeting that explores the latest research in mindfulness in education and is a wonderful place to gather with other educational leaders interested in bringing contemplative practices to their organizations or lives.

The **Contemplative Teaching and Learning Initiative**, based at the Garrison Institute in Garrison, New York, holds an ongoing annual meeting that draws teacher educators and teacher leaders from across the United States and Canada and from as far away as Israel and Colombia. Held in late November, the most recent meeting in 2013—"Mindfulness in Education: Promoting the Social and Emotional Competencies of Educators"—was an exploration of how mindfulness and other contemplative practices might be used to transform teacher education and, by extension, public education. Participants explored a variety of contemplative practices currently used by teacher educators and described the impact of contemplative practice programs like the Garrison Institute's CARE for Teachers and others around the country, including PassageWorks, SMART in Education, and the Inner Resilience Program (developed by Linda Lantieri).[22] The Garrison Institute will continue supporting and exploring the training of teachers and educational leaders in contemplative education practices designed for various settings through symposia, research, and public outreach, and perhaps your involvement!

Wake Up Schools, a worldwide educational and spiritual initiative begun by Zen Master Thich Nhat Hanh and the international Plum Village community, offers workshops, training, and programming to schools, students, and school leaders around the globe to "support the happiness and well-being of teachers, administrators, students, and parents." Wake Up Schools uses mindfulness, which it describes as "the energy of being aware and awake to what is happening inside and around us in the present moment, to nourish education communities that excel in social emotional learning, moral/ethical education, experiential learning, stress reduction, and inner resilience."[23] Wake Up Schools' vision, as described at its website, is for schools to become a family and for participants in programs to lead happy, healthy, and meaningful lives. Wake Up Schools is currently holding events worldwide. Please check the initiative's website for more information (see http://wakeupschools.org), and take a look at Shantum Seth's profile on page 201. Seth has been involved in Wake Up Schools for many years in India.

Based on the huge body of clinical research on contemplative practice and human effectiveness, dozens of **university-based, education-focused leadership research, leadership training, and leadership practice centers** and initiatives are under way or being founded at major universities around the world. Some of the most prominent with which we are familiar are the contemplative teacher education programs at Teachers College, Columbia University; the new teacher education program and research study at the Contemplative Sciences Center at the University of Virginia; Lesley University's advanced professional certificate in mindfulness studies; Naropa University's contemplative education program; and the Harvard Graduate School of Education's Inner Strengths of Successful Leaders program. Because new research centers focused on educational leadership and contemplative practice are gestating rapidly, we cannot catalogue them all, but we believe that contemplative practice as a part of educational leadership preparation will increasingly become central to teacher leadership programs and understandings of powerful leadership practice in education.[24]

Finally, although it is not exclusively aimed at educational leaders, we are very captivated by the work of **Mindful Schools** based in Oakland, California. Founded in 2007, Mindful Schools has as its mission to integrate mindfulness into education by offering professional training and other resources to schools, teachers, and school leaders. Mindful Schools has conducted training and workshops for more than 4,000 public and private school parents, teachers, therapists, and other professionals in education and social work, benefiting (it estimates) more than 100,000 youth to date. Its in-school curriculum uses mindfulness to teach concentration, attention, conflict resolution, and empathy, and has been offered to tens of thousands of children.

We love Mindful Schools' observation: "We consistently find that people are more successful learning and teaching mindfulness when they are able to share ideas and get support in groups. Then as interest builds, other community members may be inspired to get trained, further integrating mindfulness school-wide."[25] To facilitate this growth, **Mindful Schools offers group rates and need-based scholarships for educational organizations that train three or more of their staff.** These group rates apply to mindfulness fundamentals, curriculum training, and yearlong certification courses. Because we believe deeply in the value of mindfulness for youth, we are eager to encourage districts and schools to implement mindfulness training for their staff and hope educational leaders will consider one of the many fine training programs available for students and teachers.

With interest in contemplative practice growing in virtually every leadership arena, we believe the organizations and collectives above will be central to ushering in a new educational era, one that honors the profound nature of self to other and self to self in the equation of learning. We wish to support these collectives in every way possible. Now on to our final practices and portraits.

Mindfulness Practice Aids

Mindfulness Practice Aid 7.1: One Minute for Good

We want to conclude this book with a quickie practice. We truly love Rick Hanson's new book, *Hardwiring Happiness* (2013),[26] which is about developing the mental habits that allow us to compensate for the brain's natural negativity bias. In the most practical terms, Hanson describes what to do to help yourself have more frequent positive experiences—how to enrich them, absorb them, savor them, and then link positive mental experiences to negative ones to actually "replant" your mind with greater optimism, contentment, and calm.

We think this is critical mental hygiene for educational leaders, who must constantly rebalance negative experiences with more positive ones and be able to notice and appreciate pleasant events—to savor and enrich them—for a strong mental outlook. We encourage you to "grow the good" on a daily basis with this practice. Put our book down and try this right now!

One Minute for Good

- Take a minute now—let your hands drop from the computer keyboard, or put the smartphone down, or stop talking—to pause and look around you. Take a couple of breaths, being aware of what's happening, and also noting how you are and what's going on inside your body and mind. As Hanson says, "find an intimacy with yourself."
- Start relaxing, letting your breathing soften and slow down. Let worried thoughts flow away from you, and get in touch with everything that's alright with you and in your world right now. Notice that you're alright right now. Begin to take comfort in a growing sense of calm and peace.
- Bring to mind one or two things you're grateful for, or glad about, like the children who are streaming past you or the sense of being surrounded by colleagues whom you genuinely enjoy. Actually

look closely at their faces and let yourself experience your sense of connection to them.

- Be aware of the sense of warmth, caring, and connection this engenders in you. Notice you feel these things.
- Settle into a sense of peace, contentment, and love woven together into a rich moment, and rest in this like a homecoming. Imagine taking this good feeling, of connection and contentment and gladness, through your whole day.
- Finish up with another breath or two, while you sense that peace and love are sinking into you.

We thank Rick Hanson for outlining this lovely practice, and we hope you enjoy it as much as we do. We practice it whenever we can.

Mindfulness Practice Aid 7.2: Count Your Blessings Pause, Dwell in Your Victories, and Show Up as Your Bigger Self (CVS)[27]

By Jerry Murphy

We recommend this practice to many educational leaders, and they seem to truly enjoy it and notice the ways in which it sets them up to have a good day and to be grounded in themselves throughout the day. We thank Jerry Murphy, former dean of the Harvard Graduate School of Education, for this wonderful practice, and we think this is a great way to close out our mindfulness practices for educational leaders. Educational leaders often need to show up as their bigger selves, and we know this practice helps us do this.

Count Your Blessings Morning Pause

Each day many leaders arrive at work already caught up in the stresses and strains of their jobs. The **CVS Morning Pause** is meant to help you start your day on the right foot—with a balanced frame of mind that's marked by good feelings, openness to the work ahead, and ability to take what comes in stride. This three-step exercise takes about three minutes.

Step 1: Count Your Blessings

1. Take a few seconds to get grounded. You can sit, stand, or lie down. Close your eyes, if you like.
2. Imagine your whole body rooted in the earth. Feel your feet in contact with the ground or the floor.

3. Start by asking yourself, "How am I feeling right now? What emotions can I sense inside?" If you're feeling cranky, for example, acknowledge this feeling and allow it to be. Say to yourself, "I notice something in me that's cranky. I'm going to just let it be."

4. When you are ready, shift your attention to the blessings in your life. Ask yourself, "What do I feel good about? What makes my life worth living? What am I grateful for?" You might identify family members, colleagues, your health—whatever comes to mind.

5. Now identify three persons or things that you want to express gratitude for today. You might silently say, "I'm so lucky to have such a great mother. Thanks, Mom," or "We live in such a beautiful town," or "I'm so fortunate to have good health." Notice how you feel right now. For a moment more, **count your blessings** and stay with your good feelings.

Step 2: Dwell on Your Victories

1. Now, shift your attention to any **victories** at work—victories that perhaps are small and private, such as comforting a colleague in a moment of grief. Because identifying victories may not always be easy, take a moment to identify just one or two. Dwell on them, instead of dismissing them as we so often do. Take deserved pride in those things—big and small—you've accomplished. Notice how you feel right now.

2. If you have time, you might direct your attention to another V—your core **values.** Ask yourself, "What really matters to me? What do I stand for? What gives my life meaning?" Identify three core values—such as caring, fairness, and family time. For a moment, dwell on them—and notice how you feel right now.

Step 3: Show Up as Your Bigger Self

1. Now ask yourself, which part of me is going to **show up** at work this morning? My weary self? My reactive self? My small-minded self? Instead, imagine showing up as your **bigger self**—calm, clear, connected, compassionate, curious. Your bigger self is able to notice your upsetting feelings, instead of getting hooked by them. For a moment, dwell on your bigger self. Notice how you feel. Now imagine *being*

your bigger self as you walk through the front door at work later this morning.

2. Finally, thank your body and mind for all their hard work, and open your eyes.

We hope you enjoy this practice and use it frequently at the beginning of the day. For us, simply envisioning how we want to show up as our bigger selves each day is a helpful reminder to live our values and to be a little kinder, more patient, and less rushed than we might otherwise be. Let us know how it works for you.

Portraits of Practice

7.1 Shantum Seth, Teacher of Applied Ethics in Mindfulness

India

> "Happy teachers will change the world."[28]

We met Shantum Seth many years ago while attending a mindfulness retreat with Thich Nhat Hanh. Even at the time, Shantum was a well-known mindfulness practitioner and at the center of Wake Up Schools all over the world (mentioned on page 196 of this chapter). We have traveled to India with Shantum in one of his many mindful and transformative journeys, and for this book we talked with him about his mindfulness practice and his leadership work in offering mindfulness in schools throughout India.

"For about 25 years, I worked in the field of development in the United Nations. I stayed in this work because I wanted to help create a better world, and the UN has the mandate for poverty eradication and peace. I slowly realized that besides structural change, we need a shift in individual and collective consciousness. I realized that this education, especially mindfulness in the educational setting, was the best way to have a positive impact on my community in India—and that this could be a contribution of India to the global educational field. Somewhat like

Photo ©2013 by Thomas Kierok.

yoga has now become popular in countries like the United States, I can see that the software of mindfulness that exists in the India spiritual systems can be transferred into a secular setting globally.

"As a father and a husband, and not just as an educator, I was really motivated to help young people be happier and live more fulfilling lives through mindfulness. I saw how it changed my life, and I wanted to share that with others.

"When I was working as a political activist, I faced daily burnout and stress. At first, I turned to my own Hindu culture for relief. I was searching for a spiritual path. In 1987, I met Thich Nhat Hanh, and that changed my life. I began practicing engaged Buddhism—blending and embedding mindfulness in all my daily activity, including in my workday.

"Early on, when I started training Indian teachers and students in mindfulness, I saw the power of the unwritten curriculum: the presence of the teacher in the classroom. I just knew that more mindful teachers could help create more mindful students and, in turn, build a more mindful school culture, a more mindful society, making the world a better place. In fact our logo now says 'Happy teachers will change the world.'

"Practicing mindfulness is also for me about being aware of the state of my body, feelings, and mind, my thinking, my intentions. I check in with myself a number of times throughout the day to be aware of how I am feeling: calm, agitated, excited, equanimous, whatever. Often, I find that my mental state is neutral. If I feel a positive mind state, like happiness or deep contentment, I enhance it, and try and develop the conditions that make that feeling arise. I really absorb the feeling. When I do this, even mundane events and circumstances like drinking water or walking, which start as neutral feelings, get transformed to positive feelings. This is a practice of mindfulness training. I don't mean this in a narcissistic kind of way. I feel really alive and so very grateful; I don't take being alive in this moment for granted.

"It is really important to cultivate the seed, the kernel of mindfulness, in everything I do. So, I practice every day being aware of my body, my environment, how I speak, how I listen. For example, as I wake in the morning, I notice my body resting on my bed, listening to the sound of my breathing and the birds, shifting my body position, aware of my feet meeting the floor, aware of my walking as I move from the bed to the bathroom. I bring this attentiveness to everything I do: eating, being with friends and family, teaching, sitting, walking.

"The biggest challenge in my work in offering mindfulness in schools throughout India is the lack of trained teachers. Here in India, it is no longer a question of the strength or validity of the scientific research on mindfulness. Government officials and school leaders recognize the overwhelming scientific data, the research. We also know that understanding oneself is an important basis not just for pedagogy, but to lead a happy, peaceful, and ultimately free life. Here the demand for trained mindfulness teachers is much greater than the supply, especially teachers who can live this life 24/7.

"There is also a need for a global paradigm shift from the narrow view of 'How does all this benefit me personally?' and 'How can I improve my performance?' to 'How can mindfulness foster a culture of peace?' In my own life, I face challenges, too, in the practice of mindfulness. Like many people, I have a very busy life, teaching mindfulness and applied ethics in education in schools throughout India and in the United States, leading transformative journeys through my company Eleven Directions, building a mindfulness practice center in the Himalayas, consulting with the World Bank, advising the government of India, and so on. I have a very full life. With all of these activities and projects, it is sometimes difficult to remain authentic and attentive. The challenge for me is saying no and not to take on more than I can do and to stay in touch with the blue sky, the rocky mountains, the people I meet daily.

"This engaged mindfulness practice really suits me. It helps me create space in my daily life to enjoy life. I don't need to take long meditation retreats that take me away from my family; in fact, when I go on retreat, my family often comes, too. My busy schedule has me traveling a lot, and I treat the journeys that I lead through South Asia as retreats on wheels.

"I know that leading a conscious and watchful life is a possibility, and I carry the image in my mind of teachers and students practicing walking mindfully [see Mindfulness Practice Aid 3.2, "Mindful Walking," in Chapter 3, page 97], smiling and pausing to touch nature deeply. I see the look of happiness and peace on the faces of those teachers and young people, and know in that moment they are free."

Shantum Seth is an ordained teacher in the Zen Buddhist lineage (of the Venerable Thich Nhat Hanh) and has been leading transformative mindfulness journeys since 1988. He is actively involved in social, environmental, and educational programs, including teacher training through mindfulness and applied ethics in education, work being pioneered by the nonprofit trust Ahimsa (www.ahimsatrust.org). He is actively engaged in creating a mindfulness practice and learning center in the Himalayas in India.

For more information about Shantum's work, please visit his website www.elevendirections.com.

7.2 Diana Chapman Walsh, President Emerita

Wellesley College, Wellesley, Massachusetts

"The kingdom is now or never."

Diana Chapman Walsh settles back onto the large couch at the center of her living room—a piece of furniture that dwarfs her small, well-groomed frame. Formidable on paper, and well known by reputation in higher education and contemplative leadership circles, in person Diana is approachable, nondogmatic, informal, and very willing to play along with what's on offer with her conversational partner.

Settling back onto her couch cushions and rearranging herself so that she can face her interviewer directly, she says, "I don't set myself up as a mindfulness leader at all, I really don't. I'm not living the life of a quiet contemplative, at least on the surface. Since my retirement

from Wellesley, my life is very busy, by my design and my choice. I am now mistress of my own destiny, and I seem to choose to do many, many things!" she offers with delight.

Diana serves on several boards and is a formal and informal advisor to higher education leaders around the country. We fit our interview into time around a meeting she is about to attend with the Mind and Life Institute's Ethics, Education, and Human Development initiative before she flies off to California at the end of the week to visit her daughter and beloved grandson. While Diana is known for her thoughtful, integrative, profoundly principled approaches to leadership and leadership development (her *Trustworthy Leadership*[29] is a touchstone for many emergent

leaders of educational institutions), she is also frank about the challenges she has faced and mistakes she has made as a leader, as well
as the ways in which her growing contemplative practice has put
mindfulness at the center of how she conceives of thoughtful, wholehearted leadership.

"My mindfulness practice started around the work I did at the
Kellogg Foundation. From 1987 to 1990, I had a national fellowship
from Kellogg in which I traveled around the country studying
workplace democracy, the principles of leadership, and writing
poetry. During that time, poems were coming to me, and through
me, and as I tentatively showed them to people close to me to see if
they resonated with others, I began to understand those inter-
changes as part of my leadership practice." Reflecting on this shift,
Diana notes that a retreat with Parker J. Palmer began a kind of
mindfulness journey.

"It was at a retreat led by Parker Palmer that this outpouring of
poetry began. It was inspired by him. The retreat was organized by
Rick Jackson, a colleague in the Kellogg fellowship program. After
that experience, I continued to follow Palmer's work closely. Parker
became a dear friend, as did Rick, who is a co-founding director of the
Center for Courage & Renewal along with his wife, Marcy. I continued to learn with and from them. They were refining the use of
poetry, and social technologies akin to mindfulness practices, to create spaces in which teachers and leaders could reconnect with the
'inner teacher' Palmer understands we all have within ourselves, if
we can settle down and listen for it. I come from a Quaker background, so these concepts were second nature to me.

"For a long while, those wonderful Kellogg Foundation meetings,
in that cohort of extraordinary people, and spending time with
Parker, *was* my mindfulness practice. I became aware that the world
needs college presidents who appreciate poetry, and also that trustworthy leadership starts from within. I began to think about where
leadership comes from . . . who my leadership models were and what
I stood for as a leader."

Soon after, Diana was invited to consider the presidency of
Wellesley College, an office that was deeply attractive to her but also
unlike most of the professional roles she had occupied before. "My
first year as president was an incredibly steep learning curve," she
says wryly. (She also describes this in some of her vivid public
addresses.) While Diana was deepening her leadership practice, she
was also "being drawn to the East."

> "It was in contemplative practice I discovered how the contemplative disciplines could help me stabilize my mind, engage in deeper reflection, quiet my heart, manage my stress, see my blind spots, and ground in a truth I could trust, a truth based not solely in my ability to integrate knowledge, but equally in my skillfulness at integrating self as knower, mind, body, heart, and spirit. If I couldn't trust myself, I realized, how could I ask others to trust me?"

For instance, during her early years at Wellesley, Arun Gandhi, the Mahatma's grandson, was invited to spend a week on the Wellesley campus when it hosted an international conference to commemorate Gandhi's 125th birth anniversary. Another event that deepened her interest in contemplative practice happened in 1997, when Diana met His Holiness the Dalai Lama as a fellow faculty member at a conference at Naropa University in Colorado. She also recalls, with fondness, a group of Tibetan monks who made a sand mandala in a tent outside the Wellesley chapel in 2001 at a conference Wellesley hosted on education as transformation. Diana also remembers "a sweet and touching day on our campus with Thich Nhat Hanh, who led a retreat for several hundred of his followers, and closed it by painting a calligraphy and presenting it to me with a flourish. 'The kingdom is now or never,' it said in bold black ink. I had it framed and hung in a prominent spot in my office."[30]

These "unbidden visitations from the East," as Diana describes them, guided her "to the teaching that *ignorance* lies at the root of suffering and to see my evolving contemplative practice *not* as a religious or spiritual gesture but as a doorway to learning. I was learning a new way of being in the world."

Then, like many people, she discovered specific mindfulness practices—as the world was—through Jon Kabat-Zinn. "Jon, initially in disembodied form—through his writings and tapes—was for many years my meditation teacher, the mainstay who laid the foundation for me and inspired me to delve deeper and venture farther along a path that continues to declare itself ever more intriguingly to me. When I met Jon—the fully embodied version—we became friends as we participated in an informal discussion group of people who met periodically at Wellesley to envision an entirely different kind of university.

"For me, the discovery of contemplative practice was initially very much implicated in the practice of leadership—leadership that is effective or 'trustworthy.' I came of age as a leader in the field of higher education, a setting where there is an inherent distrust of authority and of people who might think they're 'in charge.' Faculty are independent, necessarily and sometimes defiantly so, suspicious of administrators, always on the lookout for the hidden agenda. Students emulate faculty. Skepticism reigns. Trustworthy leadership, I discovered in that unforgiving ecosystem, begins and ends with leaders who can question themselves."

It was in that cauldron of pressures and projections that Walsh says she learned, with the help of gifted consultant Richard Nodell, to craft a particular style of integrative leadership that combined the inner work of Parker J. Palmer with a co-commitment to carve out time to reflect with her senior colleagues about the systems they were leading, and to share insights into their strategies for going forward.

In this formative process, she says, she discovered how the contemplative disciplines "could help me do that questioning, help me stabilize my mind, engage in deeper reflection, quiet my heart, manage my stress, see my blind spots, and ground in a truth I could trust, a truth based not solely in my ability to integrate knowledge, but equally in my skillfulness at integrating self as knower, mind, body, heart, and spirit. If I couldn't trust myself, I realized, how could I ask others to trust me?"[31]

The essential practices of leadership to which Diana has publically committed—self-questioning and forthright self-inquiry, seeking out ranges of opinions in decision making and in leadership deliberation, resisting the use of force, and valuing difference as perhaps the greatest teacher of all—are universally supported by her daily mindfulness practice. Diana has a morning sitting practice of "about 20 minutes a day" and practices breathing and pausing throughout the day. Listening to podcasts and learning from new spiritual teachers—she mentions having recently discovered the podcasts of Tara Brach—help center her and remind her of her central values, moral commitments, and energies. She speaks about aging and its challenges and gifts—more time to spend with a beloved husband and life partner, more time to breathe—and of learning how to be present to the people she loves in new ways as they go through their own living and dying. "Our culture urgently needs—in all sectors [but especially education]—next-generation leaders who will be equal to today's challenges in all their complexity and who will be skillful at leading *themselves* with compassion and equanimity . . . with love." That may be the work Diana has given herself for the future.

She speaks feeling fully of giving attention to growing the next generation of leaders, through her own deepening contemplative practices and on which she shines attention: her work, her child and grandchild, the forwarding of important integrative work across disciplines that promise to reduce human suffering.

"If we can bring to our [work] qualities that stand as signposts along the path of contemplative inquiry—respect, gentleness, intimacy, vulnerability, participation, and transformation—then perhaps we can hope to begin sculpting here a . . . field unlike any other—a field that unites students of the mind in a warm and welcoming community around the world dedicated to the relief of human suffering and the enhancement of human flourishing."

Diana Chapman Walsh was the 12th president of Wellesley College, a leading college for women and one of the nation's top liberal arts colleges, from 1993 to 2007. Before assuming the Wellesley presidency, Diana was a professor at the Harvard School of Public Health. She writes, speaks, and consults regularly on a range of issues related to higher education. She is the author of Trustworthy Leadership: Can We Be the Leaders We Need Our Students to Become? *(2006) and many book chapters, invited addresses, and public forums on the challenges and touchstones of leadership.*

Please visit us on Facebook at https://www.facebook.com/TheMindfulSchoolLeader.

Endnotes

Front Pages

1. Also see page 23 of this book. http://henryjenkins.org/2010/11/multitasking_and_continuous_pa.html#sthash.v8rlCsFh.dpuf
2. www.garrisoninstitute.org/contemplation-and-education/care-for-teachers
3. Wendy Palmer and Janet Crawford, *Leadership Embodiment: How the Way We Sit and Stand Can Change the Way We Think and Speak* (San Rafael, CA: CreateSpace, 2013), i.

Introduction

1. For a complete description of formal loving-kindness meditation, please see Bob Stahl and Elisha Goldstein, *A Mindfulness-Based Stress Reduction Workbook* (Oakland, CA: New Harbinger, 2010), 145–149.
2. For the purposes of this text, we include compassion-based practices under the general umbrella of mindfulness and/or mindfulness-based practices. Many scientists, Buddhist scholars, and contemplatives would likely take issue with the conflation of these types of practices. This conflation speaks to a larger discourse about the meaning of the term *mindfulness,* and whether it refers to English translations of terms from Pali and Sanskrit texts (these translations are highly contested in Buddhist scholarship), or alternatively refers to mindfulness as a synonym for a kind of generalized "wellness" under the umbrella of positive psychology (the validity of which is also a subject of great debate). For the purposes of this book, we are simply alerting the reader to this set of discourses.
3. Jerry Murphy, "Jerry Murphy on Becoming an Effective Advocate for Contemplative Teaching and Learning," www.youtube.com/watch?v=U45x00sfwkw
4. For more on the sacrifice syndrome, see Annie McKee and Richard Boyatzis, *Resonant Leadership: Renewing Yourself and Connecting With Others Through Mindfulness, Hope, and Compassion* (Cambridge, MA: Harvard Business Review Press, 2005).
5. www.soundstrue.com/weeklywisdom/index.php?s=kabat-zinn&category=ALL&formOnly=

Chapter 1

1. Parker J. Palmer, "Introduction," in *Leading From Within: Poetry That Sustains the Courage to Lead,* edited by Sam M. Intrator and Megan Scribner (San Francisco, CA: Wiley, 2007), xxxiv.

2. Jeff Jordan, "Leaving It All on the Field," *Harvard Business Review* (May 2014): 40.

3. See, for instance, Bob Stahl and Elisha Goldstein, *A Mindfulness-Based Stress Reduction Workbook* (Oakland, CA: New Harbinger, 2010), which includes worksheets and a CD with 20 mindfulness meditations and exercises.

4. See Rick Hanson, "A Taste of Taking in the Good," *Hardwiring Happiness* (New York: Harmony Books, 2013), 62.

5. www.youtube.com/watch/?v=gXDMoiEkyuQ

6. Jon Kabat-Zinn, *Mindfulness for Beginners* (Boulder, CO: Sounds True, 2012), 17.

7. Kate Pickert, "The Mindful Revolution," *Time,* February 3, 2014.

8. Patrick Hruby, "Marines Expanding Use of Meditation Training," *Washington Times,* December 5, 2012. www.washingtontimes.com/news/2012/dec/5/marines-expanding-use-of-meditation-training/?page=all

9. Julie Watson, "Marines Studying Mindfulness-Based Training." *Yahoo News,* January 19, 2013. http://news.yahoo.com/marines-studying-mindfulness-based-training-184225539.html

10. Barry Boyce, "No Blueprint, Just Love: Interview With Jon Kabat-Zinn." *Mindful* (February 2014): 35–41.

11. Ibid., quoted on magazine cover.

12. For more information, in very simple and friendly form, see Bob Stahl and Wendy Millstine, *Calming the Rush of Panic* (Oakland, CA: New Harbinger, 2013).

13. www.forbes.com/sites/emilybennington/2013/03/28/get-off-the-treadmill-former-corporate-vp-brings-mindful-leadership-to-the-business-world

14. http://henryjenkins.org/2010/11/multitasking_and_continuous_pa.html#sthash.v8rlCsFh.dpuf

15. We love Linda Stone's image so much it inspired the book cover.

16. Ellie Drago-Severson, "The Need for Renewal: The Promise of Sustaining Principals Through Principal-to-Principal Reflective Practice." *Teachers College Record* 114, no. 12 (2012): 1–56.

17. http://scoop.intel.com/what-happens-in-an-internet-minute

18. Our leadership lives reflect a larger trend: A public interest group that researches the effects of *stress on organizational leaders* estimates that during the past decade, the number of adults in leadership positions indicating that job stress is a "major negative component" in their lives has doubled. The American Psychological Association surveyed busy Americans in 2013, and reported that 77% of us regularly experience physical symptoms caused by stress, including many of us who say "work overload" is the major cause of stress in our lives. The U.S. Department of Health and Human Services suggests that 70% of all work-related physical and mental complaints are due to, or related to, stress; and health insurance claims related to stress are estimated to cost organizations more than $300 billion yearly.

19. Kirsten Olson has written extensively about these shifts. See www.slideshare.net/kirstenolson/where-are-we-now-27414767 for a summary.

20. Tina Fey, *Bossypants* (New York: Reagan Arthur Books, 2011), 77.

21. Steve Heller, "Self Awareness in Leaders and Coaches," in *On Becoming a Leadership Coach,* 2nd ed., edited by Christine Wahl, Clarice Scriber, and Beth Bloomfield (New York: Palgrave, 2011), 75–82.

22. Alina Tugend, "A Call for a Movement to Redefine the Successful Life." *New York Times,* June 13, 2013. www.nytimes.com/2013/06/15/your-money/a-call-for-a-movement-to-redefine-the-successful-life.html?_r=0

23. Louis Cozolino, *The Social Neuroscience of Education* (New York: Norton, 2013). Throughout this powerful book, Cozolino describes the social and neurobiological processes of reflective learning in groups.

24. Parker J. Palmer, *Healing the Heart of Democracy* video, "From Effectiveness to Faithfulness." See www.couragerenewal.org/democracyguide.

25. www.youtube.com/watch?v=FXxrJEnIboM

26. Britta K. Hölzel, James Carmody, Mark Vangel, Christina Congleton, Sita M. Yerramsetti, Tim Gard, and Sara W. Lazar, "Mindfulness Practice Leads to Increases in Regional Brain Gray Matter Density," *Psychiatry Research: Neuroimaging* 191, no. 1 (2011): 36–43.

27. Britta K. Hölzel, James Carmody, Mark Vangel, Christina Congleton, Sita M. Yerramsetti, Tim Gard, and Sara W. Lazar. Mindfulness practice leads to increases in regional brain gray matter density. *Psychiatry Research: Neuroimaging,* 2011; 191 (1): 36 DOI: 10.1016/j.pscychresns.2010.08.006.

28. Massachusetts General Hospital. "Mindfulness Meditation Training Changes Brain Structure in Eight Weeks." *ScienceDaily,* January 21, 2011.

29. Rick Hanson, *Hardwiring Happiness* (New York: Harmony Books, 2013), 11–12.

30. www.mindfulschools.org/resources/healthy-habits-of-mind

31. www.lesley.edu/mindfulness-studies

32. www.tc.columbia.edu/centers/mindfulness/index.asp?Id=About+Us&Info=Our+Team

33. http://spiritualitymindbody.com/page/our-mission

34. http://uvacontemplation.org/content/applying-mindfulness-practices-support-school-leadership

35. www.nyu.edu/life/student-life/student-diversity/spiritual-life/mindfulness-project.html

36. Stahl and Millstine, *Calming the rush of panic* (Oakland, CA: New Harbinger, 2013), 13.

37. George, B. (2012, October). "Mindfulness Helps You Become a Better Leader." *Harvard Business Review* blog. Retrieved from http://blogs.hbr.org/2012/10/mindfulness-helps-you-become-a

38. www.waynekhoy.com/org_mindfulness.html

39. Anthony S. Bryk and Barbara Schneider. "Trust in Schools: A Core Resource for School Reform." *Educational Leadership* 60, no. 6 (2003): 40–45; Anthony S. Bryk and Barbara Schneider, *Trust in Schools: A Core Resource for Improvement* (New York: Russell Sage Foundation, 2004).

40. Patrick B. Forsythe, Curt M. Adams, and Wayne K. Hoy, *Collective Trust: Why Schools Can't Improve Without It* (New York: Teachers College Press, 2011).

41. Shimul Melwani and Sigal Barsade, "Held in Contempt: The Psychological, Interpersonal, and Performance Consequences of Contempt in a Work Context." *Journal of Personality and Social Psychology* 101, no. 3 (2011): 503–520.

42. www.forbes.com/2009/07/16/bad-mood-workplace-forbes-woman-leadership-solutions.html

43. George, B. (2012, October). "Mindfulness Helps You Become a Better Leader." *Harvard Business Review* blog. Retrieved from http://blogs.hbr.org/2012/10/mindfulness-helps-you-become-a

44. Stahl and Millstine (2013).

45. www.roomtobreathefilm.com/index.html

46. www.mindfulschools.org/resources/healthy-habits-of-mind

47. http://marc.ucla.edu

48. http://marc.ucla.edu/body.cfm?id=100

Chapter 2

1. Richard Hanson, *Buddha's Brain: The Practical Neuroscience of Happiness, Love, and Wisdom* (Oakland, CA: New Harbinger, 2009), 5, 18.

2. See http://vimeo.com/13179421 for a webinar from the Center for Contemplative Mind in Society. This is an excellent resource for information on contemplative neuroscience.

3. Richard J. Davidson and Sharon Begley, *The Emotional Life of Your Brain* (New York: Penguin Group, 2012), 161; Hanson (2009), 10.

4. Eleanor A. Maguire, Katherine Wollett, and Hugo J. Spiers, "London Taxi Drivers and Bus Drivers: A Structural MRI and Neuropsychological Analysis." *Hippocampus* 16, no. 12 (2006): 1091–1101.

5. Draganski Bogdan, Christian Gaser, Busch Volker, Gerhard Schuierer, Ulrich Bogdahn, and Arne May. "Neuroplasticity: Changes in Grey Matter Induced by Training." *Nature* 427 (2004), 311–312; Janina Boyke, Joenna Driemeyer, Christian Gaser, Christian Büchel, and Arne May. "Learning-Induced Gray-Matter Plasticity." *Journal of Neuroscience* 28, no. 28 (2008): 7031–7035.

6. Davidson and Begley (2012), 10.

7. www.soundstrue.com/weeklywisdom/?source=podcast&p=1172&category=IATE&version=full

8. See the article on this revolution online: Carl Zimmer. "Secrets of the Brain." *National Geographic*, February 2014, pp. 36–49; http://ngm.nationalgeographic.com/2014/02/brain/zimmer-text

9. Lisa A. Kilpatrick, Brandall Y. Suyenobu, Suzanne R. Smith, Joshua A. Bueller, Trudy Goodman, J. David Creswell, Kirsten Tillisch, Emeran A. Mayer, and Bruce D. Nailboff. "Impact of Mindfulness-Based Stress Reduction Training on Intrinsic Brain Connectivity." *NeuroImage* 56, no. 1 (2011): 290–298.

10. www.sciencedaily.com/releases/2011/01/110121144007.htm

11. www.nimh.nih.gov/health/topics/anxiety-disorders/index.shtml#part3

12. Robin Marantz Henig, "Valium's Contribution to Our New Normal." *New York Times*, September 29, 2012, p. 9.

13. Robert M. Sapolsky, *Why Zebras Don't Get Ulcers* (New York: Holt Paperbacks, 2004), 12–13.

14. Ibid.

15. Daniel Goleman, *The Brain and Emotional Intelligence: New Insights* (Northhampton, MA: More Than Sound, 2011), 20.

16. Ibid., 31.

17. Hanson (2009), 55–58.

18. Sapolsky (2004), 16.

19. Ibid., 4.

20. Hanson (2009), 54–55.

21. On a visit in February 2014 to Gandhi Smriti, Gandhi's memorial in New Delhi, India, we read this quote attributable to Albert Einstein.

22. Gaëlle Desbordes, Lobsang T. Negi, Thaddeus W. W. Pace, B. Alan Wallace, Charles L. Raison, and Eric L. Schwartz. "Effects of Mindful-Attention and Compassion Meditation Training on Amygdala Response to Emotional Stimuli in an Ordinary, Non-meditative State." *Frontiers in Human Neuroscience* 6 (2012): 292; Philippe Goldin and James J. Gross. "Effects of Mindfulness-Based Stress Reduction (MBSR) on Emotion Regulation in Social Anxiety Disorder." *Emotion* 10 (2010): 83–91; Véronique A. Taylor, Joshua Grant, Véronique Daneault, Geneviève Scavone, Estelle Breton, Sébastien Roffe-Vidal, Jérome Courtemanche, Anaïs S. Lavarenne, and Mario Beauregard. "Impact of Mindfulness on the Neural Responses to Emotional Pictures in Experienced and Beginner Meditators." *NeuroImage* 57 (2011): 1524–1533.

23. Jon Kabat-Zinn, Ann O. Massion, Jean Kristeller, Linday Gay Peterson, Kenneth E. Fletcher, Lori Pbert, William R. Lenderking, and Saki F. Santorelli. "Effectiveness of a Meditation-Based Stress Reduction Program in

the Treatment of Anxiety Disorders." *American Journal of Psychiatry* 149 (1992): 936–943.

24. Sara W. Lazar, Catherine E. Kerr, Rachel H. Wasserman, Jeremy R. Gray, Douglas N. Greve, Michael T. Treadway, Metta McGarvey, Brian T. Quinn, Jeffery A. Dusek, Herbert Benson, Scott L. Rauch, Christopher I. Moore, and Bruce Fischld. "Meditation Experience Is Associated With Increased Cortical Thickness." Neuroreport 16, no. 17 (2005): 1893–1897, available from www.ncbi.nlm.nih.gov/pmc/articles/PMC1361002/.

25. Norman A. S. Farb, Zindel V. Segal, Helen Mayberg, Jim Bean, Deborah McKeon, Zainab Fatima, and Adam K. Anderson. "Attending to the Present: Mindfulness Meditation Reveals Distinct Neural Modes of Self-Reference." *Social, Cognitive, and Affective Neuroscience* 2, no. 4 (2007): 313–222; Véronique A. Taylor, Joshua A. Grant, Véronique Daneault, Geneviève Scavone, Estelle Breton, Sébastien Roffe-Vidal, Jérôme Courtemanche, Anaïs S. Lavarenne, and Mario Beauregard. "Impact of Mindfulness on the Neural Responses to Emotional Pictures in Experienced and Beginner Meditators." *NeuroImage* 57, no. 4 (2011): 1524–1533.

26. Desbordes et al. (2012); Goldin and Gross (2010); Taylor et al. (2011).

27. Patricia A. Jennings, Jennifer L. Frank, Karin E. Snowberg, Michael A. Coccia, and Mark T. Greenberg. "Improving Classroom Learning Environments by Cultivating Awareness and Resilience in Education (CARE): Results of a Randomized Controlled Trial." *School Psychology Quarterly*, *29*, no. 4 (2013): 374–390.

28. Elliot Washor and Charles Mojkowski. "Student Disengagement: It's Deeper Than You Think." *EdWeek*, April 25, 2014.

29. Center for Creative Leadership. "What's New for Leadership? 5 Big Ideas." 2011–2012 Annual Report, available from www.ccl.org/leadership/pdf/aboutCCL/CCL2012AnnualReport.pdf

30. Linda Stone. "Just Breathe: Building the Case for Email Apnea." *Huffington Post*, February 8, 2008; *New York Times*, "Email Apnea: Holding One's Breath Unconsciously While Reading an Email." *Schott's Vocab*, September 23, 2009.

31. Donna Farhi, *The Breathing Book: Good Health and Vitality Through Essential Breath Work* (New York: Henry Holt, 1996), 16–18 and 22–24.

32. Robert W. Roeser, Kimberly A. Schonert-Reichl, Amishi Jha, Margaret Cullen, Linda Wallace, Rona Wilensky, Eva Oberle, Kimberly Thomson, Cynthia Taylor, and Jessica Harrison. "Mindfulness Training and Reductions in Teacher Stress and Burnout: Results From Two Randomized, Waitlist-Control Field Trials." *Journal of Educational Psychology* 105, no. 3 (2013): 787–804.

Chapter 3

1. Anne Lamott, *Bird by Bird* (New York: Anchor Books, 1994), 99.

2. Daniel J. Levitin, "Hit the Reset Button in Your Brain," *New York Times*, August 9, 2014, available from www.nytimes.com/2014/08/10/opinion/sunday/hit-the-reset-button-in-your-brain.html?smid=tw-share&_r=0

3. Ibid.

4. Daniel Goleman, *Focus: The Hidden Driver of Excellence* (New York: HarperCollins, 2013), 55.

5. Levitin (2014).

6. Richard J. Davidson and Sharon Begley, *The Emotional Life of Your Brain* (New York: Penguin Group, 2012).

7. Levitin (2014).

8. As an aside, when we use the word *insight,* we are referring to a colloquial sense of enhanced discernment, a quality of wisdom. We are not referring to the more technical Theravadin or Mahayana Buddhist interpretation of the term.

9. Timothy D. Wilson, David A. Reinhard, Erin C. Westgate, Daniel T. Gilbert, Nicole Ellerbeck, Cheryl Hahn, Casey L. Brown, and Adi Shaked. "Just Think: The Challenges of the Disengaged Mind." *Science* 345, no. 6192 (2014), 75–77.

10. John Tarrant, "A Beautiful Wish," *Shambhala Sun,* September 2013.

11. Lamott (1994), 28.

12. Kristin Neff, *Self-Compassion: The Proven Power of Being Kind to Yourself* (Harper-Collins, 2011).

13. Bob Stahl and Wendy Millstine, *Calming the Rush of Panic* (Oakland, CA: New Harbinger, 2013), 17–19; Bob Stahl and Elisha Goldstein, *A Mindfulness-Based Stress Reduction Workbook* (Oakland, CA: New Harbinger, 2010), 41–42.

14. Margaret Wheatley, *Perseverance* (San Francisco, CA: Berkana, 2010), 81.

15. Jon Kabat-Zinn, *Wherever You Go There You Are* (New York: Hyperion, 1994), 123.

16. Dan C. Lortie, *Schoolteacher: A Sociological Study* (Chicago: University of Chicago Press, 1974).

17. For more information about continuous partial attention, visit Linda Stone's Attention Project at http://lindastone.net/qa/continuous-partial-attention/

18. Adrian W. Savage, *Slow Leadership.* Message posted at www.slowleadership.org

19. Eyal Ophir, Clifford Nass, and Anthony D. Wagner. "Cognitive Control in Media Multitaskers." *PNAS* 106, no. 37 (2009). Retrieved from www.pnas.org/content/106/37/15583.10ng

20. http://executiveeducation.wharton.upenn.edu/thought-leadership/wharton-at-work/2011/02/emotional-contagion

21. Rick Hanson, *Hardwiring Happiness: The New Brain Science of Contentment, Calm and Confidence* (New York: Harmony Books, 2011), 31.

22. Rick Hanson, *Just One Thing: Developing a Buddha Brain One Simple Practice at a Time* (Oakland, CA: New Harbinger, 2011), 18.

23. Hanson, *Hardwiring Happiness* (2011), 13.

24. *Primal Leadership: Unleashing the Power of Emotional Intelligence,* Harvard Business Review Press. Authors: Daniel Goleman, Richard Boyatwzis, and Annie McKee, 2013.

25. Sara Eckel, "Bad Moods at Work." *Forbes,* July 16, 2009. Retrieved from www.forbes.com/2009/07/16/bad-mood-workplace-forbes-woman-leadership-solutions.html

26. Goleman (2013), 47.

27. Ibid., 47.

28. Ibid., 56–58.

29. This is a quote from a lecture presented by Amhsi P. Jha, at the 12th Annual International Scientific Conference, Investigating and Integrating Mindfulness in Medicine, Health Care, and Society, Center for Mindfulness in Medicine, Health Care, and Society/University of Massachusetts Medical School, April 3, 2014, Norwood, Massachusetts.

30. Ophir, Nass, and Wagner (2009).

31. Goleman (2013), 20.

32. Sharon Salzberg, *Real Happiness at Work: Meditations for Accomplishment, Achievement, and Peace* (New York: Workman, 2014), 49.

33. Eckhart Tolle, *The Power of Now: A Guide to Spiritual Enlightenment* (Novato, CA: New World Library, 1999).

34. See, for example, Martin E. P. Seligman, *Learned Optimism: How to Change Your Mind and Your Life* (New York: Knopf, 1991).

Chapter 4

1. Susan Scott, *Fierce Conversations: Achieving Success at Work and in Life One Conversation at a Time* (New York: Berkley, 2004), 1.
2. Mark Nepo, *Seven Thousand Ways to Listen: Staying Close to What Is Sacred* (New York: Free Press, 2012), 147.
3. www.cnvc.org
4. Gregory Kramer, a longtime meditation teacher, has developed a specific focus on mindful speaking and listening called "Insight Dialogue." In this practice, mindful attitudes (nonjudgment, allowing and opening, equanimity) are brought to the act of speaking and listening. Kramer articulates six key elements:

   1. Pause—stop to notice your thoughts and emotions; create space and silence to act differently.

   2. Relax—replace old patterns and habits with greater acceptance and receptivity.

   3. Be open—deepen awareness of yourself and others.

   4. Trust emergence—set aside "ready-made" responses, your agenda, to remain open.

   5. Listen deeply—practice active and compassionate listening.

   6. Speak the truth—use honest and compassionate speech.

   See Kramer's *Insight Dialogue: The Interpersonal Path to Freedom* (Boston: Shambhala, 2007), as well as his website at www.metta.org.

5. http://www.umassmed.edu/cfm/Training/Continuing-Education/
6. http://ojaifoundation.org/discover-council
7. Jack Zimmerman and Virginia Coyle, *The Way of Council* (Putney, VT: Bramble Books, 2009), 28–36.
8. Ibid., 28.
9. Ibid.
10. Ibid., 29.
11. Christine Riordan. "Three Ways Leaders Can Listen With More Empathy." *Harvard Business Review* (January 16, 2014); available from http://blogs.hbr.org/2014/01/three-ways-leaders-can-listen-with-more-empathy/.
12. Parker J. Palmer, *The Courage to Teach Guide for Reflection and Renewal* (San Francisco: Wiley, 2007), 118
13. Eleanor Drago-Severson, "The Need for Principal Renewal: The Promise of Sustaining Principals Through Principal-to-Principal Reflective Practice." *Teachers College Record* (2012). Available from http://www.tcrecord.org/Content.asp?ContentID=16717
14. Brené Brown, *Daring Greatly: How the Courage to Be Vulnerable Transforms the Way We Live, Love, Parent and Lead* (New York: Gotham Books, 2012), 188.
15. Susan Scott, *Fierce Conversations: Achieving Success at Work and Life, One Conversation at a Time* (New York: Berkley Books, 2004), 254.
16. Tara Brach, *Radical Acceptance: Embracing Your Life With the Heart of a Buddha* (New York: Bantam Dell, 2003).
17. Pema Chödrön, *Comfortable With Uncertainty* (Boston: Shambhala, 2002), 21–22.
18. Ibid.
19. Rick Hanson, *Hardwiring Happiness: The New Brain Science of Contentment, Calm and Confidence* (New York: Harmony Books, 2011), 106.

20. Ibid., 107.

21. This is an excerpt from the Center for Courage & Renewal's *Touchstones*. For *Touchstones* in its entirety, please contact the Center for Courage & Renewal at www.couragerenewal.org.

22. www.tarabrach.com/articles/RAIN-WorkingWithDifficulties.html. See also Brach (2003).

23. Pema Chödrön, *When Things Fall Apart* (Boston: Shambhala, 1997); *The Places That Scare You: A Guide to Fearlessness in Difficult Times* (Boston: Shambhala, 2002).

24. The Four Limitless Ones refer to Buddhist teachings on the qualities of love, compassion, joy, and equanimity. See http://pemachodrontapes.com/store/index.php?main_page=index&cPath=4.

25. Richard J. Davidson and Sharon Begley, *The Emotional Life of Your Brain: How Its Unique Patterns Affect the Way You Think, Feel, and Live—and How You Can Change Them* (New York: Penguin, 2012).

Chapter 5

1. Richard Boyatzis and Annie McKee, *Resonant Leadership* (Boston: Harvard Business School Publishing, 2005), 63.

2. Cheryl Woods-Giscombé. "Superwoman Schema: African American Women's Views on Stress, Strength, and Health." *Qualitative Health Research* 20, no. 5 (2010): 668–683, available from http://www.ncbi.nlm.nih.gov/pmc/articles/PMC3072704/. See also the research of Angela Black on black women, health disparities, and mindfulness: http://wisc.academia.edu/AngelaRoseBlack.

3. www.createwritenow.com/personal-growth-journaling-blog/bid/51559/mindful-journaling

4. Portions of these quotes are from Jonathan Beasley. "Helping to Heal." *Harvard Gazette*, November 20, 2009, available from http://archive.hds.harvard.edu/news-events/articles/2011/02/07/helping-to-heal.

5. John Welwood, *Journey of the Heart* (New York: HarperCollins, 1990).

6. Dan Huston, *Communicating Mindfully: Mindfulness-Based Communication and Emotional Intelligence* (Stamford, CT: Cengage Learning, 2010).

7. The results of this study appear in "Mechanisms of Mindfulness in Communication Training" in the *Journal of Applied Communication Research* 39, no. 4 (November 2011): 406–421.

8. Henry Emmons, *The Chemistry of Joy Workbook: Overcoming Depression Using the Best of Brain Science, Nutrition, and the Psychology of Mindfulness* (Oakland, CA: New Harbinger, 2012).

9. Jeff Gordinier. "Food for Thought." *New York Times*, February 8, 2012.

10. According to the Centers for Disease Control and Prevention, the estimated annual medical cost of obesity in the United States was $147 billion in 2008 U.S. dollars; the medical costs for people who are obese were $1,429 higher than those for people of normal weight. We know, too, that obesity affects some groups more than others.

Chapter 6

1. James Baldwin, *Notes of a Native Son* (Boston: Beacon Press, 1955), 140.

2. These EQ skills include:

- Self-awareness—the capacity to recognize, reflect, and understand your moods and emotions in the present moment and respond with clarity and compassion.
- Self-regulation—the capacity to calm yourself in the moment while under pressure, to control and redirect impulse and moods.
- Motivation—the capacity to find purpose and meaning in work that goes beyond money, power, or status.
- Empathy—the capacity to be aware of others' feelings, needs, and concerns.
- Social skill—the capacity to manage complex relationships and build networks.

3. https://www.youtube.com/watch?v=NeJ3FF1yFyc
4. Daniel Goleman, "What Makes a Leader?" *Harvard Business Review: The Magazine* (January 2004): 86; see also http://hbr.org/2004/01/what-makes-a-leader/ar/1
5. Judy Brown, *The Art and Spirit of Leadership*. (Bloomington, IN: Trafford Publishing, 2012), 147–148.
6. Daniel Goleman, "What Makes a Leader?" *Harvard Business Review: The Magazine* (January 2004): 86, p.89–90; see also http://hbr.org/2004/01/what-makes-a-leader/ar/1
7. Chade-Meng Tan, *Search Inside Yourself* (New York: Harper One, 2012), 166.
8. Ibid., 167.
9. Jon Kabat-Zinn, *Let Everything Become Your Teacher: 100 Lessons in Mindfulness* (New York: Delta Books, 2009), 90.
10. Paul Gilbert, *The Compassionate Mind: A New Approach to Life's Challenges* (Oakland, CA: New Harbinger, 2009), 4.
11. Ibid., 20.
12. Kristin Neff, *Self-Compassion: The Proven Power of Being Kind to Yourself* (New York: HarperCollins, 2011).
13. Gilbert (2009), 246–247.
14. Ibid., 246–247, 263, 288.
15. Belle Linda Halpern and Kathy Lubar, *Leadership Presence: Dramatic Techniques to Reach Out, Motivate, and Inspire* (New York: Penguin Books, 2003), 30–31.
16. Adam Grant. "The Dark Side of Emotional Intelligence." *Atlantic Monthly*, January 12, 2014.
17. Irene McHenry and Richard Brady, *Tuning In: Mindfulness in Teaching and Learning* (Friends Council on Education, 2009).
18. A mindfulness program for adolescents: http://learning2breathe.org

Chapter 7

1. www.gse.harvard.edu/news-impact/2009/09/harvard-university-to-offer-groundbreaking-doctoral-program-for-education-leaders/
2. Diana Chapman Walsh, "Cultivating Inner Resources for Leadership" (February 2005). See also https://groups.yahoo.com/neo/groups/NonprofitNetworking/conversations/messages/7381
3. John O'Donohue, *Anam Cara: A Book of Celtic Wisdom* (New York: Harper Perennial, 1998), 111.
4. http://fortune.com/2013/03/08/whole-foods-john-mackey-self-awareness-on-aisle-5
5. Chade-Meng Tan, *Search Inside Yourself* (New York: Harper One, 2012).

6. As already noted, recent research supports this idea that educational leaders have too few opportunities for reflective leadership practice, and it is more necessary than it has ever been. Please see Eleanor Drago-Severson. "The Need for Principal Renewal: The Promise of Sustaining Principals Through Principal-to-Principal Reflective Practice." *Teachers College Record* 114, no. 12 (2012): 1–56.

7. For a view of Kirsten Olson's views on this vast sectoral change, go to SlideShare (www.slideshare.net/kirstenolson/where-are-we-now-27414767) to check out "A New Era Dawns."

8. Lynne Twist, *Soul of Money* (New York: Norton, 2003), 74.

9. www.couragerenewal.org/programs

10. Antonio Machado, "Proverbios y Cantares #29," in *Border of a Dream: Selected Poems,* translated by Willis Barnstone (Port Townsend, WA: Copper Canyon Press, 2004), 281.

11. www.goodreads.com/quotes/61047-everything-that-happens-to-you-is-your-teacher-the-secret

12. Our views of wholehearted leadership are strongly influenced by Brené Brown and her work on vulnerability: www.soundstrue.com/podcast/the-courage-to-be-vulnerable/ and www.csh.umn.edu/prod/groups/ahc/@pub/@ahc/@csh/documents/bio/ahc_bio_419226.pdf. Also see Brown's work, *Daring Greatly: How the Courage to Be Vulnerable Transforms the Way We Live, Love, Parent, and Lead* (New York: Gotham, 2012).

13. www.ascd.org/publications/educational-leadership/dec08/v0166/num04/The-New-Stupid.aspx

14. Thanks to Drew Bird, of ClearPoint Leadership (www.clearpointeq.com), for some of these thoughts. ("Developing Emotionally Effective Leaders Through Coaching," Part 4 of 4.)

15. Dan Siegel, *The Mindful Brain* (New York: Norton), 256.

16. Chade-Meng Tan, *Search Inside Yourself* (New York: Harper One, 2012), 229.

17. www.umassmed.edu/cfm/leadership/index.asp

18. www.couragerenewal.org/leadingtogether

19. Brooke Dodson-Lavelle et al., *EEST Planning Year Final Report* (Hadley, MA: Mind and Life Institute, 2014), 4–5.

20. http://www.mindandlife.org/research-initiatives/

21. www.mindfuled.org/about

22. www.garrisoninstitute.org/contemplation-and-education/care-for-teachers; http://passageworks.org; www.smart-in-education.org; www.innerresilience-tidescenter.org

23. http://wakeupschools.org/about-us/

24. Daniel P. Barbezat and Mirabai Bush, *Contemplative Practices in Higher Education* (San Francisco: Jossey-Bass, 2013); Parker J. Palmer and Arthur Zajonc (with Megan Scribner and Foreword by Mark Nepo), *The Heart of Higher Education: A Call to Renewal* (San Francisco: Jossey-Bass, 2010).

25. www.mindfulschools.org/our-programs

26. Rick Hanson, *Hardwiring Happiness: The New Brain Science of Contentment, Calm and Confidence* (New York: Penguin, 2013).

27. This practice was created by Jerry Murphy, and is influenced by the work of Ann Weiser Cornell.

28. See http://plumvillage.org/audio/happy-teachers-will-change-the-world/. "Happy teachers will change the world" is now used worldwide for Wake Up Schools retreats (http://wakeupschools.org).

29. Diana Chapman Walsh, *Trustworthy Leadership: Can We Be the Leaders We Need Our Students to Become?* (San Francisco: Jossey-Bass, 2006).

30. Diana Chapman Walsh, "Gentle Emissaries for a World of Possibility; When Leadership and Mindfulness Converge," Sonnabend Fellowship Lecture, Lesley University, April 30, 2013.

31. Some of the long quoted passages in this profile are from Diana Chapman Walsh's "Mind and Life Institute First International Scientific Symposium" keynote address in Denver, Colorado, on April 27, 2012. Quoted by permission of the author.

Index

A SAGE Company

Corwin is committed to improving education for all learners by publishing books and other professional development resources for those serving the field of PreK–12 education. By providing practical, hands-on materials, Corwin continues to carry out the promise of its motto: **"Helping Educators Do Their Work Better."**